European labour movements in crisis

MANCHESTER
1824

Manchester University Press

European labour movements in crisis

From indecision to indifference

Thomas Prosser

Manchester University Press

Copyright © Thomas Prosser 2019

The right of Thomas Prosser to be identified as the author of this work has been asserted by him in accordance with the Copyright, Designs and Patents Act 1988.

Published by Manchester University Press
Altrincham Street, Manchester M1 7JA, UK
www.manchesteruniversitypress.co.uk

British Library Cataloguing-in-Publication Data is available

ISBN 978 1 5261 3664 0 hardback
ISBN 978 1 5261 4805 6 paperback

First published by Manchester University Press in hardback 2019

This edition published 2020

The publisher has no responsibility for the persistence or accuracy of URLs for any external or third-party internet websites referred to in this book, and does not guarantee that any content on such websites is, or will remain, accurate or appropriate.

Typeset by Out of House Publishing

Contents

Figures

Tables

Preface

I have tried to make this book as accessible as possible. It is primarily intended for an academic audience, yet I hope that it falls into the hands of policymakers, students and interested laypeople. Particularly with the two latter groups in mind, I have compiled a glossary which is found at the end of the book and elaborates the meaning of key terms and functions of studied organizations. Readers for whom this subject matter is new might consult it as they progress or before they start.

I at least hope that this book is easier to read than it was to write. Colleagues who were veterans of similar projects warned me of the challenges of such an endeavour and, in the years which this work has taken to complete, I have become more than acquainted with various trials. I can at least say that I very much enjoyed writing this book. I have a passion for the topic which I hope is reflected in the text, and the process of research took me to a series of stimulating locations and organizations. Regardless of these satisfactions, I often walked a lonely road. Perhaps it is an improper admission for a Welsh scholar of labour movements to make, but I was often buoyed by the timeless counsel of Sir Winston Churchill: keep buggering on.

The act of buggering on may be a lonely one, yet Churchill himself would doubtless have conceded that it cannot be done without support from others. In this sense, I am grateful to a succession of institutions and people without whom this project would not have been possible. Thanks must go to institutions. Cardiff University has provided a conducive environment for research since I joined in 2011 and Marco Hauptmeier, Ed Heery and Keith Whitfield have been particularly supportive colleagues. In this time, I have also been fortunate enough to complete stays at the Solidarność trade union, Fundación Primero de Mayo, Carlos III University of Madrid and ETUI and have received warm welcomes.

I am indebted to Tony Mason of Manchester University Press. Tony has believed in this project from the start and was instrumental in securing its publication. Special thanks must go to interviewees. In each of the four countries in which I did fieldwork, I met a series of kind people who intelligently explained to me the positions of their organizations. Interviewed organizations are listed in an appendix, though the need to preserve anonymity prevents me from naming individuals. I hope that this work does justice to the richness of their accounts.

The help of readers of drafts was no less pivotal; it is difficult to convey my gratitude to those who read early versions of this work and made detailed remarks which invariably improved the manuscript. In an order which is merely alphabetical, I thank Colin Crouch, Patrick Emmenegger, Magnus Feldmann, Bob Hancké, Martin Höpner, Paul Marginson, Guglielmo Meardi, Nick Parsons, Vera Šćepanović, Mateusz Szymański and Gareth Williams. The comments of anonymous reviewers procured by Manchester University Press also strengthened this work. Miscellaneous acknowledgements must be made. For invaluable assistance with German-language sources, I thank Sven Werner; the chapter on Germany strongly reflects his incisive analysis. Extended conversations with Michael Arghyrou, Barbara Bechter, Romaric Godin, Simon Lightfoot, Aleksandra Maatsch and Torsten Müller elucidated national contexts. Ania Gałązka helped with last-minute presentational tasks and Chloé Fortin-Bergeron and Weronika Poliszuk transcribed interviews.

Family members also helped me complete this project. My sister-in-law, Elea Belda Beneyto, provided crucial aid with finer points of Spanish grammar, while my wife, Justyna Prosser, assisted in a similar way with her native Polish. I cannot limit my gratitude to Justyna to a single line; sharing my life with her is a privilege. Thanks should also go to my multi-talented mother, Lesley Prosser, who, aside from making a maiden stand for Parliament while this book was being written, continues to be a proofreader without peer.

One of the individuals who would have read this work most enthusiastically is alas not around to do so. My father Stephen Prosser was instrumental in encouraging me to enter academia, yet passed away before I had taken many steps down the career path. I dedicate this work to his memory.

PART I
Setting up the question

1

European labour movements in crisis

Europe lies in long-term torpor. Not only is the continent recovering from a decade-long crisis, but the single currency, hitherto the crown jewel of European integration, has itself been a major cause of malaise. This crisis of Economic and Monetary Union (EMU) has been underpinned by nationalist feuds over economic policy. A core of northern European countries, led by Germany and distinguished by their solvent economies, have become exasperated by the profligacy of southern countries. These periphery countries, ravaged by years of core-imposed austerity, in turn point to the ruinous effects of reforms demanded by the core. The dispute continues to threaten a break-up of the EU. Not only do certain periphery countries remain close to exit from the Eurozone, but the genie of nationalist-populism, unbottled by the tensions of crisis, threatens to tear the EU apart from below.

In this book, I contend that this malaise can partly be located in the response of labour movements to integration. Rather than cooperating with European counterparts so as to maximize joint outcomes, movements rely on national institutions; this instigates zero-sum forms of competition between regimes in different member states, albeit through largely unintentional means. Lack of solidarity during resulting crises reinforces effects of competition. The question of the nature of the reaction of labour to European integration has long preoccupied scholars. Political economists writing after the Maastricht Treaty underlined processes of competition (Rhodes, 1998a; Scharpf, 1999; Streeck, 1996), yet scholars who stress actor agency have contended that labour behaviour often takes a cooperative form. Such work has emphasized the capacity of unions to engage in European social dialogue (Falkner, 1998), successful union cross-border campaigns (Erne, 2008) and the Europeanization of social-democratic parties (Ladrech, 2000).

Owing to recent changes to European integration, specifically the deepening of economic integration and an upturn in nationalism, there is need for an updated approach. My argument is rooted in the study of two key contemporary processes: first, the collective bargaining practices of trade unions in the first decade of the Eurozone (1999–2010); and, second, the response of trade unions and social-democratic parties to austerity measures in the periphery of the Eurozone (2010–15). The cases of four countries – Germany, Spain, France and Poland – are examined. In the first process, national bargaining practices led to divergent economic outcomes. In Germany, an archetypal core member of the Eurozone, agreements were concluded which safeguarded competitiveness vis-à-vis other member states; this contributed to significant trade imbalances and the outbreak of debt crisis in 2010. In Spain, which was considered a member of the southern European periphery, unions failed to achieve such competitiveness and the country entered crisis. Effects were less stark in other contexts. Though French unions played a limited role in collective bargaining, a state incomes policy ensured a middling level of competitiveness in EMU; France was thus spared the fate of the periphery and may be considered an intermediate case. Non-membership of the Eurozone insulated Poland from these processes, even if de-centralized bargaining structures might have allowed the country to achieve competitiveness within the single currency.

In this first process, competition between the labour market institutions in which unions are embedded took place. Though certain accounts suggest that unions consciously adopt competitive strategies (Bofinger, 2015; Johnston, 2016), limits on actor cognition and coordination capacity tended to preclude such tactics. In Spain and Poland, short-termism and restricted awareness of external pressure meant that inter-sectoral negotiators took minimal heed of European developments. This was also the case in Germany, though the complexity of sectoral negotiations represented an additional impediment. French competitiveness was planned to an unusual degree by the state, yet unions were excluded from this process.

Structural influences, which were largely independent of actor volition yet prompted zero-sum outcomes, instead came to the fore. As a result of labour market institutions which promoted retrenchment in exposed and non-exposed sectors, Germany increasingly achieved competitive advantage within EMU. Inverse developments occurred in Spain; wage guidelines agreed at inter-sectoral level were consistently overshot as a result of the fragmented form of private and public sector collective bargaining (Johnston, 2016). The middling competitiveness achieved in France was guaranteed by a state incomes policy, while in Poland non-membership of the Eurozone was the crucial variable. Strategies aiming at European bargaining coordination, which had the potential to promote positive-sum outcomes, were frustrated. As a result of long-standing problems of comparability and collective action (Glassner and

Pochet, 2011), such initiatives had little effect on bargaining outcomes; distinct competitive advantages within EMU were a further disincentive. These developments prompted divergent competitive advantages between countries. Unions did not aim at such an end, yet their reliance on national institutions and reluctance to engage in coordination encouraged such outcomes.

In a second process, which is related to the first and concerns the response of unions and social-democratic parties to austerity measures in Southern Europe (2010–15), the behaviour of labour movements also facilitated competition between regimes. *Pace* accounts which emphasize patterns of cooperation (Erne, 2008), labour movements tended to be unresponsive to attacks on counterparts in the periphery. Trade unions behaved in such a manner. Though German unions issued *A Marshall Plan for Europe*, their participation in European protests was limited. Engagement in such actions was more considerable in France and Poland, yet unions in these countries failed to emulate levels of mobilization observed in Southern Europe. Spanish unions assumed a leading role in the organization of European protests and held general strikes on the days of action arranged by the European Trade Union Confederation (ETUC); this was associated with the weak national position within EMU.

Social-democratic parties also behaved in an underwhelming fashion. The German Sozialdemokratische Partei Deutschlands (SPD) denounced austerity, yet the party often fell silent, and votes in favour of the fiscal compact and Greek emergency loan could be construed as supportive of the policy. In the French case, European political realities forced the leadership of Parti Socialiste (PS) to toe the line of the German Government, much to the chagrin of party rank and file. Domestic incapacity accounted for lacklustre reactions in Spain and Poland. The Spanish Partido Socialista Obrero Español (PSOE) had incentive to contest austerity while in opposition, yet the earlier introduction of austerity by the Zapatero PSOE Government meant that it lacked credibility. In the Polish case, the left-wing Sojusz Lewicy Demokratycznej (SLD) was particularly weak during this time, though the absence of Poland from the Eurozone ensured that opposition to austerity was a secondary priority.

Rather than engaging in the pan-European forms of solidarity which are theorized by scholars who emphasize cooperation (Erne, 2008), labour movements therefore reacted rather coolly to austerity in the southern European periphery. Austerity was an undoubted threat to workforces outside of the periphery, attacks on workers in one member state put European labour under general pressure, yet benefits associated with the status quo precluded stronger engagement. National pre-eminence within EMU ensured improvement of the employment prospects of German workers, while the middling competitiveness achieved by France involved a related, albeit weaker, effect. In addition to these advantages, the liberalization of employment protection which took place in the periphery meant that deregulation was postponed in core and intermediate contexts.

On the basis of analysis of these two processes, I develop an updated theory of the manner in which labour movements respond to European integration. Rather than being based on cooperation, the behaviour of labour tends to facilitate competition between national regimes. Owing to the nationally embedded nature of labour movements, which is itself in the interests of certain workers, bargaining processes tend to lead to an unplanned yet incremental drift towards zero-sum outcomes which benefit national workforces in stronger structural positions. Strategies which aim to correct discrepant outcomes, which become particularly necessary at times of crisis, are generally unsuccessful. Not only are attempts at European cooperation often weakly prioritized by labour movements, which is related to the tendency for certain workers to benefit from the status quo, but difficulties associated with collective action mean they can be easily vetoed.

Previous studies have emphasized the propensity of labour to compete (Rhodes, 1998a; Scharpf, 1999; Streeck, 1996), yet my argument goes beyond these accounts in three ways. First, it theorizes developments in contemporary Europe. Existing work tends to conceptualize conditions in the 1990s; this was a period in which currency integration was less pronounced and nationalism was tamer. The current stage of integration necessitates an updated approach. Introduction of the euro has heightened competition between national regimes and increased the probability of crises (Höpner and Schäfer, 2010; Streeck, 2014), while spikes in nationalism have made workers less disposed to support disadvantaged counterparts (Polyakova and Fligstein, 2016). I contend that my results are consistent with intergovernmentalist theories which emphasize the capacity of states to control integration (Bickerton *et al.*, 2015) and underscore the role of labour in such processes. Findings are also linked to theories of disintegration (Rosamond, 2016), which conceptualize the potential of the EU to fragment and have emerged in reaction to recent crises.

Second, I elaborate precise causal mechanisms by which labour movements compete. This is a flaw of previous scholarship. Though such work underlines the propensity of labour to engage in competition (Johnston, 2016; Rhodes, 1998a; Streeck, 1996), it pays limited attention to the extent to which this results from actor volition. My claim that competition between bargaining regimes primarily reflects structural influences rather than union calculation, which is rooted in case studies more detailed than existing accounts, addresses a long-standing weakness of literature. The equation of indifference with the self-interest of national movements is a further contribution. This relationship has been theorized by scholars of dualization who call attention to the nonchalance of insiders (Palier and Thelen, 2010), yet does not feature in debates which concern the reaction of labour to integration. My assertion that lack of solidarity functions as a softer, *de facto* form of competition addresses this gap.

Third, I innovate by forging associations between patterns of competition and/or cooperation and changes in labour market conditions. This is a reaction to the tendency of existing studies to make insufficient linkages with substantive outcomes (e.g. Erne, 2008; Falkner, 1998). Though such scholarship theorizes the behaviour of labour movements, little attention tends to be paid to the consequences of this behaviour; this raises the question of the significance of studied processes. I am particularly interested in two variables: levels of (i) unemployment and (ii) employment security. Change and continuity in these outcomes are tracked and links are made with the extent to which labour movements compete and/or cooperate; this allows the foundations and consequences of studied behaviours to be better understood. Selection of these variables is inspired by literature on dualization, which concerns the capacity of certain workers to shape substantive outcomes (Emmenegger *et al.*, 2012; Palier and Thelen, 2010). This scholarship is preoccupied with the processes by which insiders profit at the expense of outsiders, and my innovation is to suggest that divisions increasingly exist among member states. As a result of patterns of competition, marked discrepancies have emerged between core and periphery countries; I consequently argue that dualization is taking place on a European scale.

The book is divided into three parts. In the first part, which contains three chapters, investigated themes are set out and an analytical framework is developed. Following the current introduction, a chapter delineates scholarship concerning the reaction of labour movements to European integration. After evaluating prevailing interpretations, I contend that developments associated with the debt crisis necessitate a new approach. I then assert that existing scholarship inadequately conceptualizes the manner in which labour behaviour affects substantive conditions in labour markets, before arguing that literature on dualization provides valuable insight into this relationship. Finally, I set out the manner in which theories of European integration aid understandings of labour movements and propose that my cases provide rich material for reconsideration of existing approaches.

Chapter 3 delineates the research design used by the book. The chapter commences with an outline of my approach and conceptualization of labour movements. I contend that a framework rooted in the discipline of political economy is most appropriate and develop a definition of labour movements which includes trade unions and social-democratic parties. Operationalization of the research question is then discussed; this involves assessment of the actions of labour movements in two distinct periods. Countries selected for case study are also presented, before my research methodology and methods are set out.

Part II contains four chapters and presents developments in studied countries; these countries are Germany (chapter 4), Spain (chapter 5), France (chapter 6) and Poland (chapter 7). Germany is the archetypal core Eurozone country and its labour movement is one which is well-organized and moderate. After the launch of the euro, the capacity of German unions to control wages via well-established sectoral bargaining institutions ensured that the country increasingly enjoyed competitive advantage within EMU (Hassel, 2014). The case of Germany consequently allows assessment of the extent to which unions may use sectoral bargaining to plan competitiveness. I argue that constraints on the ability of unions to calculate precluded such strategies and that the superior competitiveness of Germany was the result of structural influences. Following the onset of crisis and the implementation of austerity in Southern Europe, German ascendancy within the Eurozone raised the question of the extent to which a core labour movement was likely to extend solidarity to benighted counterparts. Though SPD often denounced austerity, certain actions of the party could be perceived as supportive. The disagreement of German unions with austerity was more vocal, yet their commitment to concrete opposition was arguably lacklustre (Dribbusch, 2015). I contend that the lukewarm reaction of German labour was rooted in the dominant national position within EMU.

Spain is a periphery Eurozone country and its labour movement is one which is unevenly developed. After the launch of EMU, Spanish unit labour costs (ULCs) escalated; this led to a loss of competitiveness within EMU, which exposed Spain to deep recession after the onset of crisis in 2007/8 (Johnston, 2016). Owing to the existence of inter-sectoral agreements in which unions attempt to establish competitiveness, the case of Spain raises the question of the extent to which efforts to achieve moderation are feasible in a periphery country. The failure of this strategy not only points to further constraints on the ability of actors to plan competitiveness, but also demonstrates the importance of structural influences; in this case, inefficiencies associated with lower-level bargaining institutions were crucial (Johnston, 2016). Following the outbreak of crisis and the tendency for periphery labour markets to become subject to the whims of core countries, the question was raised of the ability of periphery labour movements to marshal pan-European opposition. Though Spanish unions were at the vanguard of attempts to organize European protests and general strikes were held in Spain on European days of action, the mobilization capacity of unions was constrained by their under-Europeanized profile. The earlier implementation of austerity measures by a Socialist Government also restricted the extent of social-democratic opposition, both domestically and at European level.

France occupies an intermediate position in the Eurozone and its labour movement is one which is fragmented and adversarial. Lack of corporatist tradition means unions in France have historically experienced difficulties responding to external shocks (Crouch, 1993); the French case therefore raises the question of how unions in weak structural positions can effectively react to Europeanization. Following the introduction of EMU, this was partly resolved by a state incomes policy which limited potential loss of competitiveness; the role of unions in this process was nonetheless minor. The Eurozone crisis raised a further question of the French labour movement; namely the extent to which a movement in an intermediate country was likely to extend solidarity to counterparts in the periphery. Though mobilizations in France were more impressive than in core countries, significant protests being organized in France at key points, this response had limits and was a secondary priority for unions. The disposition of PS was also lukewarm. This was particularly the case on the right of the party; after François Hollande became president in 2012, the line of the German Government was increasingly followed.

Poland is a non-member of the Eurozone and its labour movement is one which is weak and politically divided. Inclusion of Poland allows evaluation of the extent to which examined processes are tied up with euro membership. In the Polish case, a particular issue was the extent to which unions were able to use a central and eastern European (CEE) tripartite institution to respond to pressures associated with Europeanization. Challenges encountered by unions, which resulted from political division and constraints on their ability to plan, suggest that a coherent response is also difficult in these circumstances. The onset of crisis raised the question of the extent to which a labour movement in a non-Eurozone country was likely to exhibit solidarity with periphery countries. Despite the difficulties of their domestic position, the reaction of Polish labour was not insignificant. The left-wing SLD was rather uninterested, yet trade unions engaged in a series of actions in support of Southern Europe; this was remarkable given organizational weaknesses.

Part III concludes the book. Prior to answering the research question, chapter 8 assesses difference in substantive outcomes between countries; this is a potential 'smoking gun' in that it illustrates drivers and consequences of competition and/or cooperation. Consistent with literature on dualization (Emmenegger *et al.*, 2012), I contend that divisions among countries can be linked to the interests of workers in the core, even if the means by which divides have been instigated are indirect. Specifically, the advantage of core countries within the Eurozone benefits national workforces to the degree that strategies for European solidarity are weakly prioritized and consequently unsuccessful. I also suggest that such partitions evoke Marxist-Leninist theories of imperialism, though stress differences between contemporary and historical contexts.

Chapter 9 then answers the research question. It is argued that, rather than being based on cooperation, the behaviour of labour tends to facilitate competition between national regimes. Owing to the nationally embedded nature of labour movements, which is itself in the interests of certain workers, bargaining processes tend to lead to an unplanned yet incremental drift towards zero-sum outcomes which benefit national workforces in stronger structural positions. Strategies which aim to correct discrepant outcomes, which become particularly necessary at times of crisis, are generally unsuccessful. Not only are attempts at European cooperation weakly prioritized by labour movements, which is related to the tendency for certain workers to benefit from the status quo, but difficulties associated with collective action mean they can be easily vetoed. I argue that this theory may be generalized to other settings, though emphasize the extent to which it is specific to contemporary Europe. Implications for the Europeanization of social democracy and theories of institutions and the employment relationship are also discussed.

A final chapter sets out an argument about the role of labour in the process of European integration. Rather than facilitating Europeanization, as certain theories predict, relations between separate labour movements tend to be based on national interests and, within EMU, unequal relations form between strong and weak. It is argued that such developments validate intergovernmentalist theories of European integration and, consistent with an emerging agenda which underlines the capacity of the EU to disintegrate, point to the ability of labour sectionalism to undermine the European project. An agenda for future research is also outlined. I discuss the degree to which new studies might advance knowledge of asymmetric relations between labour movements, encourage investigation into the capacity of actors to prioritize competing goals and emphasize the need for further work on the manner in which non-state actors drive the (dis)integration process. Finally, it is stressed that, notwithstanding tendencies for competition, the endurance of the EU is unequivocally in the interests of labour; I end by evaluating ways in which the EU might be reformed so as to strengthen institutional grounds for labour cooperation.

2

How do labour movements respond to European integration? Surveying the field

Challenges currently facing European labour movements are novel, yet a rich literature bears witness to the historic manner in which labour has responded to European integration. In this chapter, so as to root later analysis in relevant debates, I conduct an in-depth survey of this literature. I commence with an examination of historic attempts by labour to respond to European integration. Though prominent political economists writing after the Maastricht Treaty emphasized processes of competition (Rhodes, 1998a; Scharpf, 1999; Streeck, 1996), scholars who underline actor agency have focused upon initiatives which aim at cooperation; this literature examines attempts by unions to engage in European dialogue with employers and public authorities (Falkner, 1998), unilateral efforts by unions to cooperate on a European scale (Erne, 2008) and the Europeanization of social-democratic parties (Ladrech, 2000).

Notwithstanding achievements of this scholarship, I contend that such work inadequately theorizes the manner in which labour competition and/or cooperation affect substantive conditions in labour markets. Research on dualization is therefore evaluated; this literature provides valuable insight into the relationship between labour behaviour and substantive change, though fails to conceptualize forces external to nation states (Emmenegger *et al.*, 2012; Palier and Thelen, 2010). Third, I introduce controversies regarding labour movements and the broader trajectory of European integration. The manner in which theories such as neofunctionalism and intergovernmentalism aid understandings of labour movements is appraised, before it is asserted that the reaction of labour to the crisis provides rich material for reconsideration of prevailing approaches.

European integration: a series of constraints for organized labour?

Concern for labour movements has never been a primary driver of European integration. Aside from the imperative of avoiding another war, the statesmen who initiated the European project in decades after the Second World War desired greater economic integration (Middelaar, 2014). The first significant moves towards integration, namely the European Coal and Steel Community (1951) and European Economic Community (1957), therefore involved the opening of European markets. Subsequent steps were incremental, a result of divisions among member states, yet further integration assumed a mainly economic form. From its inception, the European project thus involved constraints for labour (Scharpf, 1999). Not only did integration enhance capital mobility, but it raised the possibility of regulatory competition among member states. Such themes would prove to be perennial, though in early decades the relatively homogenous profile of founder states ensured that they were less pressing.

Following decades were to see extensive progress towards economic integration. In 1985, in response to years of stagnation in Europe and early globalization, the Delors Commission formulated a strategy for completion of the European single market (Jabko, 2006). This initiative was to prove revolutionary. Aiming for achievement by 1992, the single market project attempted to remove barriers to closer economic integration. In practical terms, this implied legislation which abolished restrictions in some fields yet harmonized standards in others. During these years, multiple regulation was introduced in spheres as diverse as taxation, competition and consumer protection. This endeavour did not end in 1992; deepening of the single market became the overriding motivation of successive European Commissions (Fligstein and Mara-Drita, 1996).

The introduction of a single currency was to prove equally transformative. There had been attempts to work towards currency integration for years, and these efforts culminated in the launch of EMU by the 1992 Maastricht Treaty (Dyson and Featherstone, 1999). The treaty established a set of criteria for those member states who wished to embark on EMU; these included a limit of government debt to 60 per cent of GDP, restrictions on budget deficits to 3 per cent of GDP and the stipulation that consumer price inflation and the long-term interest rate should be within parameters set by best-performing member states. Challenges were encountered meeting these targets, yet the euro was launched on 1 January 1999 and monetary policy became controlled by the European Central Bank (ECB).

Changes associated with the single market and EMU were therefore ground-breaking. Labour movements were particularly affected; those elements of the European project which had always threatened them had been significantly intensified. There were three specific challenges: (i) the neoliberal policies which supported the European economic regime; (ii) the freedom such a system provided to capital; and (iii) the limited potential of corrective policies. The first of these challenges was associated with both the single market and EMU. With the aim of deepening the single market, measures were implemented which abolished monopolies and liberalized barriers to competition (Nikolinakos, 2006). Preparation for euro entry involved painful reforms to public finances, while the ECB adopted a hawkish line on inflation. Such measures disadvantaged labour movements. Not only did these policies put pressure on working conditions in industries exposed to greater competition, but considerable cuts were made to welfare states and public sectors. The closure upon which national regulation was historically predicated was also undermined (Dølvik and Visser, 2009).

A second challenge was the freedom this regime provided to capital. Owing to its reduction of barriers to cross-border business, the single market involved new opportunities for firms to enter markets (Streeck, 1998). EMU enhanced this mobility; it further facilitated business between member states and cross-border financial transactions. Such mobility disadvantaged labour. As a result of increased exit options enjoyed by employers in negotiations with unions, there was a tendency for wage rises to be limited. Heightened capital mobility also discouraged public policy friendly to labour. Given that firms had greater capacity to leave jurisdictions in which regulatory environments were unfavourable, authorities had incentives not to introduce measures which were inimical to business interests.

A third challenge was the limited potential of corrective policies. Aside from the difficulties which enhanced capital mobility posed to policymakers who wished to fortify regulation, there were specific problems associated with the European polity. A key issue was that the correction of markets was more onerous than the making of markets. As Scharpf famously observed (1996), European integration was particularly conducive to deregulation given that it was easier to agree upon the removal of regulation than its introduction. Constraints on monetary and fiscal policy associated with the single currency were also decisive. Because EMU removed the devaluation option and limited fiscal autonomy, traditional means of adjustment became unviable. Policymakers were instead forced to implement internal devaluations; these involved deflationary fiscal policies and labour market deregulation (Stockhammer and Sotiropoulos, 2014).

The existence of these constraints made several political economists pessimistic about the prospects of European labour. Building on the insights of earlier literature, Streeck emphasized the extent to which European integration was inimical to the interests of labour movements

(1994; 1997). Not only were attempts to correct European markets dismissed as inadequate, but the difficulties of the structural position of labour were underlined. Many of these challenges were catholic; union density had declined across developed countries from the 1980s and there were long-standing barriers to international trade unionism. In addition to such general problems, the European project was regarded as particularly unfavourable to labour and the constraints identified above were repeatedly emphasized. European labour movements were moreover regarded as likely to respond to such challenges by competing with one another, rather than engaging in cooperation. Noting the stickiness of national institutions and collective action problems, Streeck led a school of researchers who emphasized the tendency of unions to conclude agreements which undercut counterparts in other member states.

Certain developments in the 1990s were consistent with this view. Not only were attempts at European cooperation distinguished by serious problems, but unions sometimes adopted strategies which exerted pressure on European colleagues. Scholars of European works councils (EWCs) commented upon the trend (Streeck, 1997), yet tripartite pacts which aimed to achieve greater competitiveness and/or the criteria for euro entry were particularly notable. These agreements involved wage restraint and were concluded in a series of European countries. Given differences with traditional corporatist agreements, pacts of earlier decades put greater emphasis on redistribution, the competitive character of later agreements was underlined; one study spoke of 'competitive corporatism' (Rhodes, 1998a) while Streeck labelled the agreements 'alliance[s] between nationalism and neoliberalism' (as cited in Rhodes, 1998b: 53). The agency of unions nonetheless remained under-theorized. Though studies sometimes inferred that unions knowingly engaged in such behaviour, this issue was seldom discussed overtly.

In years following the Maastricht Treaty, prominent political economists therefore contended that integration prompted competition between labour movements (Rhodes, 1998a; Scharpf, 1999; Streeck, 1996); this view emphasized structural influences and became prevalent in the discipline of political economy. Notwithstanding consensus among these researchers, scholars in fields such as social policy and industrial relations paid greater attention to cooperative strategies which involved actor agency. Such undertakings proliferated in the post-Maastricht era and may be grouped in three categories: (i) attempts by unions to engage in European dialogue with employers and public authorities; (ii) unilateral efforts by unions to cooperate on a European scale; (iii) the Europeanization of social-democratic political parties. In the following sections, I appraise each of these initiatives.

From European social dialogue to European works councils: responding to integration with dialogue

Even if the onset of a European system of industrial relations had long been forecast (Dunlop, 1958: 75), early attempts at dialogue between management and labour were tentative. Joint committees existed in those sectors in which political and economic integration was most substantial and tripartite European summits were held in the 1970s, yet the profile of these institutions was rather minor. Socially minded actors nonetheless insisted that social union should accompany economic union and, following particular concern that the European single market would expose member states to social dumping, in 1985 Commission President Jacques Delors attempted to induce dialogue between ETUC and the employers' associations UNICE and CEEP. The results of the so-called Val Duchesse dialogue, the name inspired by the château near Brussels at which the parties met, were nonetheless hamstrung by their non-legally binding character and the exclusion of the pay issue.

More concerted efforts were made to establish European corporatism at the time of the Maastricht Treaty. The Social Protocol, annexed to the Maastricht Treaty in 1992 as a result of the opposition of the UK Conservative Government to European social policy, provided social partners with the right to conclude legally binding and non-legally binding European collective agreements (Nakano, 2014). In following years, a series of agreements were implemented via legally binding Council directive. Some greeted these developments with optimism; certain scholars of industrial relations and social policy, who tended to emphasize procedures and potential for actor-led development, heralded the onset of Euro-corporatism (Falkner, 1998; Jensen *et al.*, 1999; Welz, 2008). In a work which examined the genesis and trajectory of the dialogue, Falkner (1998) asserted that a 'corporatist social policy community' had emerged.

Other responses to the European social dialogue's new competences were unenthusiastic. The dialogue attracted a series of detractors in its first decade, this school making three key criticisms. The first related to the organization of the European social partners. Aside from the limited resources which national social partners continued to dedicate to the European level, attention was drawn to the difficulty of European social partners with diverse national affiliates resolving the collective action problem (Keller, 2003; Keller and Sörries, 1999). Second, the limited legal competences with which the dialogue was endowed were also underlined. Though the Social Protocol had made the conclusion of European agreements possible for the first time, critics noted that crucial substantive issues such as pay and social security remained outside the competences of the dialogue and thus excluded from negotiations

(Streeck, 1994). A third criticism was the dependence of the dialogue on the European Commission. As a consequence of the unwillingness of European employers to enter into meaningful dialogue and the limited mobilization capacity of European trade unions, it was noticed that employer readiness to negotiate was heavily contingent on the threat of legislation (Streeck, 1994).

These critiques appeared increasingly prescient. Notwithstanding the inter-sectoral agreements produced in the 1990s, the dialogue showed little sign of the maturation foreseen by optimists. Agreements were concluded infrequently, there was little indication of deepening national social partner commitment to the dialogue and pay negotiations appeared a distant prospect. Nor did the 1998 launch of European sectoral social dialogue committees (SSDCs) do much to improve matters. Though committees became established in a number of sectors and would take on increasing importance, such institutions were marked by similar frailties (Keller, 2003). Subsequent developments would do little to allay the fears of sceptics. In reaction to aforementioned problems and impending enlargement of the EU, non-legally binding output was increasingly produced; the Telework Agreement (2002), Work-related Stress Agreement (2004), Harassment and Violence at Work Agreement (2007) and Inclusive Labour Markets Agreement (2010) were implemented by affiliates of social partners rather than European directive. Researchers tended to agree that the effects of this output were weak (Ertel *et al.*, 2010; Larsen and Andersen, 2007; Prosser, 2011).

European dialogue at the level of the firm has also been initiated by unions. Such cooperation took place in post-war decades, unions maintained intra-firm networks and councils for European dialogue existed in certain firms, yet the 1994 European Works Council (EWC) Directive represented a watershed. This measure provided employees with the right to establish EWCs in firms with 1,000 employees in the EU/ EEA and 150 employees in each of at least two member states and stipulated that 'the exchange of views and establishment of dialogue between employees' representatives and central management' should take place. The directive moreover specified that EWCs in existence prior to 22 September 1996 would enjoy exemption from certain restrictive terms. This initiated a flurry of activity among firms anxious to avoid the statutory model. Over a thousand EWCs would eventually be created, yet coverage of the directive would continue to be a disappointment; by 2012, EWCs were established in only half of eligible firms (EurWORK, 2012).

The existence of EWCs prompted considerable academic interest. Such work addressed a range of topics; several studies interrogated the compatibility of the directive with national law (Bercusson, 1996; Blanpain and Windey, 1996; Rigaux and Dorssemont, 1999), while others examined factors which influenced adoption of EWCs (Marginson,

1992; 1998; Streeck and Vitols, 1995). There was debate about the wider significance of EWCs. A first group of scholars was optimistic. Though structural impediments were recognized, emphasis was placed on the opportunities such organs provided to actors; a series of studies underlined the potential of EWCs to prompt cross-European cooperation between unions (Lecher, 1994; Martinez Lucio and Weston, 2000). Work also stressed the significance of EWCs in a European system of industrial relations. Certain scholars suggested that EWCs would encourage European collective bargaining at firm level (Bobke and Müller, 1995), while others emphasized the role of the directive in creating European corporatism (Falkner, 1996; Knutsen, 1997).

A second group was pessimistic. These authorities emphasized structural barriers to successful EWCs; such obstacles included the neoliberal nature of the European project and difficulties associated with collective action. Specific problems with the EWC Directive were also identified. According to Streeck (1997; 1998), a foremost critic who tended to benchmark EWCs against German works councils, the directive failed to guarantee sufficient participation rights and was hamstrung by its voluntary implementation model. Others identified practical problems; these included the lack of resources available to unions, challenges associated with issue aggregation and arbitration difficulties (Keller, 1996; 1997). It was even suggested that EWCs could encourage regime competition. Streeck (1997) warned of the potential of the voluntary form of the directive to prompt coalitions between central management and domestic workforces, while the capacity of EWCs to undermine national industrial relations institutions was also foreseen (Keller, 1995; Schulten, 1996).

Limitations associated with the original EWC Directive inspired calls for its fortification. After years of union lobbying, a 2009 revision better defined rights of EWCs to information and consultation and provided unions with greater influence. Scholarly appraisal nonetheless tended to be negative; most concurred that revision had done little to strengthen EWCs (De Spiegelaere, 2016). Aside from procedures for European consultation guaranteed by EWCs, the European Company Statute also sets out rights for employee involvement through board-level participation and 'representative bod[ies]'. Such provisions are not ground-breaking, yet usefully supplement existing forms of representation (Gold and Schwimbersky, 2008).

Is unilateral action more effective?

Efforts to respond to integration through dialogue with public authorities and employers have thus been beset by weakness and, given problems associated with multilateral action, unilateral initiatives have been undertaken by unions. One strategy is collective bargaining coordination. So as to combat wage dumping, certain unions in different member states share information with the aim of coordinating bargaining demands. Such initiatives have a long history. Metal sector unions established informal bodies for the exchange of information in the 1970s and, as EMU progressed in the 1990s, there was increasing interest in such strategies. Following a law that limited wage rises vis-à-vis the country's competitors, Belgian unions established the Doorn group in 1997; this association united confederations from Belgium, Germany, Luxembourg and the Netherlands with the aim of avoiding wage competition. The group met annually in years after its formation, though difficulties associated with inter-sectoral coordination led to the eventual unravelling of the initiative (Glassner and Pochet, 2011).

Less formidable coordination problems mean sectoral networks have fared better. The record of the metal sector is particularly notable. The exposed profile of the industry and higher rates of union density lend themselves to such endeavours, and in the 1990s unions established institutions which aimed to coordinate bargaining. A centrepiece of such efforts was adoption by the European Metalworkers' Federation (EMF) of a 'European Coordination Rule'; this principle aimed to compensate workers for price increases plus 'balanced participation' in productivity gains (EMF, 1998 cited in Glassner and Pochet, 2011). Research found that these networks helped impede wage dumping (Traxler and Brandl, 2009). Similar initiatives have been implemented in other European sectors. Federations such as UNI Europa Finance, European Trade Union Federation Textiles, Clothing, Leather (ETUC-TCL) and European Federation for Public Service Unions (EPSU) have developed such programmes (Glassner and Pochet, 2011), though measures are often less advanced than those in the metal sector.

Notwithstanding these achievements, the record of attempts at European bargaining coordination is somewhat modest. Such initiatives exist in a minority of sectors, are often insipidly developed and problems exist with implementation. Glassner and Pochet (2011) identify four factors which inhibit the efficacy of such endeavours. First, the extent of coverage of collective bargaining at national level is often limited; declining rates of density constrain the ability of unions to determine wages and an increasing number of workers are covered by minimum wage legislation. Second, coordination between systems which are distinguished by single-employer and multi-employer bargaining regimes is also challenging, while, third, practical differences such as variance in the duration of collective agreements and the scope of sectoral domains exacerbate such difficulties. Finally, deviation in the content of collective agreements impedes meaningful comparison between countries.

Unions have also attempted European coordination of action. Cross-border actions have long been an ambition of the international labour movement, yet there are a series of traditional problems. Not only does neoliberalism sometimes intensify chauvinistic attitudes among national workforces, but diverse organizational resources and comparative advantages mean that collective action is particularly onerous to accomplish (Jakopovich, 2011). Though such difficulties have also affected European initiatives, a number of efforts have been made to achieve European synchronization of strikes and demonstrations. Aside from the endeavours of networks such as ATTAC and Euromarch, which attempt to organize such actions, significant protests have been provoked by the European public authorities. Plans for directives on services and the liberalization of ports activated continent-wide protests and considerable success was achieved (Turnbull, 2006). The particular capacity of unions in sectors such as transport to organize such actions has not gone unnoticed; this is a result of the lack of direct competition among national transport sectors (Silver, 2008).

The most comprehensive study of pan-European union action is the work of Erne (2008). This book-length investigation, based on case studies of union reactions to transnational company mergers, was optimistic about the capacity of unions to respond to European economic integration. The propensity of unions to engage in competitive wage restraint was acknowledged, yet countervailing examples of effective European mobilizations were emphasized; in the case of ABB Alstom Power, unions successfully contested a transnational merger which threatened job losses. Though such outcomes were contingent upon favourable conditions, the prospects of European labour were considered auspicious and a tendency for demonstrations to target initiatives of the European public authorities was underlined (p. 199).

Many European protests would take place after the outbreak of crisis; these were organized in Brussels and coordinated locations and sought to unite European unions against austerity. Such actions inspired a literature which charted their extent (Dufresne and Pernot, 2013) and was sometimes optimistic about wider significance (Anduiza *et al.*, 2014), though some authorities remained unimpressed. In an article which lamented the inability of unions to organize a European general strike, Dribbusch (2015) criticized the attitude of unions in countries such as Germany. European actions can nonetheless be said to be an established habit, even if their extent and efficacy will continue to be queried by sceptics.

The Europeanization of social democracy: a frustrated project?

Despite overlap between the launch of integration and a post-war golden age of social democracy, initial movement towards Europeanization of social democracy was limited. This was not the result of hostility to integration on the part of social democrats. Though there were worries about the liberal nature of the European Economic Community, the potential of integration to achieve peace meant that the European project was widely supported. Lack of progress reflected the slow pace of integration; in early decades there was comparative national disinterest in European affairs and direct elections to the European Parliament were not held until 1979 (Ladrech, 2009). Scholarly attention on the topic lags to this day, yet the higher profile which European integration has enjoyed in recent decades has encouraged a body of literature. This scholarship has examined two main themes: (i) the emergence of a social-democratic grouping in the European Parliament; and (ii) the extent to which national social-democratic parties have Europeanized. The capacity of social democracy to perform these feats is crucial to the ability of labour to respond to integration.

A first strand of literature has resulted directly from the rise of the Party of European Socialists (PES). PES was founded in 1992 and is represented in the European Parliament by the Progressive Alliance of Socialists and Democrats. The party has enjoyed a series of accomplishments. Not only has a common manifesto been published for European elections, but internal organization has improved; PES now employs its own staff rather than seconded officials, while 2002 competitive elections for the PES presidency represented a further breakthrough. These achievements have inspired hopeful evaluations of PES. After progress in the 1990s, Ladrech expressed optimism about the potential of the party (2000). According to Ladrech, the establishment of PES provided social-democratic parties with a network which was able to coordinate national activities on a European scale.

There were nonetheless impediments to further development; weaknesses of the European Parliament and lack of a classic left–right divide at European level precluded the party system found in member states, while differences of opinion among PES members frustrated collective action. The neoliberal nature of the European project, which was at odds with the preference of social-democratic electorates, also incentivized social-democratic parties 'to steer clear of European matters and to focus instead on domestic issues' (Mattila and Raunio, 2006: 603). Following the slowing of European integration in the 2000s, investigation into PES tended to be more sceptical. Lightfoot (2005) emphasized barriers to the better functioning of PES. On the basis of case studies in the areas of employment and the environment, it was argued that, although PES fulfilled a coordinating role, the extent of its influence was exaggerated. Existing literature was also considered to underplay impediments to the development of PES, for example domestic policy imperatives and ideological differences. Increasing Euroscepticism was additionally considered uniquely unfavourable to PES; high support for the European project among social democrats left them particularly vulnerable to loss of political support associated with this trend (Külahci and Lightfoot, 2014: 74).

A second strand of literature examines the extent to which national social-democratic parties have Europeanized. As with other literatures which attempt to assess degrees of Europeanization, for example investigation on the implementation of European soft law (López-Santana, 2006), this endeavour has encountered methodological issues; such problems are related to the lack of direct European influence on political parties and the consequent need to evaluate indirect relationships. Notwithstanding these difficulties, work has emerged on the Europeanization of political parties which grapples with salient issues. This research has tackled topics such as programmatic change, organizational change, patterns of party competition, party–government relations and relations beyond the national party system (Ladrech, 2009).

Some of this work has concerned social-democratic parties, though specific investigation on the Europeanization of social-democratic parties in Western Europe has remained scarce. Interesting scholarship on the Europeanization of social democracy in East-Central Europe (ECE) has appeared. The publication of such work is related to less pressing methodological challenges associated with this region. Because ECE political parties emerged at a time when European integration was advanced and the impact of processes of Europeanization was often highly visible, establishing links between cause and effect was easier. In a study of the Europeanization of Hungarian social democracy, it was contended that processes of ideational, policy and information transfer had changed ECE social-democratic parties to a considerable degree (Ágh, 2004: 10). These conclusions indicate progress in ECE countries, though lack of scholarship in Western Europe suggests that Europeanization is underdeveloped in this region; this will concern those who aim for greater coordination of social democracy.

In recent years there has also been reflection on implications of the crisis for the Europeanization of social democracy. Following the outbreak of public sentiment hostile to political establishments and the EU, broadly caustic for social democrats, certain assessments have been sceptical. In a volume edited by Meyer and Rutherford (2012), contributors linked electoral defeats of social democrats to the embrace of liberal economic principles; it was contended that revival of the movement required a new approach. Studies of the reaction of PES to the Eurozone crisis have been pessimistic. Though Holmes and Lightfoot (2014) conceded that PES had made efforts to arrive at joint positions against austerity, it was concluded that the impact of actions was generally weak; reasons for this were associated with the obstacles which had long impeded greater Europeanization of social democracy. Notwithstanding less sanguine assessments, certain studies have sounded a more optimistic note. Taking issue with the assumption that associations between social democrats and trade unions were eroding, a work edited by Allern and Bale (2017) found significant variation in relationships across European countries. It emerged that party–union links were more robust when unions were stronger and parties had less support from the state.

European labour after the crisis: in search of a new approach

Though attempts by unions and social-democratic parties to engage in cooperation have been disparaged, often by political economists who emphasize processes of competition, much literature is therefore optimistic. The centrality of the processes examined by these researchers can nonetheless be critiqued; institutions such as EWCs and collective bargaining networks arguably have little impact upon key substantive outcomes. Work which emphasizes competition conceptualizes effects on labour markets more successfully (Rhodes, 1998a; Streeck, 1996), yet this scholarship is dated as the nature of the European project has changed markedly in recent years.

Owing to weaknesses of existing scholarship, a new theory of the manner in which labour movements respond to integration is timely. Developments associated with the European sovereign debt crisis provide rich material. Following economic crisis and burgeoning levels of debt in countries on the periphery of the Eurozone, the EU intervened in a series of indebted member states; aid was nonetheless contingent upon austerity measures which exacerbated inequality and provoked mass opposition. These events inspired debate about labour movements. Not only was there controversy concerning the achievement of wage moderation by German unions, but division among social democrats was observed; parties in core countries were sometimes accused of indifference to conditions in the periphery. Certain optimists have even revised their positions. In a 2015 work, Erne argued that the technocratic form of European economic governance diminished the likelihood of successful resistance.

Literature concerning the Eurozone crisis provides clues as to how a new approach might be operationalized. Following the trend for core countries to achieve lower ULCs than periphery countries, certain accounts located this phenomenon in the superior coordination capacity of core social partners. Hancké (2013) and Hassel (2014) advanced arguments based on varieties-of-capitalism theory, asserting that northern European coordinated market economies (CMEs) have greater ability to achieve wage restraint than southern European mixed market economies (MMEs). The most comprehensive exposition of the argument has been made by Johnston (2016). In a book-length study, it was contended that the corporatist structure of northern European labour markets provided them with advantage over southern rivals. Particular attention was paid to differences between exposed and non-exposed sectors. Even if exposed industries in certain periphery countries exercised restraint, overall competitiveness was lost as a result of indiscipline in non-exposed sectors. This did not occur in a country such as Germany; in this case, efficient wage-setting mechanisms in non-exposed industries allowed overall moderation.

Though others have queried whether differences in ULCs were at the root of the crisis (Müller *et al.*, 2015), the relationship between labour movements and the crisis raises several questions. Aside from the role of wage retrenchment in a country such as Germany, these questions include the degree of trade union intent in this process, comparative changes to the position of different labour movements and the attitude of labour movements to austerity in other member states.

The latter issue has been the subject of academic attention. In analysis of union participation in the 14 November 2012 European Day of Action and Solidarity, Dufresne and Pernot (2013) identified three degrees of input: (i) general strikes; (ii) mass demonstrations; and (iii) symbolic actions and/or messages of solidarity. The contribution of unions in periphery countries tended to be classed in the first category, whereas the actions of unions in core countries tended to be placed in the third category. Dribbusch (2015) has also been critical of the extent to which unions in the core exhibited solidarity with periphery counterparts. It is argued that not only were core unions comparatively indifferent to the plight of Southern Europe, but that more vigorous participation might have derailed austerity.

Such discussions provide auspicious material for reflection on the question of whether labour movements compete and/or cooperate in response to European integration. In chapter 3, I operationalize my research question with reference to these debates.

What are the consequences of competition and cooperation? Linking labour behaviour with substantive outcomes

Though a body of literature has chronicled the manner in which labour movements compete and/or cooperate in response to integration, a weakness of this scholarship is the unsatisfactory manner in which it links such behaviour with substantive change. Some studies concentrate almost exclusively on procedural developments; certain analyses of the European social dialogue root claims about Europeanization in new forms of actor behaviour, while remaining less interested in consequences (Falkner, 1998: 186–207). Other literature is more sensible to relevant relationships; work on competitive corporatism (Rhodes, 1998a) is concerned with wage moderation while studies of pan-European union action (Erne, 2008) attempt to establish consequences of actor behaviour, yet this endeavour is often a secondary priority. Failure to adequately theorize such links raises questions about the significance of studied processes.

In this work, I aim to establish robust links between theorized processes and continuity/change in labour market conditions. I examine influences on levels of unemployment and employment security and, through establishment of relationships between these variables and competition and/or cooperation, demonstrate the importance of studied processes. Methodological justification for evaluation of these variables is outlined in chapter 3. Given problems which established work encounters in conceptualizing such associations, it is necessary to draw inspiration from another literature. I turn to work on dualization; this scholarship theorizes the relationship between substantive change and worker agency through analysis of the propensity of labour markets to become divided among insiders and outsiders (Emmenegger *et al.*, 2012; Palier and Thelen, 2010). Such research also concerns divisions based upon unemployment and employment security, which inspires my analysis of these variables.

Concerns about insiders and outsiders in labour markets have long abounded in Europe (see Rueda, 2007, for an overview of this literature). From the 1970s, as the result of an economic crisis which saw the return of mass unemployment, economists began to comment upon discrepancies in the access of workers to employment (Lindbeck and Snower, 1987). Though the trend of unemployment at first assumed little geographical or institutional pattern (western European countries of diverse locations and business systems were all at one stage seriously affected), the development was associated with declining industries exposed to global competition. In sectors such as mining and parts of manufacturing, large-scale restructuring left millions in long-term unemployment (Ljungqvist and Sargent, 1998). These individuals often became dependent on welfare payments, tended to be concentrated in particular localities and their rates of re-integration into the labour market were disappointing. Economists contrasted the prospects of such outsiders with those of insiders. The latter, often based in more prosperous regions, were thus labelled because of their access to employment.

Many esteemed the genesis of this divide to lie in the substantial rights still afforded to European workers. In the opinion of neoliberals, the terms and conditions set by labour law and collective agreements raised the cost of labour and increased the probability of unemployment. The influence of insiders, which was exercised through trade unions (Carruth and Oswald, 1987), was considered crucial to this status quo (Lindbeck and Snower, 1988; 2001). This thesis won widespread acceptance in the 1990s. Double-digit unemployment had endured in continental Europe for many years, and rigid labour law and strong trade unions were increasingly held culpable (Esping-Andersen and Regini, 2000).

A second form assumed by insider–outsider divisions was disparate levels of protection afforded to workers in employment. As a consequence of elevated rates of unemployment and the growing perception that labour markets in Europe were over-regulated, from the 1980s the peripheries of European labour markets began to be liberalized (Esping-Andersen and Regini, 2000). The permission of non-standard forms of employment, such as fixed-term and temporary agency work, according to this rationale, was likely to prompt the integration of excluded groups into the labour market and reduce unemployment. As such reforms were introduced, peripheral workforces grew across Europe.

This second division inspired literature on dualization. This agenda, which was led by political scientists, was concerned with the provenance of contractual insecurity. Though accounts which emphasized universal processes of liberalization called attention to structural factors such as de-industrialization (Kalleberg, 2009), globalization (Standing, 2011) and feminization of the workforce (Standing, 1999), scholars of dualization concentrated on factors related to actors and policy processes. In a study of the Netherlands, Spain and the UK, Rueda (2007) proposed that such divisions were sustained by social-democratic parties acting in the interests of insiders. Because insiders represented a core social-democratic constituency and were threatened by the integration of outsiders into labour markets, left-wing parties were considered unlikely to back policies (such as deregulation of employment protection and active labour market policies) which promoted the interests of outsiders. Outsiders, by contrast, were considered likely to support parties proposing such measures.

Theoretical (Emmenegger, 2009) and empirical (Amable, 2014) critiques were made of this thesis, yet the arguments of Rueda prompted lively interest in the role of insiders in shaping dualization regimes. In a work which conceived of dualization as encompassing wider social policy outcomes, Emmenegger *et al.* (2012) asserted the provenance of insider–outsider partitions to lie in the capture of policy processes by insiders. A 2014 book by Emmenegger added a historical dimension to this argument. In the study, based on assessment of the development of dismissal protection regulation in eight countries, it was contended that dismissal protection was the result of historic power struggles between employers and unions, the outcomes of which became institutionalized. Related explanations were adopted by others. In analysis of the response of core workers to the deregulation of non-standard employment (Eichhorst and Marx, 2011), the ability of insiders to moderate their own wages was emphasized. Certain authorities also developed structural explanations. In a study of processes of liberalization in the United States, Germany, Denmark, Sweden and the Netherlands, Thelen (2014: 23–4) asserted that lower levels of interest association inclusiveness and state capacity made dualization more likely.

In contrast to scholarship which examines the reaction of labour movements to European integration, literature on dualization therefore conceptualizes relations between worker agency and processes of substantive change. Insights from this scholarship inspire my methodological approach, which is elaborated in chapter 3. Though my primary focus in this work is not dualization, my study is relevant to this literature; findings have the potential to add a supranational dimension to existing research. Scholars of dualization have paid careful attention to national policy processes, yet a weakness of literature is its insufficient theorization of forces external to nation states. Given the crucial influence of the European level on labour markets in member states, this is quite an omission. Through assessment of the manner in which processes of competition and/or cooperation lead to divergent conditions in European labour markets, I aim to contribute to debate.

Theorizing integration: time to reconsider the contribution of labour?

If the wider significance of the reaction of labour movements to integration is to be grasped, it is also vital to appreciate broader debates about the nature of European integration. Such exchanges shed light on the genesis and trajectory of integration and have informed research on labour behaviour; many of the most notable studies of the Europeanization of labour movements make extensive reference to theories of integration (Falkner, 1998; Marginson and Sisson, 2004). Given the importance of this literature and my hope to contribute to it, in the following section I delineate its achievements.

Debate about European integration is rooted in two theoretical paradigms, which continue to underpin deliberations. The first, neofunctionalism, emerged in the 1950s in an attempt to theorize the course of the nascent European project (Haas, 1958). Central to neofunctionalism was the concept of 'spillover'. As a result of the propensity of European integration to inter-lock politico-economic functions, proponents of spillover forecast that actors would incrementally transfer loyalties to the European level. Five main types of spillover have been identified (Falkner, 1998): (i) functional spillover (in which interdependence of actors in one sector leads to interdependence in another); (ii) political spillover (a shift in the political loyalties of national actors); (iii) geographical spillover (enlargement to incorporate new member states); (iv) cultivated spillover (in which supranational institutions act as 'midwives' to inter-state bargaining and gradually increase their power base); and (v) cultural spillover (in which cultural expectations of national elites shift to supranational level). Early neofunctionalists spent limited time pondering questions related to labour, yet expected that employment and social policy would undergo spillover. Dunlop predicted that integration would lead to a European industrial relations system (1958: 75).

Adherents of a second theoretical approach, intergovernmentalism, asserted that the process of European integration was primarily state-driven, and that member states were unlikely to cede substantial power to the supranational level (Hoffmann, 1966; 1982). Intergovernmentalists stressed the endurance of national sovereignty, a result of the roots of the school in realist international relations theory, and consequently hypothesized that transferal of policy competences to supranational level would be slight. The role of 'grand bargains' in the European integration process was also underscored. Such bargains, according to the intergovernmentalist argument, ceded limited sovereignty concessions which mutually benefited states and could later be revoked. Early intergovernmentalists spent little time debating the role of labour. The approach nonetheless implied that there would be limited spillover of employment and social policy; this theme would be developed by later scholars.

After a lull in debate during the 1970s and early 1980s, a consequence of the slowing of integration in these years, the reinvigoration of the European project in the mid-1980s led to a renewal in interest. Although debate assumed a less teleological tone, a rudimentary division between those who emphasized processes of spillover and those who stressed the resilience of the European nation state endured. Neofunctionalism re-emerged in a revised format. Most recognized that classic neofunctionalism, with its emphasis on preconceived outcomes and the onset of a federal Europe, was an inadequate way to conceptualize a hybrid EU in which levels of integration differed among policy areas (Marks *et al.*, 1996; Rosamond, 2000). Multi-level governance theory was accordingly conceived. This framework, developed by scholars seeking to theorize the relationship between European institutions and regional governance (Marks, 1993; Marks *et al.*, 1998), contended that autonomous relationships existed among different governance tiers which often bypassed central governments. Actor network theory, an approach which emphasized the role of policy networks in the integration process, also became popular at this time.

The return of theories which emphasized spillover encouraged related scholarship on the Europeanization of organized interests. In a work on the launch of European social dialogue, Falkner (1998) rooted the hypothesis of a 'corporatist social policy community' in neofunctionalist theory. The Maastricht Treaty was considered to be the 'Waterloo' of intergovernmentalism (p. 186); according to Falkner the achievements of the dialogue were the result of deepening government and social partner engagement with the European polity which were congruent with the spillover hypothesis. Other works on the dialogue adopted similar arguments (Jensen *et al.*, 1999; Welz, 2008). Additionally to this scholarship, there was a broader attempt to ground the Europeanization of industrial relations in theories of spillover. In a work inspired by multi-level governance theory, Marginson and Sisson (2004) proposed that trends towards Europeanization in fields as diverse as working time, wage bargaining and employee representation were the result of processes put in motion by European integration.

Renewed debate about the provenance of European integration also prompted fresh interest in intergovernmentalism. A number of authorities came to be associated with renaissance of the theory, yet the work of Moravcsik (1993) was seminal. Seeking to reconcile traditional intergovernmentalism with the reality of ever deeper integration, Moravcsik formulated a theory of liberal intergovernmentalism. Liberal intergovernmentalism was rooted in a three-fold process. At the domestic level, a level downplayed by traditional intergovernmentalism, national preferences were formed through competition between rival interest groups. Governments then advocated these preferences at European level. Finally, if governments were concerned that agreements would not be honoured, transfer of sovereignty to supranational institutions took place.

Revival of interest in intergovernmentalism encouraged related work on employment and social policy. On the basis of his theory of the joint-decision trap, Scharpf (1988) developed the concepts of negative and positive integration (1996). Negative integration was easier to achieve. It demanded the mere removal of existing regulation and the market-making in which European integration specialized tended to be rooted in its logic. Positive integration was more onerous; agreement on new measures was required. Fatefully for advocates of European social policy, development of social Europe necessitated measures based on positive integration. The work of Streeck built on such themes. In a series of studies which emphasized tendencies for actors and policy competences to remain at member state level, the likelihood of the development of a European social policy regime equivalent to national systems was disdained (1994). Specific work on the European social dialogue was also inspired by such arguments; the scepticism of Keller (2003) was underpinned by intergovernmentalist analysis.

Despite continued doubt regarding the explanatory power of grand theories, the crisis has inspired renewed attempts to understand European integration through the lens of classic approaches. There has been fresh interest in neofunctionalism. The recent fortification of EU economic governance appears consistent with the framework, and various authorities have attempted to root developments in spillover theory. In analysis of the centralization of EMU, Niemann and Ioannou (2015: 212) asserted that 'management of the crisis resulted in integrative outcomes owing to … functional dissonances that arose from the incomplete EMU architecture created at Maastricht'.

Intergovernmentalism has also undergone a renaissance. Recent disunity in the EU has been based on traditional fault lines between nation states, and there has been an increasing tendency for decisions to be taken at intergovernmental summits. Scholarship has responded to these developments and the onset of the 'new intergovernmentalism' has been claimed (Bickerton *et al.*, 2015). These authorities concede that EU activity has expanded, albeit with little new competence transfer, yet consider states to remain in control of the integration process.

Aside from the reinterpretation of existing theories of integration, a stimulating recent development is the appearance of approaches which grapple with the dynamics of disintegration. Though theories of European disintegration have been previously discussed, certain neofunctionalists debating the concept of reverse spillover in the 1970s (Schmitter, 1971), recent crises of the EU have inspired particular interest in the concept. Some authorities have been critical of the capacity of prevailing approaches to explain the process of disintegration; this has been attributed to the tendency of existing theories to be both state-centric (Vollaard, 2014) and presuppose the resilience of EU institutions (Rosamond, 2016).

Certain promising avenues for the study of disintegration have nonetheless been identified. Rosamond (2016: 867) suggests that elements of the realist/neorealist approach to international relations are auspicious, while Vollaard (2014) advocates the ideas of Bartolini (2005). Bartolini's approach is considered apt because it conceives of the external consolidation and internal structuring of states as mutually dependent; this implies that, without both control of external borders and ability to internally organize, polities are vulnerable to disintegration (p. 7). Vollaard in turn makes four propositions which are inspired by Bartolini's arguments: (i) the EU's external consolidation has remained weak; (ii) European integration is a continuous source of dissatisfaction; (iii) weak external consolidation restrains political structuring within the EU; and (iv) without full exit options outside the EU, Eurosceptic dissatisfaction induces partial exits within the EU and voice for the exit of others (pp. 9–12). With regard to the role of labour, theories of disintegration evoke concerns about negative integration; scholars have framed the phenomenon of social dumping in these terms (Scharpf, 1999).

The crisis has therefore inspired several new perspectives on European integration. The insights of traditional schools remain essential yet, given the pressure to which the European project has been subjected and the likelihood of future crises, theories of disintegration represent a particularly interesting avenue. This agenda is nevertheless at an early stage, and hypotheses such as those advocated by Vollaard (2014) require empirical testing. A key issue is that recent innovations pay little heed to labour movements. Given the traditional importance of labour to theories of European integration and the role played by labour movements in instigating the crisis, this represents quite an omission. Such a gap nonetheless presents an opportunity, and a key goal of mine is to reconsider contemporary debates about integration so that the significance of labour is recognized.

Literatures outlined in this chapter differ in their orientations, yet all are relevant to the question of whether labour movements compete and/or cooperate in response to integration. In country and analytical chapters, I present material with reference to these debates and aim to build on insights. Prior to doing this, it is necessary to develop a robust methodological approach.

3

Conceptualizing European labour movements in crisis

If I am to theorize the terms in which labour movements react to European integration, it is vital to develop a research design suitable for this task. This endeavour is undertaken in this chapter. I begin by outlining my general approach and conceptualization of labour movements. It is contended that a framework rooted in the discipline of political economy is most appropriate, given that this tradition is particularly concerned with explaining long-term socio-economic outcomes and the role of actors in such processes. A definition of labour movements is also outlined. Though there are problems with the extent to which trade unions and social-democratic parties represent certain categories of workers, I assert that these organizations are most representative and define labour movements in corresponding terms.

Operationalization of the research question is then discussed. The two periods in which the actions of labour movements are evaluated are outlined; these span from the launch of the euro to the outbreak of the sovereign debt crisis (1999–2010) and from the onset of this crisis to its apparent conclusion (2010–15). I delineate the manner in which labour movement competition and/or cooperation is appraised, before setting out studied substantive indicators: levels of unemployment and employment security.

Countries selected for case study are then presented. Four countries which exhibit different values in terms of status within the Eurozone and form of labour movement are chosen, so that deductions about the importance of these variables are as broad as possible. I outline in detail the cases of Germany, Spain, France and Poland and discuss problems presented by each country. Finally, my research methodology and methods are set out. I adopt an approach to the explanation of change which is rooted in historical institutionalism and critical juncture theory and a methodological stance which is based on the work of Blatter and Haverland (2012). Research methods are also delineated, involving semi-structured research interviews and analysis of relevant documentation.

Conceptualizing European labour movements

The goal of my study, namely to appreciate the extent to which labour movements compete or cooperate in response to European integration, is best served by an approach rooted in the discipline of political economy. This tradition is concerned with explaining long-term socio-economic outcomes and the role of actors and institutions in such processes. In the last twenty years, a body of scholarship has markedly contributed to knowledge concerning the behaviour of actors and the relationship of this behaviour with socio-economic institutions (Hall and Soskice, 2001; Streeck and Thelen, 2005). Given that the objective of this work is to conceptualize the long-term behaviour of actors (i.e. labour movements) within given institutions, adoption of a research design grounded in the political economy tradition is most apposite.

This work is concerned with the manner in which labour influences public policy; it is thus crucial to define the terms in which labour is understood. Though it is important to consider the preferences of individual workers, difficulties associated with the conceptualization of aggregate interests mean that examination of the organizations which collectively represent labour is vital. In this work, I focus on the behaviour of trade unions and social-democratic parties. The terms 'labour movement' and 'labour' are used synonymously. Though the extent to which these are the same can be disputed, they are close enough in meaning to do this.

The collective organizations which best represent the interests of workers remain trade unions. Despite years of declining density rates, millions of employees continue to be union members. Trade unions are therefore the key actor in this book; their behaviour is examined in both of the studied processes. More detail about operationalization is set out below. Notwithstanding the extent to which trade unions *are* representative of workers, there are crucial issues associated with the goals and constituencies of unions which must be taken into account. As has long been known, individual unions are distinguished by disparate politico-economic goals and membership structures (Hyman, 2001); such organizations are far from passive representatives of the interests of employees. It is consequently imperative to keep in mind the nature of individual unions and relevant profiles are delineated in country chapters.

Trade unions continue to be proper objects of study for those interested in understanding the dispositions of workers, yet declines in density mean that they are less representative than they once were. In this work, labour movements are also conceived as constituting social-democratic parties. This decision is not unproblematic; social-democratic parties have never unambiguously represented the interests of labour and, in recent years, embrace of third way politics has weakened the connections of these parties with the working classes (Piazza, 2001). As outlined in country chapters, such parties nonetheless continue to have palpable links with workers. Crucially, social-democratic parties also exerted direct influence on the intergovernmental negotiations which were used to resolve the sovereign debt crisis; trade unions tended to be at the margins of such processes. It should nonetheless be emphasized that the role of social-democratic parties is assessed only in the second studied process: the reaction of labour movements to EU-imposed austerity measures.

In recent times, there has been wider critique of the extent to which social-democratic parties are representative of workers and society more generally. This development has been associated with the rise of alternatives to established parties and, across European countries, new-left parties such as Podemos, Syriza and the Corbyn Labour Party have increasingly challenged social democrats (March, 2015). New-left parties claim to represent the will of workers more effectively than social-democratic rivals and certain scholars are sympathetic to such assertions. Though the dispositions of new-left parties are discussed in country chapters, I do not investigate their positions as comprehensively as those of social-democratic parties for two reasons. First, the rise of the new left is very recent; in the period under investigation (1999–2015), such movements were generally absent from mainstream politics. Second, the extent to which new-left parties represent traditional working classes can be disputed; the electoral bases of such parties are primarily disaffected young people and public sector professionals. It be argued that right-populists, another movement which has enjoyed a rise in support, are more representative of low-income workers.

Analysis of trade unions and social-democratic parties allows evaluation of those workers who are part of official structures and have a consequent ability to compete and/or cooperate. As a result of the peculiar memberships of these organizations, there are nonetheless several categories of employees which may be less adequately conceptualized. Such problems are inevitable in a work which compares macro-developments in four countries over a protracted time period, yet country chapters discuss the attitudes of workers who tend to be underrepresented. In chapter 9, I also reflect on the extent to which such workers shared the dispositions of better represented counterparts.

Operationalizing European labour movements in crisis

Having outlined the disciplinary tradition in which this book is written and conceptualized labour movements, it is now necessary to delineate the manner in which my research question is operationalized. This is a crucial endeavour. Labour movements react to European integration in a multitude of ways and, given the diverse nature of these responses, a single study cannot hope to conceptualize all of these processes. As one would expect, the cases selected by previous works are inextricably linked to the broader arguments of authors (Erne, 2008; Falkner, 1998); conclusions would have differed had alternative cases been selected. This work will not be free of this problem, an ambition beyond any researcher, yet I aspire to select cases which establish better links with substantive outcomes. As emphasized, existing studies can be criticized for their weak theorization of such outcomes. In the two processes which are studied in this book, namely the collective bargaining strategies of unions in the first decade of the Eurozone (1999–2010) and the reaction of labour movements to the sovereign debt crisis (2010–15), I forge links with key substantive indicators.

Previous efforts to theorize the reaction of labour to integration have examined processes of collective bargaining (Falkner, 1998; Gollbach and Schulten, 2000). Though these studies have arrived at penetrative findings, it can be contended that many of the cases examined by these works are peripheral; the European social dialogue and collective bargaining networks arguably have little effect on procedures and outcomes in labour markets. I aspire to examine bargaining practices which are not affected by this problem. As is well-known, there is longstanding controversy regarding the extent to which wage-setting practices in certain European countries instigated the crisis. Many argue that wage-moderation in core countries after the launch of the euro directly led to significant trade imbalances, which in turn prompted escalating levels of debt and eventual crisis (Hassel, 2014; Johnston, 2016). Given the centrality of such processes to debates about labour markets in Europe, they provide excellent case study material. Study of this issue necessarily touches upon arguments about the degree to which the crisis was caused by collective bargaining outcomes in core Eurozone countries (Hassel, 2014; Johnston, 2016; Müller et al., 2015), yet my goal is to appraise the extent to which the behaviour of unions was underpinned by rationales of competition and/or cooperation with counterparts in other European countries.

In each of the four studied countries, detailed examination of union bargaining strategies is undertaken via research interviews, documentary analysis and review of relevant literature; more information on research methods is outlined below. On the basis of this data, the extent to which union strategies were underpinned by rationales

Table 3.1 Defining competition and cooperation

	What constitutes competition?	What constitutes cooperation?
Period one: the collective bargaining strategies of unions in the first decade of the Eurozone (1999–2010)	The conscious attempt to obtain advantage over rivals in other European countries through wage moderation. If unions engage in this activity, evidence of it should be apparent in source material.	The conscious attempt to set wages through cooperation with European counterparts. Such cooperation can take place through collective bargaining networks, informal dialogue and/or bilateral relationships. If unions engage in this activity, evidence of it should be apparent in source material.
Period two: the reaction of labour movements to the sovereign debt crisis (2010–15)	Lack of solidarity with counterparts in Southern Europe is considered a *de facto* form of competition. Solidarity is evaluated through assessment of (i) the willingness of labour movements to undertake strikes and protests in support of southern European counterparts and (ii) the extent to which unions lobbied national public authorities and social-democratic parties aimed at legislative solutions.	Solidarity is considered a proxy for cooperation. Solidarity is evaluated through assessment of (i) the willingness of labour movements to undertake strikes and protests in support of southern European counterparts and (ii) the extent to which unions lobbied national public authorities and social-democratic parties aimed at legislative solutions.

of competition and/or cooperation is appraised (see table 3.1). Competition is conceived as the conscious attempt to obtain advantage over rivals in other European countries through wage moderation. If unions engage in this activity, evidence of it should be apparent in examined sources. Cooperation is conceived as the conscious attempt to set wages through collaboration with European counterparts. Such cooperation can take place through collective bargaining networks, informal dialogue and/or bilateral relationships. If unions engage in this activity, evidence of it should also be apparent in investigated sources. It is possible that analysis will yield little evidence of either competition or cooperation; if this is the case, the question of alternative influences will be raised.

In the second period, which spans from the 2010 outbreak of the crisis to its apparent end in 2015, the extent to which labour movements in the four countries demonstrated solidarity with counterparts in the periphery is examined. The absence and presence of solidarity are equated with competition and cooperation; this is discussed in more detail below. In these years, significant measures of austerity were implemented in countries such as Greece, Ireland, Portugal and Spain. According to some authorities (Dribbusch, 2015; Dufresne and Pernot, 2013), labour movements in certain European countries were somewhat indifferent to the passage of these programmes. Owing to such allegations and the impact of austerity on substantive conditions in labour markets, evaluation of the actions of labour movements during these years will allow for assessment of labour competition and/or cooperation. Given that this period has been considered a 'critical juncture' (Capoccia and Kelemen, 2007), a time in which deep institutional change occurs and actor agency is unusually high, analysis will yield especially rich insight into the behaviour of labour movements.

Appraisal of a notion as general as solidarity is best performed with qualitative methods, this approach having been adopted by studies with related aims (Dribbusch, 2015; Dufresne and Pernot, 2013), yet it is necessary to establish appropriate means of measuring this concept. A first element of my assessment of solidarity involves evaluation of the willingness of labour movements to undertake concrete actions in support of benighted counterparts. Key examples of such activities are strikes and protests; less obvious forms of action, such as collaborations with sister organizations in affected countries, are also considered. Dufresne and Pernot (2013) identify three degrees of input in the pan-European protests which took place in this period: participation in (i) general strikes, (ii) mass demonstrations and (iii) symbolic actions and/or messages of solidarity. This scheme inspires assessment of the degree to which labour movements supported colleagues in the periphery, though I am sensitive to peculiarities of individual cases.

A second element of my evaluation of solidarity involves assessment of the extent to which actors in the four countries pursued political resolutions of the crisis which were favourable to workers in the periphery. This is related to the willingness of actors to undertake concrete action, yet it attempts to appreciate the extent to which unions lobbied national public authorities and social-democratic parties aimed at legislative solutions. I make particular effort to look beyond rhetoric and understand the degree to which such goals were prioritized by actors.

In this period, the presence of solidarity can be equated with cooperation; both acts are supportive of counterparts in other member states. The relationship between lack of solidarity and competition is more complex. The absence of the first does not automatically entail the second; factors beyond the control of actors may constrain their ability to support threatened colleagues. I am therefore mindful that the non-presence of solidarity does not imply conscious competition, yet it is reasonable to consider non-solidarity a *de facto* form of competition, albeit a softer one. This verdict is based on the findings of dualization theorists; these scholars consider the indifference of permanent workers to the deregulation of temporary work to be indicative of competition among groups of workers (Emmenegger *et al.*, 2012; Palier and Thelen, 2010). In country chapters, I am sensitive to contingencies and arrive at judgements on a case-by-case basis.

Social-democratic parties are also considered to be part of labour movements in this period. Inclusion of social-democratic parties permit the terms in which the interests of labour are understood to be expanded; comparisons between the manner in which unions and social-democratic parties reacted to the crisis will allow for more nuanced understanding of the behaviour of both actors. This choice potentially impedes comparison of the actions of unions in the two phases, yet I am careful to distinguish between the positions of trade unions and social-democratic parties in the second period; this allows direct comparison of the actions of unions in the two intervals. As with the first timescale, investigation is based on research interviews, documentary analysis and review of relevant literature.

Degrees of competition and/or cooperation of labour movements, in the course of the two periods and as defined above, are therefore the phenomena examined by this study. As previously argued, appreciation of the significance of processes of competition and/or cooperation requires links to be made with substantive outcomes. Levels of (i) unemployment and (ii) employment security were selected for this purpose. Both are pivotal labour market outcomes and establishment of relations between these indicators and the propensity of labour to compete and/or cooperate will provide rich insight into the behaviour of labour movements. Other indicators might be examined, pay being one such variable which has been investigated by certain accounts (Rhodes, 1998a), yet I select unemployment and employment security because they are central to dualization scholarship (Emmenegger, 2014; Rueda, 2007); as previously stated, this is a literature to which I hope to contribute. In paragraphs below my conceptualization of unemployment and employment security is outlined, yet prior to this it is necessary to reflect on the relationship between the actions of labour movements and studied indicators.

Research in the social sciences can never take place in experimental conditions and, in the case of this study, its cross-national research design involves particular challenges. Specifically, I am interested in the extent to which the propensity of labour movements in single countries to compete and/or cooperate can be linked to changes in the variables of unemployment and employment security in domestic contexts *and* in other member states. To give one example, it may be that the ability of the German labour movement to engage in successful competition ensured that labour market conditions remained benign in Germany yet deteriorated in Southern Europe.

Establishing a link between the actions of one labour movement and changes in domestic and foreign labour market conditions is challenging – it involves assessment of connections between multiple variables – and such an endeavour is undertaken in each of the studied countries. Country chapters therefore consider changes to levels of unemployment and employment security in relevant periods and evaluate the extent to which variations can be linked to the propensity of domestic and non-domestic labour movements to compete and/or cooperate. This task is complicated by the existence of multiple influences on levels of unemployment and employment security. Though I am sensitive to factors which are unrelated to the behaviour of labour movements, the existence of a broad literature which links the actions of labour movements and investigated outcomes demonstrates the viability of this undertaking (Hancké, 2013; Hassel, 2014; Johnston, 2016).

The methodological debates with which country chapters engage are too specific to fully outline here, yet certain guiding principles may be delineated. As detailed below, I employ the techniques of co-variation and causal-process tracing design recommended by Blatter and Haverland (2012); such methods facilitate conclusions about the influence of variables. Explanatory principles used by Jones (2015: 819), first developed by Miller (1987), are a further inspiration. The approach of Miller is particularly concerned with causation and attempts to determine the depth of potential causes. In a first step, causal significance is assessed on the basis of necessity, sufficiency and priority. In a second step, potential narratives are evaluated on the basis of their plausibility.

Particular attention is paid to the evolution of investigated relationships. Given that a period of near twenty years is studied, a key issue is the extent to which labour movements responded to events which were partly the result of their prior actions. The question of the reaction of German labour to the crisis in the periphery, which some associated with earlier behaviour of the movement, is one example of such a relationship. As will become apparent in country chapters, there are many more such instances. This endeavour is undoubtedly challenging yet, given that the fates of EMU labour markets have been interlinked for many years, it is one which is necessary; there is arguably not enough work which theorizes member state political economies as parts of an integrated whole.

As I have argued, a most auspicious way to gauge the influence of labour movements in domestic and non-domestic contexts is through assessment of changes in two substantive indicators: levels of (i) unemployment and (ii) employment security. In each of the studied countries, changes in rates of unemployment are therefore assessed and the extent to which variation can be attributed to competition and/or cooperation in domestic and non-domestic contexts is discussed; analysis is conducted in line with the methodological principles outlined above. It should be clarified that I am interested in rates of unemployment, rather than less commonly cited rates of employment.

Changes to employment security in studied countries are also evaluated; this involves assessing evolutions in the status of permanent and temporary workers. As with the first indicator, I attempt to track the degree to which changes in the second indicator can be linked to processes of competition and/or cooperation. In terms of definition of temporary work, I incorporate non-standard contractual forms such as temporary agency, fixed-term, zero-hour and false self-employment. Distinction is also made between *de jure* and *de facto* discrepancies in the treatment of permanent and temporary workers. *De jure* differences concern the quality of legal rights granted to such employees; the OECD Employment Protection Legislation Index (EPL) usefully, albeit crudely, provides cross-national data on the degree of legal protection enjoyed by different workers. *De facto* differences concern the outcomes to which different workers are typically subject and include indicators such as fear of unemployment and involuntary temporary work. This approach is in line with the recommendation of Marx (2011) that more care is taken distinguishing *de jure* and *de facto* elements of dualization.

Selecting representative country studies

I examine the cases of four countries: Germany, a country in the core of the Eurozone; Spain, a country on the periphery of the Eurozone; France, a country in the intermediary of the Eurozone; Poland, a country outside of the Eurozone. As delineated in greater detail below, choice of cases is based on variation in status within the Eurozone and form of labour movement; this is so that deductions about the significance of particular variables may be as broad as possible. Selected countries are also large, which aids generalizability and case comparability.

The first of my countries is Germany; this is a core Eurozone country which is characterized by a coordinated model of capitalism in which labour assumes a key role. The coordinated form of German capitalism has been long observed. As a result of cooperative, long-term relations between social partners and the state, the country has historically competed in high-quality manufacturing sectors. Varieties-of-capitalism theorists consider Germany an archetypal CME (Hall and Soskice, 2001), notwithstanding concerns about the erosion of the system (Streeck, 2009). Though there are other core countries in the Eurozone, specifically Austria and Netherlands, Germany is the most significant. This is related to the economic importance of the country. Not only was the German trade surplus a major cause of crisis, but the economic power of the country meant that it was the primary author of austerity. The role of the German labour movement in both of these processes was crucial.

Trade unions occupy a vital position in the German system. Unions are comparatively moderate and organize in individual sectors in which bargaining takes place at sector level. Collective bargaining has nonetheless been partially decentralized to firms; this is a level at which a well-developed system of works councils exists (Hassel, 1999). Although German unions have been involved in corporatist pacts with employers and the state in previous decades, German corporatism has ebbed in recent years. German labour is also represented by SPD. SPD is strongly social-democratic in orientation, though its implementation of the deregulatory Hartz reforms in the 2000s led to disillusionment on the left of party; in recent times, the radical Die Linke party has attracted disenchanted SPD supporters.

Germany is the archetypal core Eurozone country. Many consider Germany to have been advantaged from the conception of the single currency; not only did the ECB adopt the anti-inflationary stance traditionally employed by the Bundesbank on the launch of the euro, but elimination of the devaluation option deprived competitors of traditional means of adjustment. In the first decade of the euro, Germany capitalized upon this advantage. As a consequence of the Hartz reforms and collective agreements which limited wage rises, German ULCs became incrementally competitive vis-à-vis periphery countries. The trend for social partners to conclude competitive pay deals was linked with the German style of capitalism; Hassel contended that there was a tendency towards wage moderation in CMEs, owing to the ability of social partners to coordinate wage bargaining (Hassel, 2014). The role of German labour during the European debt crisis has also been debated. Though austerity was denounced by unions and SPD, some commented upon the lack of vigour of this opposition (Dribbusch, 2015).

The case of Germany presents particular questions about the propensity of labour movements to compete and/or cooperate. In the first studied period, there is the issue of whether core unions are able to use sectoral bargaining institutions to plan competitiveness. Allegations exist that German unions engaged in the conscious undercutting of rivals (Bofinger, 2015); there is a consequent opportunity to assess whether such a strategy is feasible. This undertaking will also indicate whether this behaviour is practicable in other core countries, notwithstanding differences in bargaining systems which must be kept in mind. In the second studied period, the case of Germany raises the question of the extent to which labour movements in privileged structural positions are likely to support disadvantaged counterparts. This issue is pertinent to movements in other core countries, given the existence of similar relationships with the periphery.

The second of my countries is Spain; this is a periphery Eurozone country which is considered a MME (Molina and Rhodes, 2007). The form of Spanish capitalism has divided theorists. Though some have regarded the country a CME, the lack of coordination between key actors and prominent role of the state has led to criticism of this designation. Many prefer the term MME (Molina and Rhodes, 2007); this recognizes the crucial role of the state and clientelistic nature of state–social partner relations. There are other countries in the periphery of the Eurozone, namely Cyprus, Greece, Ireland, Italy and Portugal, yet there are reasons for considering Spain to be particularly worthy of study. Not only is its system representative of the MMEs which prevail in the periphery, this is not true of Ireland, but Spain was typical of other periphery countries in that its economy was devastated by crisis; this did not occur in Italy to the same extent, especially in the north of the country. Given the larger size of Spain and its proximity to the centre of Europe, the peculiarities which distinguish the smaller and more peripheral Cypriot, Greek and Portuguese cases are also not as prominent.

Trade unions occupy an intermediate position in the Spanish system. The two main confederations are divided on political lines, the Unión General de Trabajadores (UGT) being social-democratic in orientation and the Confederación Sindical de Comisiones Obreras (CCOO) more radical, while sporadic participation in collective bargaining is under-pinned by low rates of density. Notwithstanding this tendency towards fragmentation, unions bargain at sector level and are active within firms (Jódar *et al.*, 2011; Ortiz, 2002). Unions have participated in corporatism. Recent decades have seen the conclusion of key pacts which attempted to establish competitiveness within EMU, yet the limited capacity of social partners and late transition to democracy have restricted the quality of Spanish corporatism. Spanish labour is also represented by PSOE. PSOE is a social-democratic party which formed several Governments following the end of dictatorship (Andrade, 2012), though the association of the party with austerity has led to a recent decline in support. Podemos, a party which identifies with the new-left, has attracted disenchanted PSOE voters.

Eurozone membership has generally been to the disadvantage of Spain. The country traditionally used devaluation to maintain competitiveness, yet the introduction of the single currency removed this means of adjustment. Spain became uncompetitive in the first decade of the euro. As in other Mediterranean 'mixed' regimes, euro entry initiated credit-driven compensation of economic losers by the state rather than, as in core countries, efforts by social partners to achieve national competitiveness (Hassel, 2014: 5). Spanish ULCs incrementally appreciated against core countries, particularly Germany, and poor competitiveness led to an escalating trade deficit. This not only exposed Spain to deep recession on the outbreak of crisis but, given that the traditional option of currency devaluation was unavailable, meant the country faced pressure to achieve internal devaluation.

The case of Spain presents particular questions about the propensity of labour movements to compete and/or cooperate. In the first studied period, there is the issue of the extent to which efforts to achieve moderation via national pacts are feasible in a periphery country. Given the structural obstacles which stand in the way of such a feat, examination of this will shed light on the capacity of unions to compete and/or cooperate in demanding circumstances. In the second studied period, the case of Spain raises the question of the conditions in which labour movements in disadvantaged structural positions are able to marshal pan-European opposition. This issue is pertinent to movements in other periphery countries, given the existence of similar relationships with the core.

The third of my countries is France; this is an intermediate Eurozone country characterized by a coordinated form of capitalism in which the state plays a prominent role. Owing to the weakness of organized interests and their limited capacity to self-coordinate, the ambiguous status of French capitalism tends to be emphasized; Schmidt's designation of 'state capitalism' (2003), which recognizes the importance of the state, is convincing. There are few other countries in the intermediary of the Eurozone; arguably the only other is Belgium. Though the French political economy is renowned for its exceptionalism (Godin and Chafer, 2004), the size of France and its crucial role in resolving the crisis mean that it is the intermediate country most worthy of study. I am nonetheless sensitive to peculiarities of the French case.

French trade unions receive significant support from the state. This is a result of union weakness; despite the propensity of unions to engage in industrial action, French union density is among the lowest in the EU. Following the negotiation of collective agreements, which tends to take place at sector level, the French state extends agreements to uncovered parties (Parsons, 2005). France has a limited history of corporatism. Though policymakers are not hostile to the concept per se, traditional weaknesses of unions and employers have meant that attempts have been unviable (Crouch, 1993). Recent decades have seen limited success. Social partners have concluded peak-level agreements on labour market reforms which have been subsequently implemented by law, yet deals achieving wage competitiveness have proved more elusive. French labour is also represented by the social-democratic PS. PS has a more disjointed history than its German counterpart, the modern party only having been founded in 1969, and has faced strong competition from the radical left (Bergounioux and Grunberg, 1992). Failure in the 2017 presidential election, in which PS candidate Benoît Hamon received only 6.36 per cent of the vote, raised questions about the future of PS.

France occupies an intermediate position in the Eurozone. Though the inception of the euro was associated with the French national interest, effects of EMU have been ambiguous (Hassel, 2014). The French state traditionally used devaluation to maintain competitiveness, yet the introduction of the single currency deprived it of this possibility. Euro entry had an equivocal effect on French competitiveness. The terms of the Stability and Growth Pact were repeatedly flouted by the country and competitive ULCs were not achieved. Though this ensured that France failed to achieve ascendency in the Eurozone and faced repeated pressure to adopt reforms, constraints were not as acute as in Southern Europe; this peculiar status means that France can be considered an intermediate case.

The case of France raises particular questions about the propensity of labour movements to compete and/or cooperate. In the first studied period, there is the issue of the form in which unions in weak structural positions respond to Europeanization. Though few unions in Western Europe are as marginalized as those in France, examination of this problem will yield interesting results about the manner in which unions behave when unusually weak. In the second studied period, the case of France raises the question of the conditions in which labour movements in intermediate positions are likely to extend solidarity to counterparts in the periphery. Awareness of this issue will shed further light on the actions of movements in core and periphery countries.

The fourth of my countries is Poland; this is a country outside of the Eurozone which is characterized by a liberal form of capitalism (Bohle and Greskovits, 2007; Crowley, 2004). Though in this work I am primarily concerned with the influence of EMU, examination of the Polish case will allow inference of the extent to which trends are contingent upon euro membership. The nature of Polish capitalism has divided theorists. Some have suggested that the country exhibits CME-like qualities (McMenamin, 2004), yet most recognize the deregulated, non-coordinated form of the Polish business system. Bohle and Greskovits' term 'embedded neoliberalism' (2007), a designation which acknowledges the existence of higher welfare payments and dismissal protection in an overall liberal system, is definitive. Though the category of non-Eurozone member states is diverse, including countries as varied as Sweden, Hungary and Croatia, the Polish case is particularly suitable. Not only is the economy and labour market representative of other Visegrad countries, two of which have not adopted the single currency, but Poland shares the Communist past of many non-Eurozone countries. The size of the Polish economy also facilitates comparison with other cases.

Polish trade unions are rather peripheral (Ost, 2006). Despite the crucial role played by the Solidarność union in restoring democracy to Poland, industrial relations in democratic Poland is characterized by low union density and collective bargaining coverage; working conditions are primarily regulated by the labour code. The existence of internal divisions within the labour movement, between post-Communist OPZZ and anti-Communist Solidarność, also compromises union effectiveness. Polish unions have nonetheless engaged in tripartism and, although there has been a tendency for pacts to collapse, certain experiments have achieved success. There is little tradition of social democracy in Poland. Left-of-centre parties exist in the country, yet the most prominent is the post-Communist SLD. SLD emerged from the Polish Communist Party and does not enjoy the relationship with working classes which characterizes western European social-democratic parties (Tomczak, 2012). Other parties have also been active on the Polish left; one of the most recent, Partia Razem, is a new-left party.

Poland is not a member of the Eurozone. Though the terms of EU accession stipulate that the country must eventually adopt the currency, certain unfulfilled economic criteria and concerns about stability mean that Poland has yet to do this. Polish ULCs were modest in the decade following the launch of the euro (Tchorek and Krzewicki, 2014: 51). Competitiveness was superior to most CEE countries, though from the mid-2000s Polish ULCs showed signs of appreciating. Given the tendency of non-coordinated regimes to become uncompetitive vis-à-vis core Eurozone countries, this trend might have been exacerbated by euro membership. Poland nonetheless remained aloof from the processes which gripped the Eurozone. Social partners and Government took tentative positions on the crisis, employers and the centre-right Platforma Obywatelska (PO) Government favouring the core of the Eurozone and unions sympathizing with the periphery, yet such support remained rather provisional.

The case of Poland presents particular questions about the propensity of labour movements to compete and/or cooperate. In the first studied period, there is the issue of the extent to which unions are able to use a CEE tripartite institution to respond to pressures associated with Europeanization. This is a problem which often confronts unions in CEE contexts; there are tripartite institutions in many of these countries. In the second studied period, the case of Poland raises the question of the extent to which labour movements in non-Eurozone contexts are likely to exhibit solidarity with periphery countries. Awareness of this issue will shed further light on the actions of movements in Eurozone countries.

Methodology and methods

In the first studied process, which concerns the collective bargaining practices of trade unions in the first decade of the Eurozone, I use a methodological approach based on historic institutionalism. Historic institutionalism is popular among political economists (Morgan and Hauptmeier, 2014) and seeks to explain institutional change with reference to historic processes. The results of these processes consequently become institutionalized and exert profound influence on contemporary institutions through path dependency and complementarity. This approach is most consistent with my goals. In the first studied period, my argument is that existing labour market institutions exercise deep leverage on actors and constrain certain 'rational' behaviours. Such institutions are also regarded as the product of past processes of institution creation. As scholarship has shown, the character of labour markets has been indelibly shaped by past conflicts, the outcomes of which have become hardened in institutions (Crouch, 1993; Emmenegger, 2014).

In the second studied process, which concerns the response of trade unions and social-democratic parties to austerity in the periphery of the Eurozone, I use a methodological approach based on critical juncture theory. Capoccia and Kelemen define critical junctures as 'relatively short periods of time during which there is a substantially heightened probability that agents' choices will affect the outcome of interest' (2007: 348). The investigated period can be considered a critical juncture; profound reforms were implemented both in periphery countries and at European level in these years. Given the emphasis which critical juncture theory places on the role of actors, use of the approach will enrich understanding of the actions of labour movements.

My methodological stance is rooted in the work of Blatter and Haverland (2012), who propose a three-pronged approach to case study research (see table 3.2). Emmenegger fruitfully used this methodology in a 2014 study of the historical development of dismissal protection; the employment of the approach by this work is a key source of inspiration. In this book, I make major use of co-variation design. This method is predicated on selection of cases on the basis of variation in independent variables, so that deductions about the significance of particular variables may be made. In case selection, four countries are therefore chosen which exhibit different values in terms of two key independent variables, type

Table 3.2 Three explanatory approaches in case study research

	Co-variation design	Causal-process tracing design	Congruence analysis design
Research goal	Does variable X make a difference?	What makes the outcome (Y) possible?	Which explanatory approach provides more insights?
Variation	Cross-case variation	Within-case variation	Both cross-case and within-case variation
Generalization	Drawing conclusions about the causal effect of X on Y from sample to population	Drawing conclusions about the set of proven causal mechanisms	Drawing conclusions about the relevance of theories in the scientific discourse
Case selection	Variation on the independent variable and scope conditions (controlled comparison)	Theoretical relevance of cases with regard to outcome	Likeliness of cases in respect to the selected theories (most likely cases)

Source: Blatter and Haverland (2012: 27–9), though taken from Emmenegger (2014: 19).

of labour movement and status within the Eurozone, so that deductions about the importance of variables are as broad as possible.

Though co-variation design is the primary explanatory approach used in this work, the need to explain variance within cases necessitates employment of a secondary method. Causal-process tracing design is also used; Emmenegger (2014) employed this approach to compare similarities between key episodes in national histories. The fact that this work is not a historical study means utilization of the method is not pivotal, though evaluation of the resemblance between studied events and past proceedings will be fruitful. Parallels are consequently assessed between contemporary processes and historic patterns, though the latter endeavour will be based on a reading of literature rather than primary research.

The third explanatory approach identified by Blatter and Haverland is also utilized: congruence analysis design. This approach allows researchers to draw conclusions about the viability of existing theories on the basis of collected data and is employed to answer the research question. In chapters 8 to 10, I assess the extent to which labour movements compete and/or cooperate in reaction to integration on the basis of data presented in chapters 4 to 7.

This book uses two main research methods: analysis of secondary sources and semi-structured research interviews. Three types of secondary sources were analysed; these were (i) official documentation (ii) media reports and (iii) academic work directly and indirectly concerned with subject matter. The first of these forms, official documentation, included material such as position papers and reports issued by public authorities and social partners. Throughout the period under examination, public authorities and social partners published statements outlining the rudiments of their positions. Though this material suffers from limitations related to its politicized nature, such documents offered vital insight into the orientations of studied organizations. Reports on relevant labour market developments released by public authorities and social partners were also invaluable. These sources yielded crucial information on trends germane to my study, in addition to providing clues about the attitudes of the organizations issuing such documentation.

The second of these forms, media reports, included material issued or transmitted by newspapers, internet sites, television or radio. There are well-established medias in all four studied countries, and certain media sources from other countries also contained pertinent information. Using a series of key words, sources such as the *Financial Times, Le Monde, El País, Gazeta Wyborcza* and *Frankfurter Allgemeine Zeitung* were searched. Searches were also conducted on generic engines such as Google and the websites of trade unions and political parties. Though such material suffers from methodological drawbacks associated with media reports, the benefits of working with such sources outweigh disadvantages.

The third of these forms, academic work directly and indirectly concerned with relevant subject matter, is comprised of scholarly output related to developments in the studied period. Though this book is predicated upon engagement with academic literature, academic sources used specifically as research material were those which contained data pertinent to my study. A number of works have charted relevant trends (e.g. Emmenegger *et al.*, 2012), and data gleaned from these sources was invaluable. Such studies were located on academic search engines using a series of key words.

At the outset of the project, I hoped that mere analysis of documentation might provide sufficient material for my aims. As I progressed with investigations, I realized that this was unfeasible; at the core of my research was the issue of organizational objectives and, whatever the insights provided by relevant documentation, certain organizational perspectives remained obscured. I therefore resolved to undertake semi-structured research interviews in the four countries, which would complement data collected from other sources. Interviews attempted to examine organizational strategies, rather than assessing issues such as discrepancies in ULCs which lend themselves to investigation via secondary sources. Questions particularly focused on strategies for the Europeanization of collective bargaining and organizational attitudes towards countries affected by austerity.

Interviews were conducted between April 2016 and October 2017; the great majority were carried out face-to-face though a few were undertaken via telephone. Appendix 1 provides further details of interviews. Six interviews were conducted in Germany; interviewees included representatives from the trade unions DGB, IG BAU, IG Metall and Ver.di and the SPD political party. Given the critical nature of their participation in collective bargaining processes, officials from the metal sector employers' association Gesamtmetall were also interviewed. Six interviews were conducted in France; interviewees included representatives from the trade unions CFDT, CFE-CGC, CFTC, CGT and FO and the PS political party.

Four interviews were undertaken in Spain; interviewees included representatives from the trade unions CCOO and UGT and the PSOE political party. Given their insights into relevant processes, an official from the employers' association Confederación Española de Organizaciones Empresariales (CEOE) was also interviewed. Five interviews were conducted in Poland; interviewees included representatives from the trade unions Solidarność and OPZZ and the SLD political party. Owing to their participation in relevant processes, officials from the employers' association Lewiatan and the centre-right political party PO were also interviewed.

Interviews were recorded and transcribed and later coded on the basis of themes consistent with research aims. Limitations associated with interview data should be emphasized. As outlined above, interviews were undertaken to complement existing data; interview material therefore seldom drives arguments, as is the case with many studies, but rather plays a complementary role.

A note on language is also necessary. Given my reliance on foreign language sources and the interviews with non-English speaking experts which research for this book involved, a degree of competence in relevant languages was essential. I speak and read French, Polish and Spanish, and research interviews and source analysis in these languages were unproblematic. German is a language in which I possess no competence however; conducting research in this medium was therefore a particular challenge. This was partly resolved by the body of relevant material available in English, yet I also commissioned a research assistant to prepare a 3,000-word report on relevant German language sources. All of my German interviewees were able to conduct research interviews in English, apart from one for whom an interpreter was procured.

The research design outlined in this chapter is a comprehensive one, yet the test of its effectiveness will be its practical use in conceptualizing the manner in which labour movements react to integration. In chapters which follow, in which I investigate the cases of selected countries, the approach will be put to examination.

PART II
Country studies

4

Germany: Accidental neomercantilism, questionable solidarity?

> The economic situation in the whole of the EU is increasingly deteriorating. The crisis management strategy adopted by the politicians, comprising austerity mandates and cuts in wages, pensions and welfare payments, has in some countries led to a dramatic downward spiral in economic terms, and shockwaves have sent demand plummeting around Europe and the world ... To prevent the recession from developing into an all-out depression, we are pleading for politicians to break the impasse and initiate a long-term investment and development programme for Europe. (DGB, 2012)

> Voluntaristic nonsense. (IG Metall leader Bertold Huber on the 14 November 2012 European Day of Action and Solidarity)

Germany is the archetypal core Eurozone country. After the launch of the euro, wage moderation helped guarantee competitive advantage for the country within EMU. A number of authorities have associated this outcome with the efficacy of German sectoral bargaining (Hancké, 2013; Hassel, 2014; Johnston, 2016); some even allege that unions consciously undercut European counterparts (Bofinger, 2015). Given these debates, the case of Germany allows assessment of whether core unions are able to use sectoral bargaining institutions to plan competitiveness.

In this chapter, I argue that German unions did not adopt a consciously competitive strategy; such a tactic was overly complex to formulate and there is scant evidence of its existence, notwithstanding sporadic attempts by sections of the union movement. Despite this lack of calculation, structural efficiencies of the German bargaining model helped secure competitive advantage within the Eurozone and paved the way for a consolidation of labour market conditions. There was no further liberalization of employment protection after the 2002–5 Hartz reforms; unemployment fell and the competitive advantage of Germany meant that pressures for austerity and deregulation were increasingly directed towards periphery countries.

The implementation of austerity in Southern Europe raised the question of the extent to which a core labour movement was likely to extend solidarity to benighted counterparts. I submit that the German labour movement failed to show significant solidarity with periphery counterparts after the outbreak of debt crisis. Though SPD often denounced austerity, certain actions of the party could be perceived as supportive. The disagreement of German unions with austerity was more vocal, yet their commitment to concrete opposition was arguably lacklustre (Dribbusch, 2015). Even if austerity in Southern Europe posed dangers to German labour, opposition was diluted by certain benefits for the German economy.

Labour movement and labour market in Germany: historical development and contemporary shape

The German labour movement has deep roots in the history of the country. Trade unions faced a long struggle to achieve recognition from public authorities, yet became established in post-war West Germany; in these years, sectoral trade unions and the DGB confederation were founded. Contemporary legislation was also favourable. In addition to the 1952 Works Constitution Act, which established the legal basis of works councils in West German firms, a 1949 Act on Collective Agreements instituted a well-organized system of sectoral collective bargaining. Agreements concluded at this level concerned the topics of wages and working time, whereas firm-level works councils managed personnel issues. The role of the manufacturing sector was pivotal. As the industry exposed to international competition, it acted as a pattern-setter for collective agreements in other sectors. Despite the coordinated form of the German system, corporatist agreements took place to a limited degree; the successful 1967–77 'concerted action' programme was an exception (Hudson, 1980).

Recent fortunes of unions have been mixed. From the 1990s, the German system of industrial relations became liberalized; unions lost density, the coverage of collective agreements declined and firms obtained opt-outs from sectoral agreements. Attempts at corporatism bore little further fruit. A 1996 'pact for employment' lasted a mere six months, while the Hartz Commission contained no high-level representation of social partners. Notwithstanding these challenges, unions remain important actors and the rudiments of the industrial relations system endure. Manufacturing unions, who engage in restraint and are thus vital to the success of German exports, continue to be crucial.

The position of German labour is historically defended by a strong social-democratic movement. SPD was founded in 1875 and, after prolonged conflict between revolutionary and evolutionary wings, became committed to the principles of democratic socialism. SPD played a crucial role in the governance of West Germany. Participating in a succession of Governments from 1966, several SPD initiatives ameliorated living and working conditions (Miller and Potthoff, 1986). The most recent SPD-led Government nonetheless became associated with attacks on worker rights. The Agenda 2010 programme, formulated by the SPD–Green coalition and implemented from 2003 via the four Hartz laws, sought to liberalize the German labour market and welfare state with reforms which reduced unemployment benefits and deregulated temporary work (Palier and Thelen, 2010). The measures would be credited for later German success, yet were bitterly resented by the left of SPD; some disillusioned members would join the radical Die Linke party.

German bargaining under EMU: neomercantilism in action?

Germany played a critical role in the design of EMU. Many conceived of German support for the euro as quid pro quo for French backing of German reunification yet, once they were committed to the single currency, Germany attempted to ensure that the design of EMU reflected its ordoliberal approach to economic policy. The 1992 Maastricht Treaty and 1997 Stability and Growth Pact therefore set out austere conditions for membership of the single currency; the former limited government deficits to 3 per cent of GDP and levels of public debt to 60 per cent, while the latter strengthened monitoring and coordination of these limits. German influence also secured a 'no bail-out' clause in the Maastricht Treaty and guaranteed that the newly created ECB adopted a hawkish approach to inflation. Many considered the location of the ECB, in Frankfurt and a short walk from the Bundesbank, to be of more than symbolic importance.

Debates about the influence of German ULCs on the later Eurozone crisis are well-rehearsed. My interests in this book are distinct, concerning the extent to which labour movements compete and/or cooperate rather than their role in instigating the crisis, and in the German case this necessitates consideration of the degree to which German labour consciously aimed at wage moderation. Before this can be addressed, it is necessary to set out perspectives on the role of German ULCs in causing the crisis. An established view postulates that the Eurozone crisis was in great part the result of low German ULCs (see figure 4.1). According to this interpretation, superior German competitiveness ensured that southern European competitors incurred trade deficits. These deficits

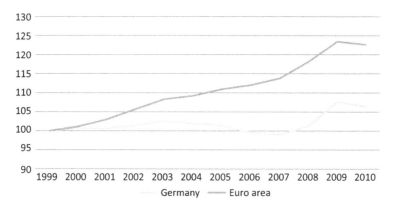

Figure 4.1 Nominal unit labour costs (ULCs) in Germany (1999–2010)
Source: Ameco; Bourgeot, 2013.

were financed by elevated levels of borrowing and, following the onset of the economic crisis, led to recession.

German unions are key protagonists for scholars convinced of this view. Though productivity increases are stressed, the wage moderation achieved by unions is considered a decisive factor. Bargaining in exposed industries such as metalworking is traditionally orientated towards restraint and it is argued that this led to competitiveness within the Eurozone. The role of agreements such as the 2004 Pforzheim agreement, which allowed certain firm-level derogations from the metalworking sector collective agreement, is called to attention. Johnston (2016) underlines the role of moderation in the non-exposed sector. Exposed sector negotiators had also been disciplined in periphery countries yet, according to Johnston, a distinguishing feature of Germany was its ability to control public sector pay. As a result of the retention of 'important veto powers in wage determination for civil servants' (p. 112), wages in the German public sector remained at competitive levels; these conditions were absent in Southern Europe and condemned the countries to wage-price spirals. Such phenomena have also been associated with the German form of capitalism. Both Hancké (2013) and Hassel (2014) assert that wage moderation is more likely to take place in CMEs such as Germany.

This view has attracted criticism. In a persuasive work, Müller *et al.* (2015) identify three problems with the argument that the crisis can be attributed to low German ULCs. First, the notion that ULCs are primary determinants of price competitiveness is critiqued; it is affirmed that, given that factors such as the profit margin behaviour of companies also determine price competitiveness, the influence of ULCs is often modest (pp. 266–9). In the case of Germany, it is contended that the export boom of the 2000s was driven by growth in export markets rather than low ULCs; the authors note that this is a fact acknowledged by the European Commission (2012; 2014, cited in Müller *et al.*, 2015: 268). Second, Müller and colleagues question the relationship between price competitiveness and export performance; it is asserted that non-price competitiveness is also crucial and played a key part in German export success. Attention is drawn to the comparative performance of Germany and France. Price competitiveness was near identical in both countries from 2000 to 2008, yet in this period sales of German exports were stronger. The authors contend that this discrepancy can be attributed to differences in non-price competitiveness (pp. 270–1). Third, the extent to which exports are significant for overall growth is queried; it is stressed that EU economies overwhelmingly depend on domestic demand rather than export demand (pp. 273–5). In the German case, it is noted that exports 'account for only one-third of overall demand for goods and services' (p. 274).

Though the points of Müller *et al.* (2015) need be taken into account when considering causes of the crisis, it is reasonable to conclude that competitive German ULCs played a significant role in ensuring German economic success. Even if other factors also explain robust German performance, it is difficult to deny that low ULCs were important; they provided Germany with a key advantage over other Eurozone countries. A well-established literature has therefore debated the extent to which German ULCs may be held culpable for the outbreak of the crisis, yet my concern in this work is distinct. I am interested in the propensity of labour to compete and/or cooperate in response to European integration and, with respect to the German case, this necessitates investigation of the extent to which German labour colluded in the process of lowering ULCs after the introduction of the euro. Investigation of this issue will allow broader assessment of whether core unions are able to use sectoral bargaining institutions to plan competitiveness.

The charge that German unions consciously suppressed wages vis-à-vis their rivals in the Eurozone, thereby conniving in neomercantilism, has perhaps circulated more widely verbally than in print. There are nonetheless certain researchers who have made such claims in writing. A notable authority is Peter Bofinger, Professor of Economics at Würzburg University and member of the German Council of Economic Experts. According to Bofinger (2015), wage moderation on the part of German unions 'is an explicit attempt to devalue the real exchange rate internally'. Certain actions undertaken by German unions are cited in support of this argument; the willingness of IG Metall head Klaus Zwickel to accept a stagnation of real wages in the 1990s, when proposing the Bündnis für Arbeit (Pact for Work), is therefore recalled (Wolf, 2000, cited in Bofinger, 2015). A January 2000 declaration by unions and employers, which stated that rises in productivity should lead to agreements which increase employment rather than real wages, is also mentioned. Flassbeck (2016) supports this argument, emphasizing pressure imposed upon unions by the Federal Government.

Other pieces of evidence suggest that German wage moderation was occasionally performed consciously and with reference to other countries. Harald Schartau, leader of IG Metall in Nordrhein-Westfalen, contended in 1999 that increases in productivity should not only lead to wage rises, but also help make German firms more competitive in a global marketplace (*Tagesspiegel*, 1999). In research interviews with metal sector social partners, it emerged that economic conditions in other countries, including ones in the Eurozone, were considered during wage negotiations.

Notwithstanding the evidence which is cited above, there are good reasons for thinking that the actions of German unions prior to the crisis did not amount to a scheme to guarantee German competitiveness through the undercutting of rivals. Even if certain individuals and organizations may have been inspired by this notion at particular times, the systematic, long-term planning required to effect such an endeavour was almost entirely lacking. Three points on this matter need be made; they concern (i) the difficulties of orchestrating such a scheme, (ii) the lack of evidence for it and (iii) the good evidence that German wage moderation resulted from structural constraints.

A first reason for scepticism concerns logistical problems associated with organizing such an endeavour. As scholars have long known, the formulation and execution of long-term organizational strategies is particularly onerous. Though the German socio-economic system is famed for its ability to secure long-term outcomes, this is promoted by institutional features rather than actor volition; the ability of German firms to plan for the long term is therefore not achieved through the ingenuity of firms, but rather by established modes of corporate governance and business financing (Wood, 2001). There are not equivalent structures which encourage moderation vis-à-vis European rivals; one is struck by the extent to which the German system inhibits such an approach. Collective agreements are short in duration, typically ranging from one to two years in length; thousands of such agreements are also concluded and negotiators possess substantial levels of autonomy. The goals of actors are often short-term. A Gesamtmetall analysis of metal and electro sector collective agreements concluded between 1990 and 2017 notes that '[IG Metall] usually reacts to previous economic development rather than expected development' (2017: 6).

In such circumstances, wage moderation which took stock of developments in other European countries would have required especially elaborate planning. Had this been executed, it is inconceivable that more evidence of it would not have emerged. The supposition that this took place also imputes semi-clairvoyance to German unions. It must be remembered that differences in ULCs only attracted significant attention after the onset of the crisis; in the 1990s and 2000s, comparatively little regard was paid to this issue. The viability of political influence prompting such a strategy is also difficult to credit. Even if Federal Governments encouraged competitiveness (Flassbeck, 2016), it is unlikely that such emphasis would have initiated systematic changes in union behaviour; this is particularly the case given the lack of a formal incomes policy and the tradition of collective bargaining autonomy.

A second grounds for doubt is the lack of empirical evidence for this process. As contended above, had such a project been undertaken it would have required sustained coordination; one may surmise that there would be widespread proof. The fact that evidence does not exist, and that there is little corroboration beyond that which has been presented, is therefore positive proof for the non-existence of such a scheme. When asked about the allegations, German unions also denied them outright. British readers may think of the famous words of Mandy Rice-Davies,[1] yet the difficulties of keeping organizational secrets mean that these denials are plausible. A DGB representative said the following:

> German unions have often been accused, by the left in Europe in partic-
> ular, of engaging in deliberate and conscious wage dumping; this is non-
> sense ... [Awareness of developments in other European countries and the
> need to achieve German competitiveness in the Eurozone were built into
> the objectives of DGB] to no extent at all. It was just not on the agenda.
> Nobody had realized that EMU would lead to different consequences as a
> result of the different behaviour of economic agents.

Significantly, respondents from outside of the German union movement denied that such a process had taken place. An official from the metal-working employers' association Gesamtmetall echoed the comments of union respondents:

> I have the feeling there was no masterplan. As always we decided year by
> year what to do. We used the normal factors, productivity from the point
> of view of employers and the trade unions spoke about the inflation rate.
> Productivity plus the inflation rate were added together, plus some redis-
> tribution ... At the end it was no masterplan but it was the result of high
> productivity at that time, higher than we have nowadays ... and maybe a

---

1 In a well-known British trial of the 1960s, Rice-Davies is famous for replying 'He would, wouldn't he?', when told that Lord Astor denied relations with her.

kind of moderate wage rise. Both together led to this falling and declining unit labour cost.

In the course of research interviews, little evidence also emerged of either long-term planning or comparisons with other European countries during processes of wage bargaining; unions concentrated on short-term objectives and paid limited heed to developments in other Eurozone member states. Representatives from Ver.di asserted that local and regional industrial relations contexts felt remote from the European level. Arguments about wage rises to increase domestic demand, so as to correct imbalances within the Eurozone, even featured in union strategies. A Ver.di official asserted:

> It's clear that wages in Germany are too low and that the increase of wages in the past was too low. Our argument is that, because of the low increase of wages, demand is too low. So because of the weak domestic demand the export surplus is so high … If higher wages were achieved it would lead to an increase in domestic demand, which would lead to a rise in imports, which would lead to a fall in the export surplus.

Documentary data also yield little indication of conscious moderation. A Gesamtmetall analysis of metal and electro sector collective agreements concluded between 1990 and 2017 makes no mention of European developments in forty pages, while references are similarly scarce in reports by Hans-Böckler Foundation (WSI, 2000), IG Metall (2004) and chemical sector social partners. It is possible that the goal of competition may have become internalized by actors, such an instinct being scarcely discouraged by EMU, yet this is methodologically impossible to establish. Even if this had been the case, problems associated with coordination would have remained; accomplishment of a tacit objective is particularly unfeasible. There are also more plausible explanations for wage restraint, as I now discuss.

A third reason for scepticism is the existence of good evidence that German wage moderation resulted from structural constraints. Use of the principle of Occam's razor, which states that entities should not be multiplied unnecessarily, is here elucidative. As we have seen, the notion that German unions consciously moderated wages is beset with problems. An alternative explanation, namely that moderation resulted from institutional constraints, involves fewer multiplications. Literature emphasizes two main forms of structural influences which limited wage rises in decades preceding the crisis: (i) difficult economic conditions and (ii) liberalization of the German industrial relations system. With respect to the first factor, difficult economic conditions, the range of challenges which confronted Germany in the 1990s and early 2000s must be recalled. In this time GDP growth was sluggish and unemployment high; this was the result of difficulties responding to globalization and the challenge of reunification. There were few pressures for wage rises in such circumstances; unions preferred to conclude agreements which safeguarded employment. In a work which aims to exculpate German unions from the charge of conscious moderation, Horn (2016) puts emphasis on the role of high unemployment in forcing unions to accept unfavourable deals.

Liberalization of the German industrial relations system also exerted downward pressure on wage increases. As a result of processes associated with globalization, trade union density and collective bargaining coverage declined in decades prior to the crisis. These developments, in addition to factors such as increased opt-outs from collective agreements and the Hartz reforms, allowed firms to set wages more flexibly (Garz, 2013). In interviews, respondents also stressed influences such as the existence of exit options for employers and public sector wage cuts. It need also be remembered that wage increases were lower for employees uncovered by collective agreements; from 2000 to 2015 real wages declined by 17 per cent for these workers, whereas in the same period employees covered by collective agreements enjoyed a 12 per cent rise (Schlecht, 2015). This not only indicates the impact of structural factors on wages, but underlines the role of unions in exerting upward pressure on wage growth.

Evidence is therefore insufficient to conclude that German unions engaged in conscious moderation after the introduction of the euro. Limits to this interpretation should nonetheless be emphasized. Given the multiple points at which negotiations take place in Germany, it is more than conceivable that the goal of moderation inspired certain actors at certain times; select statements of unions, which are cited above, are consistent with this. Some of these strategies may have generally targeted international rivals, while others may have picked out European competitors. The complexity of this issue makes a definitive conclusion impossible. Even if there were sporadic instances of this behaviour, dearth of evidence and the salience of competing interpretations nonetheless make it difficult to regard such actions as part of a movement-wide strategy.

A related question concerns the extent to which German unions engaged in coordination of collective bargaining after the introduction of the euro. Notwithstanding the lead which German unions have taken in the establishment of European networks, the influence of such initiatives was minor. This is confirmed by academic studies (Glassner and Pochet, 2011) and interview data. Though an IG Metall official underlined union participation in these networks, respondents made little reference to impact upon bargaining processes. Given the prominent role of German unions in such endeavours, not to mention extensive participation in

EWCs (Lecher *et al.*, 1999) and European social dialogue (Prosser and Perin, 2015), this is disappointing. Such an outcome is related to general problems with bargaining coordination. As Glassner and Pochet (2011) note, issues with coordination and comparability prevent greater influence. Fear of loss of competitive advantage may also preclude deeper involvement from German unions. This would be understandable given the comparative efficacy of collective bargaining in Germany, though such an interpretation is at odds with the leading role of German unions in these initiatives.

The ascendancy of Germany within the Eurozone, which cannot be separated from developments in the German labour market during this time, had a beneficial effect upon levels of employment within the country. This chiefly resulted from the correlation between GDP growth and employment. Owing to the superior competitiveness of exports, German firms were able to establish long-term markets for their products and secure employment for workers. Statistics attest to this relationship. Though unemployment grew in the first half of the 2000s, levels exceeded 11 per cent in 2005, there were incremental falls from the second half of 2005; by mid-2011 the rate was under 6 per cent (see figure 4.2).

This relationship is nonetheless complex. There were a number of influences on unemployment in this period; one of these was the programme of *kurzarbeit*. This system, which subsidized wages and social security contributions of employees with reduced working hours, encouraged firms to shorten working time rather than dismiss employees (Crimmann *et al.*, 2010). Renowned economist Hans-Werner Sinn even asserts that euro membership handicapped the German economy in the early 2000s (2013). Owing to the export of German capital, savings tended not to be invested domestically and a slump was endured. Just

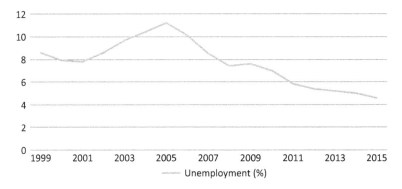

Figure 4.2 Unemployment rates in Germany (1999–2015)
Source: Eurostat.

as the later pre-eminence of Germany might be associated with lower unemployment, processes called to attention by Sinn may be linked with higher unemployment in earlier years.

Notwithstanding these caveats, it is difficult to deny that there is a relationship between German ascendency within EMU and lower levels of unemployment. After initial hardship in the single currency, which although tangible was not as considerable as that later experienced by Southern Europe, German predominance within EMU underpinned low levels of unemployment in the country.

German economic success also discouraged reform of dismissal protection regulation. Calls for liberalization of such regulation, which had been vehement just a few years earlier, abated as the German economy became among the most successful in Europe; in the second half of the 2000s, there was no deregulation of the dismissal protection of permanent or temporary employees. There was a consensus that the Hartz reforms had alleviated labour market rigidities and that further liberalization was unnecessary. Some fortification of legislation even took place; a number of 2013 Federal Labour Court decisions strengthened protection afforded to temporary workers. The numerical ascent of non-standard employment also relented. From 2008 to 2013 the percentage of workers employed on contracts of limited duration declined from 14.7 per cent to 13.4 per cent, while the proportion of fixed-term contracts converted to permanent rose from 30 per cent to 39 per cent between 2009 and 2012 (Vogel, 2013).

German ascendancy within the Eurozone can therefore be linked to the interests of workers in the country. Though wage moderation was endured and certain employees faced contractual precarity, effects which were associated with EMU, later predominance guaranteed employment and relented pressure for deregulation. Once such a state of affairs had developed, the German labour movement was loath to relinquish this advantage; this would be demonstrated by conduct after the onset of crisis.

The argument that workers can profit from national success within EMU is at odds with the verdicts of radical scholars. Bieler and Erne (2015) assert that 'this is not a struggle between different countries … [but] about class struggle between capital and labour' (p. 20). Such a position is insightful, yet I am sympathetic to pluralist analyses of the employment relationship and regard the advantages for German workers, which I have outlined above, as palpable. I reflect further upon distinctions between radical and pluralist understandings in chapter 9. Whatever such differences in interpretation, the extent to which German success benefited different types of employees within the country should not be ignored. The insiders about whom dualization theorists write, namely those workers in permanent employment, can be considered the most significant beneficiaries. Employees in such a position tend to gain from the status quo, a point long appreciated by scholars (Palier and Thelen, 2010). Even if these workers had faced wage moderation, German pre-eminence within EMU consolidated their secure status. There were also benefits for German outsiders. These employees worked in precarious conditions, perpetuation of the existing situation therefore not benefitting them to the same extent, yet economic success improved their prospects of permanent employment.

The European sovereign debt crisis: solidarity or selfishness?

Germany was a key protagonist in the sovereign debt crisis which gripped the Eurozone from 2010. The country was itself solvent and economically successful, yet its economic strength and status as the largest Eurozone economy meant that it played a crucial role in resolving the crisis. Following the bankruptcy of a series of countries on the periphery of the Eurozone, German consent was instrumental in the provision of emergency loans. Such programmes were highly controversial. Right-populists within Germany resented the provision of loans to countries they considered irresponsible, while there was wider debate in Europe over the measures of austerity and deregulation upon which the loans were conditional. According to critics, such programmes constricted economic growth, pauperized periphery societies and fuelled resentment of Germany (Blyth, 2013). Images in the Greek press depicting Angela Merkel as Hitler, widely circulated in Germany, scarcely endeared the German public to the region.

Austerity was repeatedly denounced by German trade unions. Aside from the motivation of solidarity with counterparts in periphery countries, there was also a fear that, in the longer term, such measures would be employed in Germany. Individual unions consistently issued declarations against austerity and suggested alternative courses of action based on fiscal stimulation; in 2011 both IG Metall and Ver.di issued statements to this effect. The most notable such contribution was the December 2012 *A Marshall Plan for Europe.* This document, published by DGB and backed by cross-union support, outlined a Keynesian vision for European regeneration on the basis of detailed economic calculations. Working on the premise that austerity was ineffective, the plan argued for a programme of investment in areas such as energy, transport and education and training. It was affirmed that these measures would not only help stabilize European economies, but also go some way to restoring trust in the European project. *A Marshall Plan for Europe* attracted widespread support among German unions, yet especially telling was the reaction of unions in other countries; an official from the Spanish UGT described it as 'a fantastic document' (see chapter 5).

Though German unions engaged in protests against austerity, an interesting finding was that some unionists perceived the approach taken by *A Marshall Plan for Europe* to be more effective than demonstrations. A DGB official said:

> *A Marshall Plan for Europe* I believe is, without being too modest, a real masterplan … For a simple reason we thought, okay we could protest against austerity. We could protest against the institutions that were there, but we wouldn't change anything. So we could go on the streets and declare our solidarity with Greece, with Portugal, with Italy, with Spain, with Ireland … but it wouldn't change anything.

Notwithstanding the existence of rhetorical solidarity with counterparts in Southern Europe, the actual support of German unions can be critiqued on two grounds. First, there was little participation in anti-austerity demonstrations. Though unions partook in the Europe-wide protests which took place from 2010, the degree of German participation was inferior to levels in other European countries. Particularly illustrative is the reaction of German unions to the 14 November 2012 European Day of Action and Solidarity. On this day, there were general strikes in Portugal and Spain, strikes in Greece and Italy and large protests in France, Belgium and certain CEE countries. By contrast, support in Germany was largely rhetorical; it was confined to limited protests in towns and messages of solidarity from works councils (Dufresne and Pernot, 2013: 19). In an analysis of union participation in the 14 November action which identifies three levels of input – (i) general strikes, (ii) mass demonstrations and (iii) symbolic actions and/or messages of solidarity – Dufresne and Pernot judge the contribution of German unions to have been in the third category (2013: 20).

Political strikes are admittedly banned in Germany, yet levels of mobilization fell way below degrees requisite for such actions. Dribbusch, a researcher at the DGB-supported Hans-Böckler-Stiftung institute, calls attention to failed efforts. An autumn 2012 attempt by Ver.di, along with Austrian and Swiss unions, to organize actions in towns and regions therefore 'largely failed to find active support among local union organizations in Germany' (Dribbusch, 2015: 180). It is also stressed that, had significant protests against austerity taken place in Germany, they would have achieved greater effect than actions in Southern Europe (Dribbusch, 2015: 181). The cases of campaigns against the port services and Bolkestein directives, which are called to attention, underline the potential of coordinated actions to derail the plans of European public authorities. Such a perspective is difficult to reconcile with the argument, made by my DGB interviewee, that documents such as *A Marshall Plan for Europe* were a more effective manner of opposing austerity.

Second, German union support for increased funding of the European Financial Stability Facility (EFSF) might be equated with support for austerity. Prior to a Bundestag vote in September 2011 to increase EFSF funding, the head of DGB issued a common statement with the head of the BDA employers' association, which advocated increasing the fund so as to maintain a united Eurozone. Union leaders also featured in several newspaper advertisements which promoted this course of action. Though the centre-left asserted that this was a necessary step to prevent collapse of the single currency, my social-democratic sympathies leading me to concur with this position, more radical figures argued that it amounted to endorsement of austerity. Andres Wehr, a member of Ver. di and founder of Marx-Engels-Zentrums in Berlin, criticized the DGB leadership; in the opinion of Wehr, endorsement of the EFSF was inseparable from support for austerity (Wehr, 2012). The stance of Die Linke, which is discussed below, was also based on such a rationale.

Certain proclamations of union leaders can be interpreted as rather close to the line of the German Government. IG Metall head Berthold Huber, whose familiarity with Chancellor Merkel was commented upon by some unionists (*Stuttgarter Zeitung*, 2013), asserted that unions were responsible for inflexibilities in the Spanish labour market and advocated the achievement of competitiveness through restructuring (Bieler and Erne, 2015: 12; Völpel, 2013). Huber had a history of such declarations; he dismissed the European strikes of 14 November 2012 as 'voluntaristic nonsense' (Bieler and Erne, 2015: 12). Though it is important to note that such views were not shared by all in the union movement, even attracting opposition within IG Metall, it is fair to conclude that they represent a significant strand of opinion. The attitude of German unions to Eurozone reform might also be considered disappointing. Unions lobbied for greater social regulation and intra-European fiscal redistribution, yet less attention was paid to the issue of German undervaluation.

The opposition of German unions to austerity, though regularly expressed rhetorically, was therefore somewhat equivocal. This prevarication may be attributed to two factors. First, German unions were constrained by the state of public opinion within the country. After the outbreak of debt crisis in 2010, the German public were generally unsympathetic to southern European countries; the view prevailed that the troubles of these countries were of their own making and that they were undeserving of German aid. Such sentiments were encouraged by a tabloid press which depicted southern Europeans as feckless and lazy. The *Bild* tabloid, which declared that 'Greece, but also Spain and Portugal have to understand that hard work – meaning ironfisted money-saving – comes before the siesta' (Henkel, 2015), became notorious. In such circumstances, it was difficult for German unions to move past rhetorical unity with periphery countries. There was little popular appetite for demonstrations of solidarity and members may have been hostile to concrete acts of support. Union leaders were also not immune to sentiments which were unsympathetic to the periphery, as the comments of Berthold Huber demonstrate.

A second constraint was the desire of German trade unions to maintain good relations with the Government. This is a goal which is shared by all moderate unions; when relations with public authorities are cordial there is more chance of policy objectives being advanced. In the German case, unions are renowned for their moderation and the Merkel Governments were committed to austerity. Given these two conditions, unions tended not to oppose austerity as vocally as they might have done; if one were to be uncharitable, it might be concluded that they prioritized national goals over solidarity with southern European counterparts. This appears to have been particularly true of IG Metall, a union renowned for having good relations with the German Ministry of Labour. Concerns about the position of leader Berthold Huber on austerity, articulated by many within the union movement, should be understood in the context of broader apprehensions about his relationship with Chancellor Merkel.

The attitude of SPD towards austerity was also complex. The party abstained from 2010 votes on a first emergency loan to Greece and establishment of a euro rescue fund, yet in 2012 voted in favour of a second emergency loan. Following rebellions in the governing CDU/CSU/FDP coalition, the passage of the package relied on the votes of SPD and Green Members of Parliament (MPs). In this case, the parties were motivated by the need to maintain a united Eurozone. The policy of austerity was nonetheless the target of frequent SPD criticism. Not only did the party initially favour the introduction of Eurobonds in 2010, but in December 2011 SPD published a crisis action plan with the Green Party. This paper condemned the Merkel Government for its narrow focus on austerity measures and advocated the establishment of a fiscal union with a common tax policy; it was contended that such measures would be more likely to build confidence in the Eurozone and stabilize its economies. Greater role and funding for the European Stability Mechanism were also proposed; the authors argued that this would avoid the necessity of the ECB performing the work of politicians. After they entered coalition Government in 2013, SPD continued to make the case for greater European solidarity and called attention to the deterioration of social standards in Southern Europe.

Though SPD regularly criticized austerity, two qualifications regarding the extent of opposition need be made. First, as with the German union movement, SPD was constrained by the state of public opinion within Germany; popular hostility to Southern Europe meant that positions favourable to the periphery were likely to incur disapprobation. Given the particular sensitivity of political parties to public opinion and the need of SPD to attract centrist voters, it was difficult for the party to communicate solidarity with periphery countries; SPD dropped its 2010 advocacy of Eurobonds after it emerged that the idea was opposed by supporters (Fleischhauer, 2012).

SPD leaders were not immune to rhetoric popular among the public. In the summer of 2015, at a time of heightened debate between the German coalition Government and Greek Syriza Government over Greek membership of the Eurozone, SPD head Sigmar Gabriel was critical of the actions of the Greek Government. In an interview he asserted that, 'We will not let German employees and families pay for the excessive campaign promises of a partly communistic Government' (*Frankfurter Allgemeine Zeitung*, 2015). This statement was controversial among the SPD left, yet was supported by more conservative members.

Second, the passage through Parliament of austerity packages was often contingent upon SPD support. Not only did the Merkel Government rely on SPD and Green votes to secure parliamentary approval for a second loan to Greece, but SPD supported the European fiscal compact; it was argued that support for the programmes was justified by the need to prevent a collapse of the Eurozone. I have signalled that I am sympathetic to these arguments, yet the fact remains that SPD voted in favour of austerity; many on the German left would not let them forget it.

The stance of the Die Linke party demonstrates the extent to which the position of SPD was rejected by others on the left. Die Linke, formed in 2007 by a coalition of radical movements, consistently opposed the Merkel Governments on parliamentary votes concerning the euro-crisis. This opposition was underpinned by a wider critique of austerity. In a 2011 position paper, the party demanded an immediate cessation of cuts to wages, pensions and other employee benefits in Europe. In order to resolve the crisis, the introduction of Eurobonds, transfer payments to states who 'are under the dictatorship of the financial markets' and tighter regulation of the finance sector was advocated. So as to implement these proposals, Die Linke supported a 'restart for Europe' through rewriting of the founding contracts of the EU, introduction of more democratic decision-making and minimum EU social standards. Die Linke also consistently criticized the position of SPD; for Die Linke, the stance of SPD amounted to a betrayal of European workers.

When considered generally, the reaction of German labour to the plight of counterparts in periphery countries was rather modest. Sections of the movement may have acted consistently with the solidarity dimension of labour behaviour (Hyman, 2001); many of the anti-austerity declarations issued by German unions were impressive while the opposition of Die Linke was unequivocal. There was nonetheless a broader failure to confront austerity in a committed manner. Not only did demonstrations in defence of the periphery attract poor levels of support, but the actions of SPD were often ambivalent.

As I have contended, the notion that the interests of German labour are not bound up with the ascendancy of Germany within EMU is problematic. An associated argument can be made for austerity. Radicals are correct to assert that the policy threatens German labour in the long term, yet certain benefits of austerity for the German economy should not be ignored. Not only does a weak euro aid exporters, but cheaper borrowing costs, which result from the 'safe haven' status of German bonds, help the German economy; the Leibniz Institute for Economic Research associated this effect with savings of more than 100 billion euros between 2010 and mid-2015 (Dany *et al.*, 2015). In an August 2015 analysis of austerity, Oxford economist Simon Wren-Lewis concluded that the measures were related to German self-interest.

It is true that national economic success does not necessarily advantage workers; radicals underline unequal patterns of income distribution. Gains associated with austerity may have favoured richer citizens, yet there were also benefits for workers; economic success guarantees employment and postpones painful domestic restructuring. The latter point is made by Wren-Lewis. The lukewarm reaction of German labour to austerity should be understood in these terms. Workers may well have been excited by the right-populist tabloid press which radicals call to attention, yet explanations which ignore overlap between austerity and German economic success are incomplete. Such dispositions were arguably short-sighted, austerity was a threat to workers in the longer term, yet I have emphasized elsewhere the short-term orientations of labour behaviour.

Conclusion: Accidental neomercantilism, questionable solidarity?

The question of whether unions in a core economy are able to use sectoral bargaining institutions to plan competitiveness must therefore be answered in the negative. Not only was such a scheme overly difficult to orchestrate, but there is lack of evidence for it and good reason to believe that German wage moderation resulted from structural influences. This finding that structures forestall certain actor strategies is one which will reappear in other country cases and underpins the theory of labour movement behaviour which I advance in chapter 9. In terms of the extent to which results from Germany may be generalized to other core countries, caution is advisable; bargaining in Austria takes place at peak level. The cases of Spain and Poland, in which agreements are also negotiated at inter-sectoral level, will hold lessons for this context, notwithstanding obvious differences between the countries.

The German case indicates that labour movements in core countries have difficulty extending solidarity to benighted counterparts. Though sections of German labour occasionally mounted impressive resistance to austerity, there was a wider failure to wholeheartedly oppose attacks on the periphery. This was related to benefits of German ascendancy within EMU. Given that labour movements in other core countries are in comparable positions, results are likely to be similar in these contexts; studies demonstrate this to be the case (Dufresne and Pernot, 2013). In chapter 8, I contend that such actions are indicative of the creation of a European insider–outsider division, which is broadly in the interests of insiders in core countries.

I should add that my intention in this work is not to apportion blame to Germany. Acts of genuine solidarity are difficult to achieve and, had they been in the position of German counterparts, I have little doubt that labour movements in Southern Europe would have acted in a similar fashion. Long-standing domestic insider–outsider divisions in Southern Europe, which are associated with the agency of insiders (Rueda, 2007), demonstrate the propensity of labour movements in these countries to act in such a manner. Given the constraints they faced, one might even argue that the degree of solidarity which the German labour movement *did* extend to colleagues in periphery countries was not unimpressive.

5

Spain: Going under

Tomorrow we approve the reform of the labour market and you will see
that it's going to be extremely, extremely aggressive. (Spanish Economy
Minister Luis de Guindos to Olli Rehn, European Commission Vice-
President and Commissioner for Economic and Monetary Affairs and the
Euro. Brussels, February 2012)

Spain is a country on the periphery of the Eurozone. After the introduction
of the euro, Spanish unions concluded inter-sectoral agreements which
attempted to secure competitiveness within EMU. The case of Spain
consequently raises the question of the extent to which competition via
such pacts is feasible, particularly in the context of a periphery country.
As with Germany, constraints on the ability of actors to plan meant that
these efforts were comparatively fragmented. In contrast to Germany, the
structures of the Spanish labour market damned the country to loss of
competitiveness. Difficulties associated with the achievement of moderation at lower levels, a problem over which actors had limited control, led
to incremental rises in ULCs and the onset of recession in 2008/9.

The outbreak of crisis raised the question of the ability of periphery
labour movements to marshal pan-European opposition. Though
Spanish unions were at the vanguard of attempts to organize European
resistance, these efforts met with limited success; this was primarily the
result of reasons external to Spain, yet also reflected the low priority that
Spanish unions traditionally placed on cooperation with European sister
movements. Nor were Spanish social democrats able to forge successful
alliances. PSOE was compromised by its support for austerity while in
office and was neither able to establish effective opposition to austerity
within Spain, nor marshal a common front of European social-democratic
parties. Problems such as this reinforced trends towards unemployment
and insecurity.

Labour movement and labour market in Spain: historical development and contemporary shape

Spanish trade unions are traditionally weak. This is partly the result of belated development; Spain industrialized later than other western European countries and the Franco dictatorship criminalized independent trade unions. Factors such as contestative industrial relations traditions and union attachment to anarcho-syndicalism also forestalled organizational growth (Crouch, 1993). In post-Franco Spain, unions have enjoyed democratic freedoms; in this time the two main confederations have been the social-democratic UGT and radical CCOO.

The Spanish system of industrial relations is remarkable for its statist character. So as to compensate for the weaknesses of social partners, the state extends collective agreements to uncovered workers and thereby guarantees a coverage rate which is approximately 90 per cent (Eurofound, 2018). Wages are traditionally negotiated at the level of the sector, yet inter-sectoral agreements exist which establish non-legally binding guidelines; such agreements have been used to safeguard Spanish competitiveness within EMU. The existence of provincial sectoral agreements, which grant considerable autonomy to lower levels, nonetheless make the system fragmented. In recent years, there have been demands for further decentralization so as to improve competitiveness. A controversial 2012 labour reform, which provided companies with greater scope to opt-out of sectoral agreements and stipulated that collective agreements were to expire one year after their signature, sought to address these concerns.

The political wing of Spanish labour is PSOE. A number of radical movements existed at the time of the transition to democracy, yet the social-democratic PSOE became hegemonic on the left (Andrade, 2012). PSOE was in government for twelve years from 1982. Under the leadership of Felipe González, the party played an instrumental role in the modernization of Spain and presided over the 1986 accession of Spain to the European Communities. PSOE returned to government in 2004 with José Luis Rodríguez Zapatero as prime minister, yet a May 2010 decision to implement austerity made it highly unpopular. This not only led to electoral defeat in November 2011, but was a key factor behind the emergence of the new-left Podemos party. Podemos claims the mantle of the genuine Spanish left and is popular with the young, yet by 2016 support for the party appeared to have plateaued. The challenges facing PSOE nonetheless remain severe; many consider the party to be in long-term decline.

Spain and the euro: the road to perdition?

European integration was a key foreign policy goal of democratic Spain. After joining the European Communities in 1986, there was a subsequent desire to be at the heart of the European project. Spain therefore agreed to the 1992 Maastricht Treaty and committed itself to convergence criteria for entry into the single currency. Fulfilment of these criteria represented a particular challenge. Not only was the 1989 entry of the country into the Exchange Rate Mechanism (ERM) late, but the peseta was repeatedly devaluated by the Bank of Spain in the early 1990s (Johnston, 2016: 144). A lack of capacity to moderate wages underpinned many of these problems; Spain had struggled to control wages during the 1980s as a result of weak employer organization in the non-exposed sector (Johnston, 2016: 146). Despite these challenges, impressive labour market performance in the 1990s facilitated Spanish entry into the Eurozone. This was the result of a 1994 law which increased flexibility in pay determination. Though the measure was opposed by unions, it appears to have helped achieve the moderation desired by public authorities; productivity growth exceeded wage growth by 15 per cent between 1994 and 1998. Unions would temper their position and eventually agreed to pacts with employers which complemented Government strategy (Johnston, 2016: 147).

Social partners continued to attempt to moderate wages after the introduction of the euro. A series of inter-sectoral pacts, concluded throughout the 2000s, aimed to guarantee Spanish competitiveness (EurWORK, 2005; Johnston, 2016). Trade unions consented to such a strategy, though prioritized investment and quality employment over the cutting of wages and temporary employment.

Care must nonetheless be taken when assessing the extent to which this represented a conscious strategy to achieve competitiveness vis-à-vis other Eurozone countries. The general goal of Spanish competitiveness preoccupied unions, employers and state, yet this was formulated in somewhat vague terms; reference to general European and international challenges, rather than ones specifically related to the need to achieve competitiveness within the Eurozone, tend to appear in declarations of the parties at this time. A 2003 inter-sectoral agreement makes brief reference to the need to keep inflation at levels similar to other European countries (BOE, 2003: 7541), yet the remainder of a detailed document says nothing which is more specific and discusses challenges related to competitiveness in very general terms. A key tripartite declaration of 2004, concerning competitiveness, stable employment and social cohesion, also makes no precise references to challenges related to European

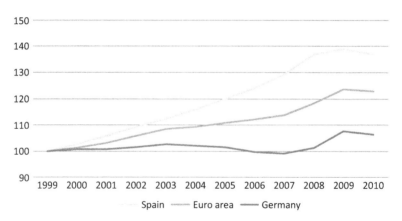

Figure 5.1 Nominal unit labour costs (ULCs) in Spain (1999–2010)
Source: Ameco; Bourgeot, 2013.

economic governance in eight pages of text (Gobierno de España *et al.*, 2004). As with the case of Germany, it is reasonable to attribute such lack of preparation to difficulties associated with long-term planning. It is easy to suppose in hindsight that the specific goal of competitiveness within the single currency exercised key influence on the minds of unions, yet in the distinct context of the pre-crisis years this was merely one consideration among others.

Whatever the extent to which competitiveness within EMU was pursued consciously and consistently, those agreements which were concluded during the 2000s failed to stem the growth of ULCs (see figure 5.1). In the opinion of Johnston, this was related to fragmentation and poor articulation in other areas of the collective bargaining system. Because of the regionalized nature of private and public sector bargaining, it is argued that wage guidelines agreed at inter-sectoral level were consistently overshot (Johnston, 2016: 139). The extent to which such factors led to crisis in Spain from 2008 is discussed below, yet a wider issue associated with the Spanish system of collective bargaining, related to the argument of Johnston, is the limited extent to which lower-level negotiators take heed of European developments. Though union interviewees referred to the existence of discussions within ETUC about wage negotiations and general stock taking of the European and international context, the extent of European influence on sectoral and firm-level bargaining is limited. This is partly for the same reasons why this does not occur in other countries; there are differences in industrial relations structures and economic contexts which make Europeanization of collective bargaining unfeasible.

Regardless of impediments to Europeanization which affect labour movements across the continent, there are grounds for considering Spanish unions to be Europeanized to a particularly small degree. In the area of collective bargaining coordination, the participation of Spanish labour has been notably lacklustre. A key IG Metall collective bargaining coordination network, which was initiated in the late 1990s and involved unions from fifteen European countries, included no Spanish unions (Gollbach and Schulten, 2000: 168). The European social dialogue is another sphere in which the record of Spanish labour is undistinguished; studies have found that Spanish engagement with SSDCs is marked by unenthusiastic participation in meetings and weak implementation of output (Prosser and Perin, 2015).

Particularly well-documented is the limited degree of Spanish union participation in EWCs. At the time of EU enlargement, there were EWCs in a mere 11 per cent of eligible Spanish firms; by contrast the European Economic Area average is around one-third (Köhler and González Begega, 2007: 135). To a large extent, structural features account for this poor take-up; many Spanish firms covered by the directive are small 'pocket multinationals', Spanish MNCs often orientate their activities towards Latin America and the structure of industrial relations in Spain is underdeveloped and adversarial (Köhler and González Begega, 2007: 136–7). Weak participation in EWCs is nonetheless related to the attitudes of Spanish unions. According to Köhler and González Begega, unions have made insufficient effort to participate in EWCs (2007: 138).

The economic crisis: all changed utterly

The Spanish economy performed robustly after the launch of the euro. Partly as a result of low borrowing costs, associated with membership of the single currency, GDP grew steadily and public finances remained healthy. Benign economic conditions encouraged labour market stability. Unemployment was comparatively low in the first half of the 2000s and, prior to the outbreak of crisis in 2008, had fallen to 8 per cent (see figure 5.2). In this time there was also little reform of dismissal protection legislation. OECD assessment of the strictness of protection for permanent workers remained constant between 1995 and 2010, while corresponding figures for temporary workers only underwent limited change. The segmented Spanish labour market continued to be the subject of debate, yet national economic success, linked to Spanish membership of the Eurozone, made reform a lower priority.

This equilibrium would soon change utterly. Following the outbreak of global crisis in 2007/8, it became apparent that Spain would be heavily exposed to adverse effects. The economy quickly went into recession;

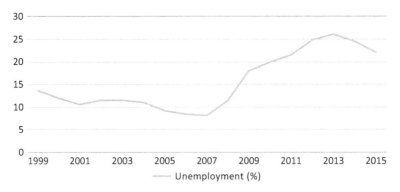

Figure 5.2 Unemployment rates in Spain (1999–2015)
Source: Eurostat.

GDP grew negatively for six consecutive quarters. Unemployment also burgeoned, a result of the high number of workers employed on temporary contracts, and would eventually exceed 25 per cent. A corresponding burden was imposed upon public finances. The Spanish budget deficit, which in 2009–12 reached around 10 per cent, was a key reason why markets later lost confidence in the country (Muñoz de Bustillo and Antón, 2011).

The causes of the crisis in Spain prompted vivid debate. One view, which focuses on the role of ULCs in instigating the Eurozone crisis, holds inefficacies associated with the Spanish model of collective bargaining culpable. This opinion has not only been advanced by neoliberals, who emphasize the need to cut ULCs so as to achieve internal devaluation, but also by political economists who underscore the inability of bargaining systems in periphery countries to replicate wage moderation achieved by countries in the core of the Eurozone (Hancké, 2013; Hassel, 2014; Johnston, 2016). The most comprehensive exposition of this view has been made by Johnston (2016). In the case of Spain, Johnston contends that the problem lay at lower levels. Though peak-level bargainers continued to aim for competitiveness after the introduction of the euro, via the agreements outlined above, lower-level fragmentation meant that targets were overshot. This led to a wage-price spiral which ultimately rendered the country uncompetitive.

There are nonetheless reasons to treat this interpretation with caution. As outlined in chapter 4, Müller *et al.* (2015) identify three problems with the argument that discrepancies in ULCs were the primary cause of the crisis; the points of these authors also pertain to Spain. With respect to the criticism of the notion that ULCs are principal determinants of price competitiveness (pp. 266–9), it is affirmed that 'the main problem for Spanish price competitiveness was not so much excessive wage developments but the profit margin behaviour of companies' (p. 267). Concerning the relationship between price competitiveness and export performance, it is asserted that Spanish non-price competitiveness offset loss of price competitiveness prior to the crisis (pp. 269–72). Finally, with regard to the relationship between export performance and overall growth (pp. 273–5), it is noted that domestic demand comprised 75 per cent of total Spanish demand in 2013 (p. 275).

It is worth taking heed of these points; they provide a counterweight to arguments which put excessive emphasis on the importance of ULCs in instigating the crisis. On the other hand, this does not mean that the arguments of authorities such as Johnston (2016) should be discarded. Not only was the weakening of Spanish competitiveness significant, but this deterioration can be linked with rising wage costs and the role of lower bargaining levels. The objections of Müller *et al.* (2015) should thus be read as important qualifications of the standard view, rather than denial that wage differentials performed any initiating role.

Whatever the exact relationship between bargaining practices and the outbreak of recession, an undisputed effect of the crisis was a worsening of conditions in the labour market. There were significant consequences in a number of spheres, yet effects on unemployment and employment security were particularly severe. Rises in unemployment were acute. As a result of the elastic relationship between GDP and unemployment in Spain, which is associated with the high proportion of temporary employees in the workforce, unemployment burgeoned from 2008. A level of 17.8 per cent was reached by July 2009, whereas in January 2008 it had been 9.6 per cent, and rates would eventually exceed 25 per cent (see figure 5.2). As a result of their propensity to be dismissed more easily, temporary workers were especially affected; the share of temporary employment declined as joblessness increased. The young were also disproportionately touched. Youth unemployment surpassed 50 per cent by 2012 and, as the crisis wore on, young citizens played key roles in protest movements.

Inauspicious economic conditions also encouraged reforms to dismissal protection legislation. Two key reforms of 2010 and 2012, advanced by the Spanish Government with the support of Spanish employers, liberalized protection afforded to permanent workers and moved the labour market towards the universal precarity commonplace in liberal systems of capitalism. A first reform was implemented by the Zapatero PSOE Government which, though initially adopting a Keynesian response to the crisis, introduced austerity after a May 2010 U-turn. This reform expanded use of the 'permanent employment promotion contract', a contract which set compensation for wrongful dismissal at a reduced thirty-three days' pay per year of service (p.y.o.s), and introduced provisions which permitted 'objective dismissal for economic reasons' with compensation of twenty-five days' pay p.y.o.s.

The second reform was introduced by the centre-right Rajoy Government. Following a decisive 2011 election victory, the new Government attempted to assuage the fears of financial markets through liberalization of a labour market which it considered sclerotic. The Rajoy reform built on measures introduced in 2010. The grounds on which workers could be dismissed for economic reasons was expanded, collective redundancy procedures were liberalized, a more flexible open-ended contract for firms with fewer than fifty employees was introduced and permanent employee compensation for wrongful dismissal was cut from forty-five to thirty-three days' pay p.y.o.s. The treatment of temporary workers was more ambiguous. Though the 2010 law aimed to make permanent employment more attractive to firms by restricting the time duration for which fixed-term contracts could be utilized and increasing redundancy payments, both reforms relaxed the regulation of temporary agency work.

A remarkable feature of these reforms was their provenance from without. Though liberals in Spain had for years demanded deregulation of the protection afforded to permanent employees, it was generally agreed that the measures implemented from 2010 could not be understood without reference to the precipitating influence of financial markets and the European public authorities. Such forces tipped the balance in favour of employers and politicians desirous of reform and paved the way for the weakening of the position of permanent employees. The role of financial markets was crucial (Bentolila *et al.*, 2012: 16–17). As bond markets speculated against a succession of indebted European countries, policymakers in Spain were compelled to implement the deregulatory reforms favoured by markets (Prosser, 2014).

The influence of the European public authorities was scarcely less pivotal. Informal pressure for deregulation was exerted upon the Spanish Government by the European Commission and core countries; many Spaniards were embarrassed when, in an episode which was discussed widely, Economy Minister Luis de Guindos was filmed in 2012 assuring Commissioner Olli Rehn that the forthcoming labour reform would be 'extremely, extremely aggressive'. A similar incident had taken place the previous summer when, in a secret letter later leaked to the press, the ECB made purchase of Spanish bonds contingent upon further deregulation of employment protection.

The nature of reforms inspired by European pressure, Meardi claimed (2014), was so radical as to exceed the demands of Spanish employers. The implementation of such measures was indicative of a wider overhaul of periphery institutions which was driven by external forces. In analysis of the effects of the sovereign debt crisis in Greece, Ireland, Italy, Portugal and Spain, Armingeon and Baccaro (2012) contended that common external restraints had prompted neoliberal revolution of national institutions. Conservative elites in these countries generally supported and often initiated such reforms, yet a precondition for their success was the existence of external pressure. A distinguishing mark of the Spanish case was nonetheless the lack of resistance offered by the Rajoy Government; one interviewee asserted that, had the Troika directly intervened in Spain, a more radical programme could scarcely have been implemented.

A further effect of the crisis was intensification of the *de facto* precarity which had long characterized the labour market. A first symptom of this was the high proportion of new workers which continued to be hired on temporary contracts. Though the proportion of temporary workers declined after the outbreak of the crisis, the rate of new hires employed on temporary contracts remained above 90 per cent (*El País*, 2012a). A spike in employee fear of dismissal was also registered. As a consequence of liberalization of dismissal protection and the unrelenting march of unemployment, by June 2012 41 per cent of Spanish employees feared losing their job in coming months (ABC, 2012). Other indicators of labour market precarity also increased. From 2006 to 2011, rates of involuntary temporary and part-time employment rose by 5.8 per cent and 22.3 per cent (Heyes and Lewis, 2014: 599).

Following the outbreak of crisis, a considerable deterioration of conditions in the Spanish labour market therefore took place; unemployment and insecurity markedly increased. A clear link can be drawn between such processes and Spanish status in the Eurozone. Because Spain was unable to achieve competitiveness within EMU, pressures for adjustment fell on employees. The crisis was also related to the behaviour of labour; unions were unable to compete or cooperate successfully in the first decade of the single currency and the position of Spain deteriorated. As argued above, doubt should nonetheless be expressed about the extent to which there were sustained attempts by Spanish labour to compete and/ or cooperate. The degree to which wage negotiators considered the situation in the Eurozone when attempting moderation was unexceptional and little effort was made to achieve coordination. The picture that emerges is one in which the role of structures is paramount. Because attempts to compete and/or cooperate were unfeasible, for reasons similar to those which precluded conscious competition in Germany, the straits in which Spain found itself resulted from structural influences. Inefficiencies associated with the bargaining system, particularly at lower levels (Johnston, 2016), contributed far more substantially to the loss of Spanish competitiveness than any act undertaken (or not) by unions.

Notwithstanding the inauspicious position which confronted them, Spanish unions contested attempts to reform Spanish and European labour markets. Unions had supported the PSOE Zapatero Government until 2010, yet attempts to reform the economy after this point were met with opposition, especially those measures introduced by the centre-right Rajoy Government. Underpinning union resistance to Spanish and European public authorities was a distinctive vision of competitiveness. Rather than policies which cut spending and deregulated the labour market, a recovery based on investment and high quality employment was advocated. Linked to this analysis was the impression that, because of its position in the Eurozone, the Spanish economy was becoming an increasingly low-quality one and stood in a 'colonial' relationship to economies in the core. A UGT official argued that this involved three processes. First, the 2012 labour reform had weakened the ability of workers to bargain collectively by prompting a shift in the balance of power towards firms. Second, owing to the improved position of firms in bargaining processes, there was a devaluation of salaries which took place in the name of competitiveness. Third, related to growing societal discontent provoked by reforms, there had been the passage of legislation which constrained the ability of unions to protest. The Citizens' Security Law (*Ley de Seguridad Ciudadana*), introduced in 2015 and criticized by both the UN and Council of Europe, criminalized certain forms of protest which were popular in Spain. Unions condemned this measure; my interviewee highlighted the cases of protestors who faced large fines and prison sentences.

Despite later imposition of limits on their right to protest, a key element of the repertoire of Spanish unions was the organization of actions against Spanish and European public authorities; these protests combined traditional forms of national agitation with more innovative efforts to articulate pan-European resistance. Attempts to construct European opposition were made at an early stage. A general strike of 29 September 2010, held in reaction to a labour market reform introduced by the Zapatero Government, was timed to coincide with an ETUC day of action (*El País*, 2010a). Protests were held across Europe on this day, yet Spain was the only country in which strike action took place (ETUC, 2010).

Further attempts at European cooperation would be undertaken by Spanish unions. At the 2011 ETUC Congress in Athens, a proposal from CCOO and UGT to examine the possibility of coordinating European strikes, including a European general strike, was accepted. The following year a European Day of Action and Solidarity, called by ETUC partly at the behest of Spanish unions (Balbona and Begea, 2016: 64), was held on 14 November. A general strike was organized in Spain on this day which, although focusing on issues specific to

Spain, made significant references to European challenges. Spanish observance of the European action again withstands comparison; Portugal was the only other European country in which a general strike took place. Participation in European protests was enthusiastic partly because such actions dovetailed with national goals. In addition to aforesaid actions, there was a third general strike on 29 March 2012; this was held in opposition to reforms introduced by the Rajoy Government. Involvement in all of the general strikes held in these years appears to have been impressive. Participation was uneven, yet unions claimed that approximately ten million workers partook in each of them; there was also a marked decrease in use of electricity on the days of the actions (*El País*, 2010b; 2012b).

When the active role undertaken by Spanish unions in European protests is reviewed, it is common to find fault with the contributions of movements in northern countries; Dribbusch (2015) is dismissive of the willingness of German unions to participate in such actions. Despite these pessimistic appraisals, which I share to an extent (see chapter 4), interviewees from Spanish unions were complementary about levels of support which they received from German counterparts. A CCOO official noted that German unions had consistently denounced austerity at European level and affirmed the good state of relations between CCOO and German colleagues. A UGT representative was enthusiastic about *A Marshall Plan for Europe*. This document, which was issued by DGB in December 2012, called for a European programme of economic stimulus and investment. The official explained:

> I can only say that the German unions ... prepared in 2011 a fantastic document which was called *A Marshall Plan for Europe*. The attitude of the German DGB towards austerity, and the attitude of the constituent unions of DGB, has been very similar ... to the attitude of Spanish unions. The DGB and German workers know who is consuming German products. And if the Spanish don't have money to buy cars, vacuum cleaners, washers and other German products then the German economy will weaken. Germany is the motor of Europe but it is a motor which relies on gas from the rest of Europe. And in this respect, DGB has always had a very clear and specific vision regarding austerity. I don't know a document of the DGB, nor a statement of the DGB – at least it would shock me – in which there is not criticism of the politics of austerity, and in which there is not criticism of the policies of Mrs. Merkel towards the other countries of Europe.[1]

---

1 'Yo solo puedo decir que los sindicatos alemanes ... presentó en 2011 un documento fantástico que se llamaba "Un plan Marshall para Europa" ... La visión del sindicato alemán, de la DGB, con respecto a la austeridad, y también de los distintos sindicatos que

The discrepancy between the verdict of Dribbusch (2015) and the responses of interviewees is rather stark, though it must be remembered that the latter are accustomed to dealing with higher-ranked German unionists. The issue of differences in the outlooks of the leadership and grassroots of German unions is nonetheless illuminating and, in later chapters, I assess it in depth.

Spanish unions therefore organized significant opposition to austerity after 2010; these actions were distinguished by consistent attempts to articulate national and European forms of protest. Despite the vigour of this opposition, two qualifying remarks need be made. A first is that, notwithstanding certain large-scale actions, figures for strikes in the years 2010–14 were comparatively modest; previous periods in democratic Spain had seen higher levels (Balbona and Begea, 2016: 56). Second, many protests which took place in this period were organized by new movements rather than unions. A group such as the Indignados, which mobilized young Spaniards disaffected with the establishment, were the driving force behind several key demonstrations. Unions nonetheless found ways to work with such movements, despite a cynicism towards established unions which was expressed by certain Indignados.

The reaction of Spanish labour to the crisis is also bound up with the actions of PSOE, the main social-democratic party in Spain. PSOE is traditionally pro-European. Not only did a PSOE Government preside over the 1986 accession of Spain to the European Communities, but during the years of transition from dictatorship the party established strong links with other European social-democratic parties, especially the German SPD. Research confirms PSOE commitment to European integration (Pardo, 2012; Rodríguez-Teruel *et al.*, 2016).

The onset of the economic crisis posed grave challenge to PSOE. Though the May 2010 decision of the Zapatero PSOE Government to introduce austerity may have helped avert direct EU-IMF intervention, it made the Government extremely unpopular and contributed to electoral defeat in November 2011. The introduction of austerity also had implications for the effectiveness of PSOE in opposition. In the first years of the conservative Partido Popular (PP) Government, which

componen la DGB ha sido muy similar … que la de los sindicatos españoles. La DGB, los trabajadores alemanes, saben quien consume los productos alemanes, y si los españoles y las españolas no tienen dinero para comprar coches, aspiradoras, lavadoras y productos alemanes, la economía alemana se resiente. Alemania es el motor de Europa, pero es el motor de Europa que se alimenta de la gasolina del resto de los europeos. Y en este sentido, la DGB siempre ha tenido una visión muy clara y muy específica con respecto a la austeridad. Yo no conozco ningún documento de la DGB, ni ningún pronunciamiento de la DGB – no lo conozco, a lo mejor hay, me extraña -, en el que no sea crítico con las políticas de austeridad, y en el que no haya sido crítico con las políticas de la señora Merkel con respecto al resto de los países europeos' (my translation).

implemented a programme of cuts and deregulation, PSOE was highly critical of PP policies; the 2012 labour market reform and cuts to sectors such as education and health were particularly condemned (PSOE, 2012a; 2013). Despite the vigour of PSOE objections, the ability of the party to arraign the Government was constrained. This was a result of the implementation of austerity by the Zapatero Government. Even if many of the reforms introduced by PP were more radical, earlier actions of PSOE meant that their criticisms lacked legitimacy. One of my interviewees, a former high-level functionary of the Zapatero Government, summarized this problem:

> I believe that [PSOE criticize the Rajoy Government] to a very small degree. The policies of the Government of Mariano Rajoy were based on austerity and devaluation of salaries ... these are barely criticized by the Socialist Party. Why? Because PSOE had implemented such measures itself. Starting from the middle of 2010, when you have the first crisis of borrowing costs and a 180 degree change in economic policy, [the Zapatero Government] goes from a policy of spending to a contrary policy ... a policy of cuts to public spending. There are many cuts in all services: cuts in pensions, cuts in the salaries of civil servants ... [so PSOE] can't really criticize the politics of austerity because it had done the same![2]

Difficulties experienced by PSOE in condemning austerity were symptomatic of a deeper crisis within the party. After the 2011 election, in which the number of PSOE MPs fell from 169 to 110, the shock of the result triggered a period of introspection. Aside from the inability of the party to authoritatively critique the programme of the new Government, PSOE faced a challenge of an existential nature: the emergence of the new-left Podemos party. The rise of Podemos, related to disillusionment with the introduction of austerity by the Zapatero Government, presented PSOE with a challenger to its left. Were the party to move to the left, to appeal to voters attracted to Podemos, the party risked losing support in the centre. The position of PSOE was also weakening in Catalonia; this was related to growing support for independence and the popularity of Podemos in the region.

---

2 'Yo creo que (el PSOE) las criticó relativamente muy poco. Las políticas del gobierno de Mariano Rajoy, estaban basadas en la austeridad y en la devaluación de los salarios ... éstas son muy poco criticadas por el Partido Socialista. ¿Por qué? Pues porque las habían hecho ellos aquí. A partir de mediados de 2010 ... se produce la primera crisis de la prima de riesgo y se produce un cambio de 180 grados en la política económica; se pasa de una política de gasto a una política contraria ... Una política de recortes del gasto público. Muchos recortes en todos los servicios, recortes en las pensiones, recortes en los salarios de los funcionarios ... entonces no podían criticar mucho las políticas de austeridad porque las habían hecho ellos' (my translation).

Such challenges not only hampered the ability of PSOE to effectively oppose austerity within Spain, but also constrained the capacity of the party to help create a European social-democratic front against austerity. PSOE continued to have links with European sister parties in these years and, together with partners from these networks, often condemned austerity. PSOE Secretary General Alfredo Pérez Rubalcaba called for a 2012 meeting of European social-democratic leaders at which a change in economic policy could be discussed (PSOE, 2012b), while in the summer of 2015 PSOE economy spokesperson Juan Moscoso del Prado announced the intention of the party to discuss progressive economic reform with European partners (PSOE, 2015). Notwithstanding such associations, the difficulties of PSOE within Spain appear to have impeded more substantial collaboration with European sister parties, including with movements in southern European countries also affected by austerity. My interviewee explained:

> During the crisis, with regard to countries affected by austerity like Greece and Italy, I think that there was very little connection [between PSOE and social-democratic parties in these countries]. I believe that between the Socialist Party [PSOE] and PASOK, for example, there is none … I believe that there are no relations nor interest in relating with one another. PSOE went through great trauma with the elections of 2011 … This loss of confidence of its own electorate, due to the U-turn which Zapatero performed in the middle of the parliament, provoked the appearance of Podemos and provoked … a crisis of identity and of self-confidence in PSOE … In these conditions, PSOE didn't know how to react, it didn't have the capacity to criticize PP [Partido Popular, the governing party] because it had introduced similar policies … So PSOE is really preoccupied with its own problems and this produces a policy of insularity, not of concern for the problems of other socialist parties [in Europe] or for a common front or pro-active policy … There is the opposite: political passivity.[3]

3 'Durante la época esta de la crisis y, en cuanto a los países afectados por las políticas de austeridad, como Grecia e Italia, yo creo que ha habido muy poca conexión. Yo creo que el Partido Socialista, por ejemplo, con el PASOK, yo creo que ninguna … creo que no hay unas relaciones, ni un interés en relacionarse. El PSOE sale traumatizado de las elecciones de 2011 … Esa pérdida de confianza de sus propios electores, debido al giro que hace Zapatero a mediados de esta legislatura, es lo que provoca la aparición de Podemos y es lo que provoca … una crisis de identidad y auto-confianza del Partido Socialista … En esas condiciones, el PSOE no sabe cómo reaccionar, no tiene elementos para criticar al PP porque ellos han hecho la misma política … Eso le llevaba a una política de ensimismamiento, no de preocupación, de vinculación con los problemas de otros partidos socialistas, de frente común, una política pro-activa … Era todo lo contrario, la pasividad política' (my translation).

Levels of solidarity from countries in the core of the Eurozone also had limits. There are long-standing links between PSOE and the German SPD, the latter providing unusually strong aid to the former during the transition to democracy (Muñoz Sánchez, 2012), and for years connections endured via organizations such as Fundación Friedrich Ebert Stiftung, a German social-democratic cultural centre which operates in Madrid. The orientations of PSOE and SPD nonetheless diverged in later years. After PSOE came to office in 2004, the movements became divided by discrepant priorities; the approach of PSOE to the labour market was more consensual, whereas SPD was implementing the Hartz reforms. During the crisis, certain wings of PSOE were also suspicious of SPD. Not only was there was a perception that SPD had supported austerity, but it was feared that the party had pressured the Zapatero Government to implement the policy.

The stance of Podemos contrasted with that of PSOE. Owing to its consistent resistance to European austerity, Podemos was able to oppose such measures in a more cogent fashion. As austerity was implemented across Southern Europe, the capacity of Podemos to harness popular anger made it a major political force in Spain. Podemos also had vibrant relationships with sister movements. Opposition to austerity united Podemos with parties such as Syriza and La France Insoumise; as the crisis progressed, close contact was kept and mutual support was provided. These associations were more vigorous than those maintained by PSOE; this was attributable to the rising profile of the European new-left and related problems faced by social democrats.

The developments which have been reviewed raise broader questions about the reaction of Spanish labour to the crisis. On the one hand, there is the issue of whether attempts were made at European cooperation. This was a challenge which Spanish labour generally met. Notwithstanding the comparative passivity of PSOE, which was linked to the context the party faced after defeat in 2011, Spanish unions made repeated efforts to achieve European cooperation. Unions were at the vanguard of attempts to arrange a European strike and their observance of organized actions was exemplary. This behaviour doubtless reflected commitment to European solidarity on the part of Spanish labour, yet is also rooted in the disadvantaged position of Spain in the Eurozone. Owing to subsequent consequences for the labour market, there were incentives for European cooperation which did not exist in other countries.

On the other hand, there is the question of the efficacy of this response. As a preliminary remark, it should be conceded that the forces against which labour were pitted were formidable. Not only did the EU exert severe pressure on Spain to implement austerity, but bond markets repeatedly speculated against the country. The disposition of the Rajoy Government towards the demands of European public authorities was also unusually compliant, some would say supine. Though these

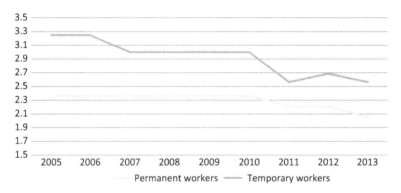

Figure 5.3 OECD Employment Protection Legislation (EPL) evaluations for permanent and temporary workers in Spain (1999–2013)

Source: OECD (later data are unavailable).

forces were not incontestable, their vigour was of a different kind to any European initiative hitherto inflicted upon labour. Successes of Spanish and European opposition should also not be ignored. The Spanish labour market was not entirely deregulated during the crisis; EPL scores, for both permanent and temporary workers, remained above 2.0 (see figure 5.3) and therefore superior to levels in the Anglosphere. This is to the credit of organized labour. In countries in which there was very little opposition to austerity, paradigmatic examples being found in the Baltic states, deeper measures were implemented.

Notwithstanding these achievements, the European opposition which was initiated by periphery labour movements was generally unsuccessful. Measures of austerity and deregulation were not halted, rather they progressively eroded the rights enjoyed by southern European workers. Reasons for this failure are varied. As argued elsewhere in this work, this can be primarily attributed to the disappointing reaction of labour movements in other European regions; because effects of EU austerity were ambiguous in these contexts, workers had diminished motivation to resist.

Explanations can nonetheless be found in the periphery. Despite the efforts of Spanish unions to initiate European resistance, later disappointments can be located in earlier failures. The extent to which the Spanish labour movement is Europeanized has long been underwhelming; this is the result of structural influences, though also reflects past choices (Köhler and González Begega, 2007: 138). If Spanish unions had participated in initiatives such as EWCs and European collective bargaining networks more actively in previous decades, their ability to instigate European protests might have been greater. Had German or French unions been threatened by significant European reforms, it is difficult to believe that movements in these countries, which possess greater resources and superior networks of European contacts, would not have resisted more effectively. Shortcomings of European opposition can also be attributed to failures of social-democratic parties in the periphery; in the Spanish case, the post-2011 insularity of PSOE was key.

Conclusion: The revenge of structures

Attempts by Spanish labour to respond to European pressures were consistently frustrated by influences external to actors. The efforts of Spanish unions to achieve competitiveness within EMU, which were also constrained by restricted awareness of external pressures, were thwarted by institutional problems associated with the Spanish system of collective bargaining. The case of Spain thus indicates challenges faced by periphery actors attempting to establish competitiveness. Findings from the country are generalizable to other periphery contexts; actors elsewhere in the region encountered difficulty achieving restraint (Johnston, 2016).

Progress towards pan-European resistance to austerity encountered related problems. Though Spanish unions were at the vanguard of attempts to articulate European opposition, which partly compensated for the passivity of PSOE, the lukewarm reaction of counterparts in other European countries ensured that these efforts were often unsuccessful. The finding that Spanish unions wholeheartedly resisted European austerity is unsurprising, it is generalizable to other periphery countries, yet the troubles of PSOE indicate that the actions of social-democratic parties are likely to be context-dependent.

As with the case of Germany, a key theme which emerges is the importance of structures. The agency of actors in Spain cannot be wholly denied as decisions made by unions and PSOE had important consequences, yet the ability of Spanish labour to compete and/or cooperate in response to European integration was consistently constrained by structural influences. This finding raises interesting questions concerning the influence of structures upon the behaviour of labour movements, which I examine in chapter 9.

To this point, I have examined the case of one core country, Germany, and one periphery country, Spain. The question is raised of the extent to which principles gleaned from these cases can be applied to other contexts. I now examine a country which occupies an ambiguous place in the Eurozone and is therefore a crucial test case of principles outlined thus far; this country is France.

6

France: Au milieu

My project is socialist and I am a Socialist. I am neither vulnerable to the sirens of neoliberalism nor the supporter of a state which decides everything above the heads of citizens, society and the social partners. I am not a moderate Socialist nor moderately socialist. I am simply a Socialist. (PS presidential candidate François Hollande, 16 March 2012)

The truth is that the French voted for the left and found themselves with the programme of the German right. (Former PS Economy Minister Arnaud Montebourg, September 2014)

France occupies an intermediate position in the Eurozone. Trade unions in the country are weak and divided, which raises the question of the manner in which unions in inauspicious structural positions respond to Europeanization. After the introduction of EMU, such incapacity meant that unions tended not to participate in wage moderation. Challenges associated with the single currency were partly resolved by a state incomes policy which limited potential loss of competitiveness; from the 1980s, French public authorities planned competitiveness to a degree which was unusual in other European countries. The French case is therefore one in which lack of labour capacity precluded a coherent response to integration, notwithstanding limited endeavours in spheres such as EWCs and collective bargaining coordination.

French competitiveness within the Eurozone was unexceptional and the labour market was habitually deregulated, though the country was not struck by recession to the same extent as Southern Europe. The crisis in this region raised a further question of the French labour movement, namely the extent to which a labour movement in an intermediate country was likely to extend solidarity to periphery counterparts. The reaction of French labour was lukewarm. Unions opposed austerity and voiced opposition to policies in available forums, yet concrete measures were less extensive; levels of participation in EU-wide actions against austerity were small compared to numbers protesting against French reforms. The response of PS was also mixed. There was considerable grassroots support for countries such as Greece, yet external realities meant that President Hollande increasingly toed the German line. I contend that the ambiguous response of French labour was related to the position of France in EMU; the existing form of the Eurozone had certain benefits for French labour and solidarity with southern European movements was consequently slighter than it might have been.

Labour movement and labour market in France: historical development and contemporary shape

France has long been renowned for its weak trade union movement. Unions developed historically late in comparison to other countries, partly the consequence of the monopolization of political space by the strong French state (Crouch, 1993), and resulting debilities endured throughout the twentieth century; union density was always low and today stands at below 8 per cent. French unions are also politically divided. Confederations of different ideological and religious stripes exist, yet the most salient division is between radical (CGT and FO) and moderate (CFDT and CFTC) unions. These problems have been compounded by the weaknesses of employers and mean that a coordinated bargaining system has encountered serious developmental difficulties.

The system of industrial relations which emerged was one which relied on state intervention. A 1950 law established the principle of state extension of collective agreements, and bargaining came to be characterized by the conclusion of agreements, usually at sectoral level by numerically weak social partners, which were passed into law (Parsons, 2005). Efforts were made to stimulate collective bargaining from the 1980s. The 1982 *Lois Auroux*, which established a duty for firm-level social partners to negotiate annually on wages and working time, encouraged collective agreements at this level. Underpinning these arrangements was the principle of the *hiérarchie des norms*; this forbade lower-level derogations less favourable to employees and ensured that firms could not circumvent minimum standards.

There have also been attempts to initiate peak-level dialogue between social partners, though wage negotiations at this level have remained elusive. The state has consequently intervened in wage bargaining so as to guarantee competitiveness; this has often been done in conjunction with large firms. Despite lack of participation in wage bargaining, French unions exert considerable public influence. Aside from membership of key committees, the ability of unions to mobilize protests is unparalleled in Europe. This capacity has allowed the successful contestation of numerous reforms.

The French labour movement is also represented politically, albeit in a more fragmented manner than in many other western European countries. This is partly the result of the historic strength of radicals; Parti Communiste Français (PCF), in addition to a number of similar parties, has attracted comparatively high levels of support. A moderate tradition nonetheless exists in France and this section of the left has been represented by PS. Formed in 1969, PS has played a key role in the politics of modern France (Bergounioux and Grunberg, 1992). The figure most associated with the party is François Mitterrand, who twice served as president of France between 1981 and 1995, yet PS has also provided a series of prime ministers. Recent fortunes have been mixed. Following the victory of PS candidate François Hollande in the 2012 presidential election, president and party endured crises which culminated in heavy defeat in 2017 elections. The scale of these losses prompted speculation about the end of PS (Courage, 2017).

France in the Eurozone: the enduring shadow of the state

France consistently supported the creation of the euro. Deepening integration was considered synonymous with French interests in postwar decades; successive governments therefore pursued the goal of currency integration and supported pre-euro initiatives such as the 'snake in the tunnel' and European Monetary System (EMS). The eventual form of EMU was not entirely consistent with the national interest. The anti-inflationary orientation of the ECB and austere nature of convergence criteria, both prices of German support for EMU, sat uneasily with the more expansive approach of French policymakers.

Preparation for euro entry triggered a range of reforms which attempted to make the French business system more competitive. Efforts were undertaken to reduce the long-standing budget deficit, a centrepiece of such attempts being cuts to early retirement schemes, and reforms were made to working time and unemployment insurance which attempted to promote job creation. Social partners participated in reforms which prepared the ground for introduction of the euro; reform of unemployment insurance was based on a June 2000 agreement between employers and moderate unions.

Following the introduction of the euro, the extent to which unions were able to respond to pressures associated with Europeanization was nonetheless minor. In contrast to many European countries, there were no tripartite agreements which attempted to establish competitiveness; this was a result of low rates of union density. The contestative dispositions of French unions, particularly the radical CGT and FO, were also scarcely conducive to such pacts. In that such factors had frustrated the historic emergence of corporatism in France (Crouch, 1993), these developments were foreseeable. Such barriers also impeded the conclusion of equivalent sectoral agreements, as occurred in Germany. Agreements at sector level may have been formally concluded, yet the weakness of unions ensured that they exercised little influence during processes of negotiation.

Strategies to achieve wage-restraint were consequently atypical. From the 1980s, the French state developed wage policies which aimed to secure French competitiveness within Europe. Following the Mitterrand decision to stay in the EMS, problems with wage inflation led public authorities to implement austere measures; the central bank, which was run by the Treasury, adopted a constricting monetary policy and pressures for wage rises relented (Hancké and Soskice, 2003: 14–15). The state would continue to play a key part in wage policy after the introduction of the euro. A small committee of experts, comprised of members of the Central Bank, Ministry of Finance and *Commissariat général du Plan*, communicated its views on acceptable wage rises to social partners (Hancké and Soskice, 2003: 49). The functioning of this institution was somewhat opaque, with little documentary evidence of its workings available, yet its centralized nature and the tradition of statist planning suggests that it adopted a comparatively calculated approach; in a work which examined processes of wage-setting within the Eurozone, Hancké and Soskice (2003) assert that the committee was keenly aware of developments in Germany. This strategy had parallels in other countries; a 1996 Belgian law limited wage rises vis-à-vis neighbouring countries (EurWORK, 2009).

The role of large firms during this time should not be ignored. As a result of aforementioned union weakness, large firms in France set wages with reference to relative productivity in French MNC sites. These rates are then presented to unions in processes of sector-level bargaining, before the Ministry of Labour extends agreements to uncovered parties (Hancké and Soskice, 2003: 43–4). Such a process also involves the public sector; rates agreed in the private sector act as benchmarks for public sector bargaining (Johnston and Hancké, 2009: 16). Given the fate of countries in the periphery of the Eurozone, in which indiscipline in the non-exposed sector contributed to loss of competitiveness (Johnston and Hancké, 2009), this practice was to prove crucial in the longer term.

Reductions in working time were a further method used by the French state to limit wage costs. In the second half of the 1990s, the French public authorities encouraged agreements which restrained wages in exchange for diminutions in hours. The first Aubry Law of 1998 was among the most significant of these reforms; this measure established a statutory working week of thirty-five hours and encouraged firm and sector-level negotiations which exchanged working time reductions for salary moderation. A second Aubry Law, which elaborated definitions and set out additional rules for lower-level negotiators, stimulated this process further. Social partners responded to these measures; following the passage of the Aubry laws, thousands of agreements were concluded which reduced working time and moderated wages. It is nonetheless difficult to link such agreements with conscious attempts to establish competitiveness within Europe; there is little evidence of this and, consistent with knowledge of lower-level union behaviour, it is reasonable to conclude that negotiators were preoccupied with more prosaic goals. Despite this lack of union intention, these agreements have been linked with the control of ULCs. In a work which compared wage moderation in France, Germany, Italy and Spain, Yakubovich (2002) asserted that measures taken by French public authorities to reduce working time could be compared to the formal pacts which were concluded in other countries.

Notwithstanding the involvement of unions in measures to reduce working-time, the extent of union participation in wage moderation was comparatively limited; this task was largely undertaken by the French state. Despite these initiatives on the part of the state, which were particularly calculated compared to efforts undertaken by unions in other countries, French performance within the Eurozone was unexceptional. The country registered a series of budget deficits in the 2000s, EMU fiscal rules were at times broken, and unemployment stayed close to 10 per cent. French ULCs also remained at mediocre levels (see figure 6.1). Though never as elevated as countries such as Greece and Spain, labour costs were consistently higher than those in Germany and remained above the Eurozone average.

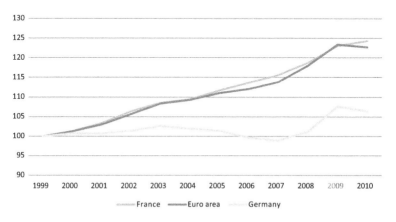

Figure 6.1 Nominal unit labour costs (ULCs) in France (1999–2010)

Source: Ameco; Bourgeot, 2013.

The record of the French economy after the introduction of the euro has inspired debate about the role of unions. In a work which contended that CMEs were likely to outperform MMEs within the Eurozone, Hassel argued that the performance of France implied that it should be considered an MME (Hassel, 2014). It was asserted that the country was characterized by 'weak trade unions with high political influence' (p. 15) and that there was a tendency for the state to protect and compensate actors; these traits were considered synonymous with MMEs and associated with weak competitiveness.

The place of France in typologies of capitalism is a broader question, yet this analysis of unions requires clarification. As I have emphasized in this chapter, unions played a secondary role in wage-setting processes after the introduction of the euro. Assertions that unions were positively associated with loss of competitiveness may therefore be disputed; their lack of capacity merely meant that they were unable to perform the role assumed by counterparts in the core. There is also clear dissimilarity between France and the southern European countries which incrementally lost competitiveness. According to Johnston and Hancké (2009), a key reason for this was restraint within the French public sector. Because pay-setting in the sector was successfully controlled by authorities, the spirals which characterized periphery countries were averted. Given the existence of moderation in the public sector, which did not occur in the periphery, the thesis of state compensation of unions also appears at odds with the case of France. Emphasis on differences between France and core countries is nonetheless valid. Though the French system shares similarities with core regimes, bargaining predominantly taking place at sector level in France and Germany, lack of union capacity in France precluded the retrenchment which transpired in the core. The role of firm-level opt-outs from sectoral agreements should also be noted. Though the French labour market was later reformed to permit certain opt-outs, such innovations had existed earlier in Germany and were crucial to the achievement of competitiveness (see chapter 4).

If the response of French labour to integration is to be fully appreciated, it is also necessary to review other forms of Europeanization in which unions are engaged. Certain kinds of European activity have long characterized the French labour market. French firms were among the first to institute organs for the consultation of European workforces and, following the introduction of the EWC Directive, a considerable number of EWCs were established. According to the European works councils database, there are currently 129 EWC bodies active in France; Germany is the only European country with more (EWCDB, 2018). French unions are also involved in networks which aim to coordinate bargaining; CFDT, CGT and FO have participated in such initiatives in the metalworking sector. Engagement has never been as considerable as the degree observed in Germany, this partly reflecting weaknesses discussed above, yet participation in such endeavours has been more extensive than levels in periphery countries.

Crisis and reform

France was significantly affected by the economic crisis. The country entered recession following the onset of crisis in 2007/8, the economy contracting by over 2 per cent in 2009, and growth thereafter was underwhelming. Unemployment also increased and levels eventually exceeded 10 per cent. Though this performance was not as poor as that registered by countries in the periphery of the Eurozone, it led to years of challenging labour market conditions. Such difficulties were compounded by the debt crisis which struck the Eurozone from 2010. Though France remained solvent, its own public debt and budget deficits were nonetheless considerable; these problems prompted ratings agencies to downgrade the country on a series of occasions. Wider disorder in the Eurozone, exacerbated by the fact that much periphery debt was owned by French banks, was also unconducive to growth.

In these years, partly as a result of the manner in which French labour had responded to European integration, levels of unemployment and employment security underwent changes. There was an increase in unemployment. Levels had been below 8 per cent in 2008, yet incrementally rose after the outbreak of crisis and exceeded 10 per cent by 2013 (see figure 6.2). As with other European countries, the young were badly affected; youth unemployment eventually reached 25 per cent. Effects by contract type were more difficult to discern. Though the percentage of employees in temporary work changed little in these years, certain statistics indicated that temporary workers were more vulnerable to unemployment (Chastand, 2014).

There was also a rise in employment insecurity. A series of measures, effected to improve the flexibility of the labour market and often with the explicit goal of enhancing French competitiveness within the Eurozone, were implemented in this time. A law of 2008, based on the *Modernisation du marché du travail* agreement between employers and four unions, extended trial periods and introduced the possibility of employers and employees terminating contracts by mutual consent. The 2015 Macron Law was based on similar rationales and simplified procedures during employment disputes. The 2016 El Khomri Law[1] was particularly controversial. This measure, bitterly contested by unions and agreed to only by

---

1 Though this law falls just outside of the studied period of 1999–2015, its importance to the Hollande presidency and the scale of union reaction means that I consider it.

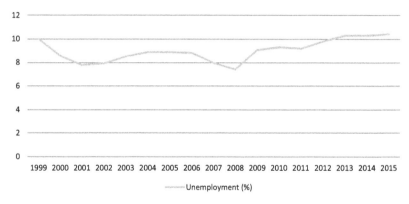

12
10
8
6
4
2
0

1999 2000 2001 2002 2003 2004 2005 2006 2007 2008 2009 2010 2011 2012 2013 2014 2015

Unemployment (%)

Figure 6.2 Unemployment rates in France (1999–2015)
Source: Eurostat.

CFDT, included the introduction of new economic conditions in which workers could be dismissed. A cap on levels of compensation awarded by employment tribunals was planned, yet amounts were eventually made indicative. There was also considerable *de facto* precarity; by the third quarter of 2013, the proportion of temporary contracts in new hiring was 82.6 per cent. This figure had been high for years, though the mid-2000s average of 72 per cent was lower.

Aside from reforms to dismissal protection, French labour was also weakened by a series of other measures. A 2008 law stipulated representative criteria for unions involved in collective bargaining and liberalized the thirty-five-hour week, while the possibility of limited derogations from collective agreements to firms in financial difficulties was introduced in 2013. In addition to its implications for employment security, the 2016 El Khomri Law extended maximum daily and weekly working time and permitted further derogations from *la hiérarchie des normes*. The cumulative effect of these measures was marked. In the course of a decade, as a result of reforms which provided firms with greater flexibility, the position of French labour was significantly debilitated. An official from the FO trade union summarized:

> France has a reputation for a lack of reform, but that is actually false. The labour market has been subject to enormous reforms and I believe that the labour market of 2016 is very different to the labour market of 2006. We have had some very important laws. One could call these laws 'holdalls' which concern an enormous range of subjects, whether it is the law on the securing of employment in 2013, another law in 2014 … or again in 2004 and 2008 … In 2015 there was also the Macron Law which especially

concerned working on Sundays, and now we have the new law [the 2016 El Khomri Law]. We really are in a very different context today, in which both the labour market and negotiation have changed.[2]

It is crucial to establish the relationship between such measures, the status of France within the Eurozone and the behaviour of labour. The reforms which have been identified above cannot be separated from the position of France in the single currency; membership of the euro deprived public authorities of the possibility of devaluation, limited fiscal autonomy and left labour market reform as the primary means of achieving competitiveness (Hancké, 2016). Some form of deregulatory agenda would have likely been pursued by public authorities had France not been in the single currency, this being made plain by developments in non-Eurozone labour markets, yet such processes were hastened by EMU. Links between these measures and the behaviour of labour are more complex. As I have contended, French unions played little role in wage-setting after the introduction of the euro. The question of whether the behaviour of unions can be linked with later substantive changes, which was examined in Germany and Spain, is thus of less relevance to the French case; structural weaknesses precluded significant competition and/or cooperation. Notwithstanding this lack of participation, the intermediate position achieved by France in the Eurozone was to have crucial implications for the manner in which French labour reacted to the debt crisis.

Despite the intermediate position of France, the labour market was also subject to European pressures for reform in these years. The solvent state of the economy ensured that these pressures were less invasive than in countries which received emergency loans, yet the EU Semester became a continual constraint. From 2011, country-specific recommendations were issued which advised French public authorities to deregulate employment protection, develop firm-level derogations from collective agreements and suppress social security spending (Clauwaert, 2013). Given the less secure position of France in the Eurozone, these measures tended to be deeper than those advocated in core countries. In

---

2 'S1: Malgré tout, on décrit la France comme un pays qui ne s'est pas réformé, ce qui est quand même faux on a quand même … Il y a énormément de réformes du marché du travail et je crois que le marché du travail de 2016 il n'a plus grand-chose à voir avec le marché du travail de 2006.

S2: On a eu des grandes lois. Qu'on a appelé un peu les lois "fourre-tout" qui traitaient d'énormément de sujets. Que ça soit la loi de sécurisation de l'emploi en 2013, en 2014 on a encore eu loi sur … Encore 2004 et 2008 … en 2015 on a eu la loi Macron qui a notamment traité du travail du dimanche. Et là encore, projet de loi travail.

S1: donc on est vraiment dans un contexte très différent qui a beaucoup bougé à la fois le marché du travail et puis la négociation' (my translation).

contrast to emergency interventions in the periphery, which were typically unilateral, unions were consulted about such reforms. A CFDT official nonetheless asserted that the capacity of unions to resist was limited:

> Unfortunately in the last stage of the Semester process, which is the most important and in which recommendations to the member states are issued, we are consulted a lot less often [than in previous stages]. We nonetheless present our opinion and often contest decisions taken ... On the recommendations we get angry, because every year the recommendations repeat the things which we contest and once again say to us that it is necessary to reduce deficits, that it is necessary to review company size thresholds, facilitate sacking and then things on taxes with which we do not agree at all ... The policy of the European Commission is to put countries in competition with one another. Spain has lowered its cost of work, so it is necessary that France lowers its own cost. Then when France does this, it will be said that Spain has to lower its costs again. In the end, everyone will find themselves receiving Chinese salaries![3]

French unions opposed attempts to deregulate national and European labour markets. Disparate effort was nevertheless expended on these tasks and, if the behaviour of French labour is to be understood, it is vital to appreciate the nature of these reactions. Contestation of domestic reforms was a key priority for unions. From 2008, consistent with the long-standing ability of French unions to mobilize wide sections of society, a range of protests were undertaken against planned reforms. Over a million took part in marches against increases in the retirement age in 2010 and further rallies against pension reform were organized in 2013, though this time they were smaller (*Le Monde*, 2013). Protests against the El Khomri Law were also extensive. In the course of 2016 over ten marches were held in opposition to the law and, although the extent of the actions were disputed by unions and authorities, participants could be numbered in hundreds of thousands. Following nation-wide

3 'Et puis malheureusement sur la dernière phase qui est quand même la plus importante qui sont les recommandations aux États membres on nous consulte beaucoup moins, mais on donne quand même notre avis. On intervient pour contester les décisions qui sont prises ... et sur les recommandations alors là on s'est fâché, parce que les recommandations tous les ans, il nous répète les mêmes choses disant on conteste et une fois de plus ils nous ont encore dit qu'il fallait qu'on réduise les déficits ... qu'il fallait remettre en cause les seuils d'entreprise, faciliter le licenciement et puis des choses sur les impôts sur lesquelles on n'est pas du tout d'accord ... La politique de la commission européenne vient mettre les pays en concurrence les uns contre les autres. L'Espagne a baissé sont coût du travail, donc il faut que la France baisse le sien. Lorsque la France aura baissé le sien, on dira à l'Espagne il faut que vous baissiez aussi. À la fin, tout le monde se retrouve au salaire chinois' (my translation).

demonstrations on Bastille Day, CGT claimed that a total of 1.3 million protestors had participated; estimates from police and public authorities were more modest.

French unions also protested against European reforms, though less energy tended to be dedicated to this goal. General objection was made to austerity. In a series of statements at key points in the Eurozone crisis, French unions advocated Keynesian solutions which were similar to those outlined in *A Marshall Plan for Europe* (see chapter 4). Consistent with their radical orientation, CGT and FO adopted especially vociferous stances. Despite their milder tone, moderate unions such as CFDT were nonetheless unwavering in opposition. The EU Semester system, because of its association with austerity and labour market deregulation, was also viewed warily.

This opposition was expressed directly to national public authorities. In a domestic context, French unions possess advanced institutional means, compared to certain European countries, to indicate disagreement with European developments. A CFDT official stated:

> There are structures for concertation between the state and social partners, through what you would call the CDSEI: the Committee for European and International Social Dialogue. It is the French Government which is responsible for initiating meetings of this committee ... There are many ministers who are represented and who present to us the European Semesters, the latest developments in the European Council of Ministers for labour, and so we are regularly consulted on appropriate matters by the French Government. People working on the European Semester, as with the Commission, come to France to work with the French Government on the NRP [National Reform Programme] ... They consult with us on NRPs ... in the CDSEI, but sometimes also at the Commission, because there is a representation of the European Commission in Paris.[4]

Interviewees also stressed the extent to which resistance to austerity was articulated via European confederations. In these years, French unions

---

4 'Il a des structures mises en place pour une concertation entre l'État français et les partenaires sociaux, ce qu'on appelle un CDSEI, comité de dialogue social pour les affaires européennes et internationales ... C'est le gouvernement français qui prend l'initiative de le réunir ... Il y a donc plusieurs ministères qui sont représentés et qui nous présente: les semestres européens, les ordres du jour du conseil des ministres européen du Travail et donc on est consulté sur tous ces domaines régulièrement par le gouvernement français. Ce semestre européen, comme la commission, vient en France pour travailler avec le gouvernement français, sur le PNR ... Ils nous consultent également sur ce PNR ... dans le cadre de ces CDSEI, mais aussi parfois à la commission, parce qu'il y a une représentation de la commission européenne à Paris' (my translation).

perceived membership of such organizations as mainly fulfilling their obligations to oppose European reforms and tended to support relevant confederations. The anti-austerity lobbying strategies of organizations such as ETUC were consistently endorsed, while French unions participated in protests which were organized in Brussels. Parsons (2018) nonetheless expresses ambivalence about the extent of union interest in European affairs. In a work which theorizes the relationship between French and European social dialogue, the tendency for unions to abdicate European affairs to confederations is underlined; it is also noted that the Committee for European and International Social Dialogue meets for a mere half day every year. The Economic, Social and Environmental Council, which is endowed with consultative powers, is therefore a more important forum for debate of European questions. In this institution, the presence of multiple civil society actors nonetheless makes the achievement of consensus challenging.

Notwithstanding the existence of constraints, French unions developed bilateral links with unions in other member states and, in the context of these relationships, worked with unions in countries affected by austerity. In addition to moral support, certain forms of learning resulted from such connections. An FO official asserted that, owing to links with Spanish unions, the union had learnt much about developments in Spain; this proved to be useful given that Spanish reforms of 2010 and 2012 were perceived as anticipating later reforms in France. It was added that this represented an inversion of the usual practice of trends affecting France before spreading to Spain.

French unions also engaged in demonstrations against European austerity. In addition to events in Brussels in which unions participated, protests in support of European counterparts were held in France. On the European Day of Action and Solidarity of 14 November 2012, more than 130 actions took place (Dufresne and Pernot, 2013). Levels of participation were not insignificant. Demonstrations in cities such as Paris, Marseille and Bordeaux attracted thousands and a nation-wide figure of 113,000 protestors was reported (Dufresne and Pernot, 2013). The actions also enjoyed considerable political support; not only were a range of unions involved, including CGT and CFDT, but prominent radical politicians such as Jean-Luc Mélenchon were present.

The extent of engagement can nonetheless be overstated. At the French actions which took place in November 2012, one report described participation as 'often sparse' (Gonzalez and Khalip, 2012). It should also be remembered that no strikes were held. This was not the case in Southern Europe; in Greece, Italy, Portugal and Spain, calls for European solidarity inspired general strikes (Dufresne and Pernot, 2013). Days of action admittedly function as a substitute for strikes in France, workers using time-banked leave to partake in demonstrations, yet this caveat does not explain mediocre levels of participation.

The middling commitment observed in France is conspicuous in a country in which hundreds of thousands habitually take part in demonstrations against domestic reforms, even if one takes into account the diminished ability of French public authorities to shape policy in countries such as Greece. French unions indeed perceived such matters to fall within the domain of unions in affected countries. When asked about the issue, a French trade unionist remarked that it was important not to intrude in the affairs of counterparts. As observed when considering the reaction of German labour (see chapter 4), it should also be remembered that more decisive action from French workers could have helped achieve the dilution of austerity. Given the slighter importance of the French Government to the resolution of the crisis, in contrast to Germany, limits to the influence of French unions should nonetheless be borne in mind.

If the reaction of French labour to austerity is to be more fully conceptualized, it is also vital to take into account the position of PS. PS has been accused of embracing neoliberalism, yet in these years the party can be considered reasonably representative of French workers (Berruyer, 2012). Following the outbreak of debt crisis, PS was comparatively united in its opposition to Government policy. President Sarkozy was perceived as differing little from Chancellor Merkel in his attitude to austerity; at this time the appellation 'Merkozy' was popular. PS MPs abstained in a February 2012 vote on the creation of the European Stability Mechanism; this distinguished them from the German SPD, which supported this measure. In an incident which foreshadowed future divisions within the party, twenty MPs on the left of PS nonetheless voted against the policy. Opposition to the Government featured strongly in the 2012 presidential election campaign of PS candidate François Hollande. In an interview which was conducted jointly with SPD leader Sigmar Gabriel, Hollande condemned austerity and denounced neoliberalism while declaring himself a true socialist (*Libération*, 2012). Such sentiments underpinned a key Hollande promise during the 2012 campaign; this was to renegotiate the European fiscal compact to incorporate goals of growth and employment.

Following the victory of Hollande and his assumption of office, European political realities soon drove a wedge between the president and party grassroots. The issue of the European fiscal compact was a particular sticking point. Regardless of pledges made by Hollande during the campaign, German refusal to renegotiate meant that the terms of the treaty remained unchanged. The role of SPD in this process should not be ignored. Despite the earlier stand of PS and SPD against austerity, later attempts by Hollande to achieve an understanding with SPD ended in disappointment. Following a cool reception from Chancellor Merkel, Hollande held talks with SPD leaders in the summer of 2012; some of these were secretive and were eventually divulged by WikiLeaks. Such discussions appear to have borne little fruit. Not only did SPD vote in favour of the fiscal compact, but the party tended not to discuss European affairs as the 2013 federal elections approached (Stierle and Mayer, 2014).

Hollande managed to secure the concession of a growth pact, though some dismissed this as insignificant and agreed simply to save the face of the French president (Volkery, 2012). Many in PS were deeply disillusioned by this failure and there were escalating tensions within the party. When a parliamentary vote was taken on the ratification of the treaty in autumn 2012, twenty PS MPs joined Green and Communist colleagues in opposing the text; this was despite the fact that PS leadership had made it clear that there would be no freedom of vote. Such rebels were outnumbered by PS colleagues who were in favour, yet their stance would have profound implications in the longer term.

Rebellions on such lines would become a recurring feature of the Hollande presidency. PS rebels became known as 'frondeurs'.[5]. There were approximately twenty core members of this faction though it could include around fifty depending on the issue, and the Government was defied on a series of occasions. President Hollande preferred a government in which various strands of PS were represented, yet tensions among wings meant that this became impossible. Matters came to a head in August 2014. Following continued reluctance to toe the party line, Economy Minister Arnaud Montebourg declared that the 'obsessions of the German right … [were leading France down] a blind alley'. Hollande responded by forming a new Government from which Montebourg and his allies Benoît Hamon and Aurélie Filippetti were excluded; Le Parisien reported that Prime Minister Manuel Valls had instructed the president to choose between himself and Montebourg (*Guardian*, 2014).

Strained relations between Government and grassroots, which resulted from the impossibility of reconciling European imperatives with popular demands, thereafter were exacerbated. Following the purging of Montebourg and his allies, the orientation of the Government moved to the right; during the Greek crisis of the summer of 2015, the line of the German Government was closely followed. Such a position worsened tensions with the left of the party. In this time, figures such as Montebourg openly criticized Government policy and sought alliances with anti-austerity movements in other European countries; the visit of former Greek Finance Minister Yanis Varoufakis to Frangy-en-Bresse in August 2015, during which Varoufakis spoke at a festival

---

5 This French term refers to a political rebel.

with Montebourg, was covered widely in the media (*Le Monde*, 2015). The stance of Montebourg and his allies tended to be shared by PS grassroots. As the Government position converged on the German one, there was increasing unhappiness among rank and file. Relations with sister parties brought little relief. Notwithstanding long-standing links with social-democratic parties in other member states, which endured in these years, there is little evidence that PS used such associations to achieve the European solidarity initially desired by Hollande. Aside from the failed 2012 talks with SPD, which can be regarded as casting a subsequent shadow, a PS interviewee opined that links with southern European counterparts had been weak during this time.

The tensions which racked PS in these years would lead to disaster in 2017 elections. As a result of disillusionment with the Hollande presidency, which was in great part rooted in opposition to the closeness of the Government to Chancellor Merkel, veteran left-winger Jean-Luc Mélenchon attracted considerable support in the presidential election. Mélenchon had been consistently against austerity. Though the choice of the left-wing Benoît Hamon as PS candidate for president led many to believe that the party would not struggle to attract radical support, Mélenchon proved to be the more successful candidate; Hamon eventually obtained a mere 6.36 per cent of the first-round vote. The collapse of PS was also a result of competition from the centre. Following the creation of the centrist En Marche party by Economy Minister Emmanuelle Macron, many moderate PS voters defected to En Marche. Parliamentary elections were just as disquieting; PS won a mere thirty seats as En Marche made sweeping gains. At the time at which I write (the start of 2018), the future of PS is uncertain; it can nonetheless be concluded that the debt crisis played a key role in the 2017 collapse. The party was unable to reconcile the demands of government with the sentiments of its base and was consequently squeezed between resurgent centrist and radical movements.

If the picture is considered overall, the extent to which French labour exhibited solidarity with counterparts in the periphery was therefore mixed. Unions engaged in moderately sized actions and the left of PS rebelled against the Government, yet it is reasonable to conclude that more could have been done; French unions failed to engage in strike action on 14 November 2012 and the Hollande presidency increasingly adopted the line of Chancellor Merkel. President Hollande was admittedly pushed in this direction by external realities, yet the degree to which a hard-line position was advocated by the French public (including workers) must not be ignored. In 2015, 58 per cent of the population advocated ejecting Greece from the Eurozone should the country fail to make loan repayments; this position was shared by 41 per cent of PS voters. In 2011–12, support for such a course of action had been even higher (IFOP, 2015).

These developments raise the question of the extent to which the behaviour of French labour was underpinned by the national position within the Eurozone. On the one hand, the somewhat precarious status of France meant that labour had an interest in challenging the prevailing shape of EMU. Union protests and PS revolts against President Hollande, the equivalent of which did not occur in Germany, can be understood in these terms. Notwithstanding these acts, the status quo was not entirely counter to the interests of French workers. France secured a degree of competitiveness in the single currency, which implied that increases in unemployment and insecurity were not as considerable as in periphery countries. The measures of austerity which were implemented in the periphery were also not completely at odds with French economic interests; periphery debt was owned by French banks and a cheap euro helped exporters. Advantages associated with austerity admittedly tend to accrue to richer classes, repayment of Greek debt being most palpably in the interest of French banks, yet the extent to which workers also benefited should not be ignored; national economic success has important implications for employment. Given the less secure position of France in the Eurozone, this relationship was nonetheless weaker than in Germany. In chapter 8, I examine in detail the degree to which different labour movements gained from the existing character of EMU.

Conclusion: The French exception?

Following the introduction of the euro, the extent to which French labour reacted to integration in a coherent manner was therefore very slight; this was a result of union weakness and meant that the position France obtained within the Eurozone cannot be regarded as the result of labour intent. As in Germany and Spain, external influences were more profound; in France, the role of state incomes policy was critical. The French case demonstrates that, in contexts in which unions are weak, challenges associated with Europeanization can be resolved by external actors. Such a discovery provides additional indication of the importance of structures and this theme is assessed further in chapter 9. Given that unions were involved in tripartite and/or sectoral agreements in most European countries following the launch of EMU, it must be acknowledged that the case of France is rather anomalous. In that developments in France are illustrative of union marginalization, which is an increasingly common phenomenon in Europe, these principles are nonetheless instructive.

The case of the reaction of French labour to the debt crisis is invaluable; it allows theorization of the extent to which an intermediate labour movement is likely to extend solidarity to periphery counterparts. Though the behaviour of French labour cannot be divorced from national peculiarities, the middling reaction which was observed is consistent with an intermediate context. This finding informs my conceptualization of the response of European labour movements to crisis, which I undertake in chapter 9.

Thus far I have examined the cases of core, periphery and intermediate countries; presented data are nearly sufficient for my research question to be answered. This is an endeavour I undertake from chapter 8, yet prior to this it is necessary to consider developments in a country outside of the Eurozone. The case of Poland, which I now present, is such a context and allows the influence of euro membership on labour behaviour to be better isolated.

7

Poland: Splendid isolation?

'Razem expresses solidarity with the society and Government of Greece in their fight for democracy and social justice ... The politics of cuts and reduction of demand does not work, because it cannot work. Consistent with the predictions of economists it is bringing Greece to economic collapse. (Razem statement on the Greek crisis, June 2015)

We don't want to be on benefits, we want to work, we want the creation of jobs. Today we want to have benefits from work like the Greeks, Spanish and Portuguese have benefits for the unemployed. (OPZZ leader Jan Guz on the 14 November 2012 European Day of Action and Solidarity)

Poland is a non-member of the Eurozone. Despite this, the Polish labour movement was exposed to pressures associated with Europeanization. This was particularly the case at tripartite level; scholars at one point predicted that Polish tripartism would ready the country for membership of the euro (Meardi, 2006). Given this concern, a key issue is the extent to which Polish unions were able to use a CEE tripartite institution to respond to pressures associated with Europeanization. This happened to a limited degree, which reflected political division and the restricted planning capacity of actors.

Polish absence from the Eurozone nonetheless pre-empted a subsequent deterioration of conditions in the labour market, as occurred in countries on the periphery of the Eurozone. Partly as a result of monetary autonomy, the Polish economy stayed competitive and conditions in the labour market remained comparatively benign. Polish non-membership of the euro also precluded a second scenario, namely a situation in which, as in Germany, conditions in the labour market were consolidated at the expense of periphery countries. The onset of the crisis also raised the question of the extent to which a labour movement in a non-Eurozone country was likely to exhibit solidarity with periphery countries. The reaction of Polish labour was fairly substantial. Though the left-wing SLD party was rather unconcerned, trade unions engaged in a series of actions in support of Southern Europe; this was especially noteworthy given organizational weaknesses of Polish unions.

Labour movement and labour market in Poland: historical development and contemporary shape

The historical emergence of Polish trade unions was disjointed. Not only was Poland partitioned into German, Russian and Austro-Hungarian territories prior to the First World War, thereby ensuring that unions developed in distinct manners in the three districts, but independent unions were outlawed under Polish Communism. In opposition to Communism, the Catholic-populist NSZZ Solidarność union emerged in 1980 and the official Ogólnopolskie Porozumienie Związków Zawodowych (OPZZ) was soon founded in retort. Following the fall of Communism, Solidarność and the post-Communist OPZZ became the two main unions in democratic Poland; at times rivalry has been bitter.

Industrial relations in democratic Poland is decidedly neoliberal. Rates of trade union and employers' association density are low and collective bargaining tends to be performed on a single-employer basis, where there is a trade union presence. Though certain sectoral agreements exist, predominantly in the state sector, these cover less than 3 per cent of workers (Meardi *et al.*, 2015). Economic policy has also tended to be neoliberal, most egregiously during a period of 'shock therapy' in the early 1990s, yet certain elements of the Polish system are based on state intervention. The labour code survived the fall of Communism and comparatively generous social welfare, in the spheres of pensions, unemployment benefits and health, have distinguished democratic Poland. Bohle and Greskovits (2012) emphasize the propensity of Polish capitalism to compensate 'losers' and contrast the case of Poland with the more neoliberal Baltic states.

One achievement of contemporary Poland has been its sustained use of tripartism. A number of pacts have been concluded since the start of the transformation, though the politicized nature of union-relations has meant that tripartism has been prone to collapse (Meardi *et al.*, 2015). The most recent failure occurred in 2013 under the centre-right PO-PSL Government, though tripartism was soon reinstituted by the right-populist PiS administration.

Social democracy has a weak foundation in Poland. This is primarily a result of the Communist past; the socialist nature of the regime ensured that opposition to it tended to assume a Catholic and/or liberal form. In democratic Poland, the left has been dominated by the post-Communist

SLD (Tomczak, 2012). SLD has enjoyed electoral success and emphasizes social goals to an extent, yet the party tended to adopt neoliberal policies while in government (Woś, 2014) and failed to forge the bonds with lower-income voters which characterize western social-democratic parties. The 2015 general election was a serious disappointment for the Polish left. Not only did an alliance which included SLD fail to attract the 8 per cent support required to enter Parliament, but the new-left Razem party was unable to meet the 5 per cent threshold for individual parties.

Poland and the euro: a dalliance never to be consummated?

Membership of the EU was a key long-term goal of post-Communist Poland. This was to take over a decade to be realized, yet, when Poland acceded to the union in 2004, the terms of membership committed the country to eventual adoption of the euro. At the time of Polish accession to the EU, policymakers in Poland considered the rapid realization of this goal to be desirable. National Bank of Poland (NBP) governor Leszek Balcerowicz at one time regarded 2007 as a plausible adoption date (Bohle and Greskovits, 2012: 173), while in 2007–8 the PO-PSL Government aimed to introduce the euro by 2012 (Meardi and Trappmann, 2013: 198). These ambitions were not to be achieved. Not only was a 2005–7 nationalist-populist Government less keen on membership, but the debt crisis made the prospect of joining the Eurozone temporarily unattractive. Poland remains committed to adopting the single currency, yet it is uncertain when this will occur.

Accession to the EU had a range of consequences for Polish labour. Though there were challenges associated with the intensification of competition, implementation of European regulation introduced a series of rights for workers. Changes in union competition and/or cooperation was another question. Sectoral bargaining, which predominates in most western European countries and is a level at which processes of Europeanization commonly occur, is underdeveloped (Meardi, 2002). The firm level, at which pay negotiations predominantly take place, is a level which does not lend itself to Europeanization. Pay is set unilaterally in the majority of firms and, in those firms in which negotiations take place, European influences are taken into account to a limited degree. Though interviewees reported that there was awareness of developments in other countries and that wage demands in MNCs had been moderated by the perception that Polish competitive advantage lay in low labour costs, such considerations tend to be secondary. As in other European countries, the goals of negotiators revolve around the economic situation of the firm. The predominance of concerns specific to the Polish context, such as the preservation of employment, is a further barrier. These patterns have characterized the Polish labour market for many years, are well-attested by literature and are typical of the CEE region (Bohle and Greskovits, 2012).

Processes of Europeanization are more feasible at tripartite level; as in other CEE countries, tripartite negotiations have long taken place in Poland. Dialogue at this level concerns macro challenges and is therefore more likely to reflect the need of labour to compete and/or cooperate in response to integration. In a 2006 article, Meardi expected that Polish tripartism would assume an important role in preparation for adoption of the euro. This work nonetheless looked forward to this development, as opposed to reflecting upon the extent to which it had taken place. Despite subsequent preoccupation of policymakers with adoption of the euro, the extent to which European goals were pursued by tripartite negotiators turned out to be limited. Polish tripartism concerns itself with issues related to wages, minimum wages are set and recommendations on ceilings for rises are made, yet European considerations appear to have had slight effect on negotiations. Analysis of forty-three resolutions made by the Tripartite Commission between 2001 and 2010 reveals that very little attention was paid to European influences (Trojstronna komisja ds społeczno gospodarczych, 2017). Certain working groups occupied themselves with subjects such as the European structural funds and social charter, yet the work of such committees did not lead to any Europeanization of wage negotiations.

Nor did the Tripartite Commission concern itself with the aim of euro membership; assessment of documentation mentioned above reveals no preoccupation with this ambition. Given that the objective of euro membership was not a pressing one for Polish policymakers prior to 2007, this is perhaps understandable. In the period 2007–10, in which euro entry was a key aim for the centre-right PO-PSL Government, lack of Tripartite Commission work on this goal can be attributed to poor relations between PO and Solidarność. Animosity among the parties, rooted in their fundamentally different outlooks on socio-economic and cultural questions, meant that tripartism decayed in these years before temporarily collapsing in 2013. The tendency for Polish tripartism to fall victim to partisanship, long noted by scholars (Meardi *et al.*, 2015), therefore partly explains the failure of tripartism to help prepare Poland for euro membership.

Engagement in the forms of cooperation which take place in other countries is also traditionally limited in Poland. Not only is participation in European social dialogue rather lacklustre, a study finding that Polish involvement in SSDCs was minimal (Prosser, 2018), but Polish engagement in EWCs is also slight. A single EWC is headquartered in Poland; Liechtenstein and the United Arab Emirates register the same figure (EWCDB, 2018). Strategies for collective bargaining coordination are also underdeveloped; Polish engagement in the bargaining networks found in Western Europe has been limited. Though these levels of participation reflect structural influences, a trend for actors to be unenthusiastic about European cooperation should not be ignored. This is associated with perceptions of Polish comparative advantage. Given lower labour costs in Poland, unions have been tempted to avoid initiatives which make the country less attractive to capital.

Notwithstanding these historic limits, there is an increasing tendency for Polish unions to engage in coordination. This trend is associated with Polish subsidiaries of MNCs. A Solidarność official emphasized the extent to which the union was in favour of greater Europeanization of bargaining in this domain; it was reported that Solidarność shared information with other unions within MNCs and that this led to increased expectations concerning wage rises in Poland. Reference was also made to changes in the attitudes of Polish unions. Though it had been traditionally thought that a precondition for the continuing presence of MNCs in Poland was comparatively low wages, this view had evolved. This was partly the result of Fiat's relocation of employment from Poland to Italy; the episode had taught unions that, if Fiat was prepared to move production to a country in which labour costs were higher, there was little point in acquiescing to low pay.

Interviewees also placed emphasis on other attempts by Polish unions to Europeanize wage bargaining. An OPZZ official asserted that not only did the union support attempts by the European Commission to guarantee equal pay for posted workers, but that OPZZ campaigned for a European minimum wage. Interesting reference was made to resistance to such efforts within the European trade union movement. A Solidarność official commented upon the tendency of Scandinavian unions to object to the Europeanization of pay regulation, underlining the opposition of unions from these countries to European minimum wages and Europeanized negotiations within MNCs. Despite the existence of such obstruction, the tendency for Polish unions to be more amenable to cooperation with sister movements is noteworthy. This can be associated with the increasing development of the Polish economy and, especially if the trend is replicated in other CEE countries, is likely to improve the quality of European coordination.

The crisis: continuity through autonomy

The economic crisis affected Poland relatively lightly. The country had low public and private debt and export dependency and was consequently the only EU member state not to enter recession. Though Polish economic success was related to low public debt and high external investment, there were good reasons for considering Polish non-membership of the euro to be a further crucial variable. Unlike in countries such as Spain, Polish absence from the single currency permitted monetary and fiscal policies which guarded against the effects of recession. In a study which assessed implications of Polish non-membership of the euro, it was asserted that 'independent monetary policy and, in particular, the flexible exchange rate played an important stabilizing role for the Polish economy' (Brzoza-Brzezina *et al.*, 2014: 66).

Polish economic success was associated with a relatively low level of unemployment. Unemployment rose to around 10 per cent yet, compared to rates in certain EU countries and the 20 per cent unemployment which Poland endured at the turn of the millennium, this was somewhat mild (see figure 7.1). There was also little debate over the reform of permanent and temporary dismissal protection. A 2009 measure temporarily removed limits on the permissible number of consecutive fixed-term contracts, though in tandem introducing regulation which limited fixed-term contracts to a maximum of twenty-four months, yet the success elsewhere of measures hoarding labour meant policies liberalizing labour markets became temporarily unpopular (Meardi and Trappmann, 2013: 198).

European-level pressures for reform were also very slight. Not only was Poland spared the European interventions which took place in Southern Europe and involved significant labour market reforms, but the implementation of the European Semester tended not to involve deregulation. A Solidarność official asserted that, rather than urging reforms which Polish unions opposed, the Semester often encouraged improvements in areas such as labour market dualism, civil law contracts and the working

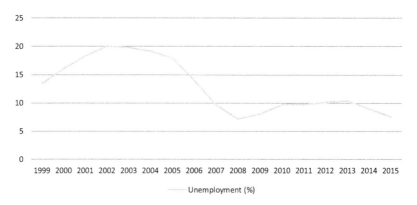

Figure 7.1 Unemployment rates in Poland (1999–2015)
Source: Eurostat.

poor in which unions also desired action. More serious consequences of the crisis included an upturn in the long-standing problem of false self-employment (*Forsal.Pl*, 2013). One authority believed the phenomenon to affect 1.5 million workers in 2011 (*Forsal.Pl*, 2013), this representing a 200 per cent increase on the 2002 estimate of 500,000 (Portet, 2005: 280).

This lack of change to unemployment and dismissal protection can be associated with Polish non-membership of the euro. Though establishing a tight link is challenging, one consequence of Polish non-membership may have been a forestalling of pressure on ULCs. Poland was more competitive than many CEE countries in the 2000s (Tchorek and Krzewicki, 2014: 51), yet from the middle of the decade ULCs showed signs of appreciation (see figure 7.2). Given the tendency of non-coordinated regimes to become uncompetitive vis-à-vis core countries, this trend might have been exacerbated by euro membership. In the Polish case, the crucial structural influence was therefore absence from the single currency. Polish labour was unable to achieve a coherent response to Europeanization, as was the case in other countries, yet non-membership of the euro ensured that consequences were less significant.

Difficulties associated with lower-level wage moderation might have left Poland vulnerable to loss of competitiveness. The capacity of Polish labour to achieve moderation is limited. Not only are social partners too weakly organized to secure such a feat, but the labour code forbids the lower-level derogations which are increasingly employed in Western Europe. Had Poland been in the Eurozone, lower borrowing costs associated with euro membership may have provoked loss of competitiveness and indebtedness, as occurred in Southern Europe. Policymakers

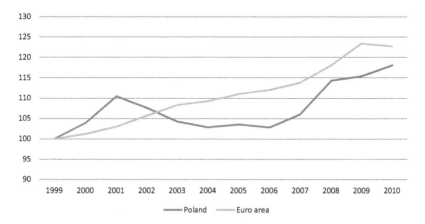

Figure 7.2 Nominal unit labour costs (ULCs) in Poland (1999–2010)

Source: Ameco; Bourgeot, 2013.

were not unwise to such a possibility; a 2009 NBP report on the costs and benefits of single currency entry emphasized the risk of wage and price rises and a consequent worsening of the competitive position (NBP, 2009: 171).

Such a development would nonetheless have been far from inevitable. Had Poland joined the Eurozone in the 2000s, it is plausible that the decentralized and weakly unionized Polish system would have delivered wage moderation. According to the hump-shaped hypothesis of Calmfors and Driffill (1988), both centralized *and* decentralized systems are able to achieve restraint. In the Polish case, tripartite pacts could also have limited wage rises, had problems with planning and political division been overcome. There are further factors in Poland, namely high unemployment, poor socio-economic development and the perception that the competitive advantage of Polish MNC subsidiaries lay in low wages, which historically constrain wage rises. Such a discussion is admittedly hypothetical; in comparison to the other countries I have reviewed, it is challenging to establish links between the behaviour of Polish labour and later outcomes.

Notwithstanding the protection monetary autonomy afforded Poland, there was recognition that the Eurozone crisis had key implications for the country. At European level, the Polish Government was extensively involved in the preparation of measures which sought to resolve the crisis. Poland held the presidency of the Council of the European Union in the second half of 2011, at a time when the crisis raged particularly strongly, and assumed a critical role in the design of policies which reformed the Eurozone. The governing PO party took this opportunity to mould the EU's response to the crisis in the image of the centre-right PO's conservative economic philosophy. The EU economic governance 'six pack', designed at the time of the Polish presidency, incorporated points related to debt brakes and the importance of debt levels which reflected long-standing PO concerns. The broader dispositions of PO towards the sovereign debt crisis were more cautious; although the sympathies of PO tended to lie with core countries, the party claimed to be sensitive to social degradations undergone in the periphery.

Polish trade unions generally defended periphery countries; at a formal level, austerity measures were consistently opposed. Such resistance was articulated at European level. Through membership of ETUC and other European sectoral confederations, unions subscribed to declarations which criticized austerity. An OPZZ official emphasized how, in the course of dealings with the European public authorities, the union had raised the issue of conditions in countries touched by austerity and lobbied for greater social regulation. Associations were also developed with unions in affected countries; the respondent underlined partnerships with unions in Southern Europe and the involvement of

OPZZ in European protests. Interviewees from Solidarność also stressed how the official programme of the union, last articulated in 2014, condemned austerity.

Though the formal stance adopted by Polish unions towards the crisis was unambiguous, the situation was complicated by the dispositions of union members and lower-level officials. As in Germany, such individuals were influenced by right-populist interpretations which prevailed in the media. During the crisis, tabloid papers such as *Fakt* (2011) and *Super Express* (2015) underlined the role of high social spending in instigating the crisis and dismissed Greeks as feckless and lazy. In the Polish case, such interpretations were encouraged by inferior levels of socio-economic development. One *Fakt* article (2015) itemized the superior conditions in which Greek pensioners, minimum wage workers and recipients of unemployment benefit lived, in comparison to Polish counterparts; a popular social media meme was based on a similar theme. A Solidarność official elaborated:

> Quite a few unionists ... rely very heavily on information transmitted by the media. Information transmitted by the mainstream media was unambiguous concerning the situation in countries such as Greece: 'Greece has been living on credit ... look at the pensions they have compared to Polish pensions.' ... There was a narrative, on the one hand, about the lazy Greek who took siestas through half the day. On the other hand, there was a more correct narrative about the falsifying of statistics, which concerned how Greece had done something to the European Union, which was some kind of fiddle ... and now there were consequences to this ... [also according to this view] whatever the changes to the labour market and labour law which had occurred ... it would still be better than in Poland.[1]

As in Germany, Polish union leaders were not immune from sentiments which excited their members. The declaration of OPZZ leader Jan Guz that Polish unions wanted benefits from work like the Greeks, Spanish and Portuguese had for the unemployed (Polskie Radio, 2012), expressed

---

1 'Spora część związkowców, w zakładach związków branżowych korzystała, korzysta i korzystać będzie z informacji przekazywanych przez media. Informacje przekazywane przez media głównego nurtu, dotyczące sytuacji na przykład w Grecji były jednoznaczne: "Grecy żyli na kredyt ... patrzcie jakie emerytury mają, a jakie wy macie emerytury" ... To znaczy to była ta narracja trochę, z jednej strony leniwy Grek tak, sjesta przez pół dnia, potem taka narracja, no oczywiście słuszna narracja ta druga fałszowanie statystyki tak, które szły z Grecji do Unii Europejskiej, no jakiegoś takiego przekrętom ... no i właśnie no to teraz są konsekwencje tego ... A poza tym należy pamiętać, że jak się rożne elementy tych zmian na rynku pracy, prawa pracy, które tam zachodzą,. będą i tak lepsze niż w Polsce' (my translation).

at the time of the 14 November 2012 European Day of Action and Solidarity, might be phrased differently on reflection.

Notwithstanding occasional rhetorical looseness, the extent to which Polish labour engaged in displays of support for counterparts in periphery countries was not insubstantial. In 2011–12, Polish unions undertook a series of actions which were partly or wholly motivated by the desire to express solidarity with the periphery. On 30 June 2011, on the eve of the Polish assumption of the EU presidency, Solidarność led a large protest in Warsaw to which other Polish and European unions were invited; Solidarność claimed that 80,000 partook in the demonstration (*Polska Times*, 2011), though a lower figure was reported in the press (*Gazeta Wyborcza*, 2011). The overwhelming motivation of protestors appears to have been concern with Polish issues, a Solidarność official even emphasizing to reporters that the event pertained solely to affairs in Poland (Katka, 2011), yet the European dimension to this action should not be ignored.

A union demonstration which was more European in motivation took place in Wrocław on 17 September 2011. This was organized by the ETUC and coincided with a meeting of European finance ministers in the city, at which issues concerning the debt crisis were to be discussed. Representatives from almost thirty unions affiliated to ETUC were present at the protest, though members of OPZZ and Solidarność were most heavily represented (EurWORK, 2011). The leaders of OPZZ and Solidarność spoke at the event, explicitly denouncing EU policy and underlining the threat it posed to workers. Organizers claimed that a minimum of 50,000 protestors were present, yet police estimated that the figure was around 20,000. Whatever the exact scale, this still represents a substantial degree of participation. One analyst suggested that the action 'was the biggest trade union demonstration in Poland since 1989'. It is conceivable that this was the case, though the Solidarność figure for the June 2011 event is higher (EurWORK, 2011).

Other protests with a European focus were undertaken in these years. Polish unionists were present at the 29 September 2010 European Day of Action in Brussels, and a demonstration was held in Warsaw on the same day (Solidarność, 2011). Union protests were also held in Polish cities to mark the 14 November 2012 European Day of Action and Solidarity, though the absence of Solidarność on this day drew comment (TVP3 Warszawa, 2012). In analysis of union participation in the 14 November action which identified three levels of input – (i) general strikes, (ii) mass demonstrations and (iii) symbolic actions and/or messages of solidarity – Poland was classed in the second category (Dufresne and Pernot, 2013: 20). Other CEE countries were assigned to this grouping; there were similar demonstrations in the Czech Republic, Romania and Slovenia.

If we are to understand the reaction of Polish labour to the debt crisis, it is also crucial to take into account the position of SLD; this is the main left-wing party in Poland. Despite its prominent role on the Polish left, the commitment of SLD to social goals has been disparaged; there is an accusation that the party has been too ready to embrace neoliberalism (Woś, 2014). SLD also faced major constraints at the time of the crisis. Not only was the party in opposition, the last SLD Government having left office in 2005, but a crisis of declining support was underway; this culminated in the loss of all parliamentary representation in 2015. Such difficulties encouraged introspection and, in these years, SLD tended to focus on domestic issues.

The response of SLD to the crisis reflected such challenges. The party preferred a resolution which involved strengthening of European political structures, yet little action was taken at national or European level which supported workers in periphery countries. Searches of press and documentary sources yield limited indication that this was the case. SLD leader Leszek Miller published a July 2015 article which was sympathetic to Greece and criticized neoliberalism, while the SLD website featured articles by journalists which articulated opposition to austerity. In general, there is nonetheless a dearth of such material; SLD appears to have been equally disposed to use the crisis as occasion to caution that the absence of Poland from the single currency was leading to the marginalization of the country (SLD, 2013), or to warn about the sustainability of Polish public finances (SLD, 2012). In an interview, an academic expert asserted that SLD was also concerned about the proper use of EU funding in Southern Europe.

A further reason for SLD reticence may have been the desire not to sour relations with social-democratic parties in the core of the Eurozone. The relationship between SPD and SLD is an important one. At the height of the debt crisis, party leaders Sigmar Gabriel and Leszek Miller visited one another in Berlin and Warsaw (*Wprost*, 2012), and the significance of this association may also explain the comparative inaction of SLD. Such influence can nonetheless be overstated; the expert stated that SPD did not attempt to impose its European policies upon SLD. It was also reported that SLD relations with other European social-democratic parties were similarly informal and focused upon internal issues such as the rights of minorities. A previous SLD leader had dealings with José Zapatero, yet these meetings did not lead to discussion of the economic problems faced by Poland and Spain; they were chiefly personal exchanges.

The somewhat uncommitted attitude of SLD is thrown into relief by the disposition of Razem, a radical party which was founded in May 2015 by citizens unhappy with the existing Polish left. Razem made the following declaration on the subject of the Greek crisis in June 2015:

Razem expresses solidarity with the society and Government of Greece in their fight for democracy and social justice ... The politics of cuts and reduction of demand does not work, because it cannot work. Consistent with the predictions of economists it is bringing Greece to economic collapse. Public debt has become impossible to pay, the economy has shrunk by a quarter and unemployment stands at 27%. Millions of Greeks have been pushed into poverty.

Such language is stronger than anything used by SLD and suggests that, had it been in the Polish Parliament, Razem would have forcefully lobbied for policies favourable to the periphery. The existence of a prominent press interview with an economist affiliated to Razem (*Gazeta Wyborcza*, 2015), in which sympathy with Greek society is clearly expressed, also indicates the depth of the conviction of Razem; an equivalent source cannot be found for SLD.

Notwithstanding the comparative inaction of SLD, the reaction of Polish labour to the debt crisis was not insignificant. In addition to declarations of support for colleagues in the periphery, unions exhibited solidarity via a series of well-attended demonstrations. Such protests may also have been motivated by unhappiness with Polish public authorities, yet their European dimension should not be denied. The occurrence of these actions is notable in a country which is not only not in the single currency, but in which unions are weak and industrial relations is Europeanized to a slight degree. These circumstances mean that the reaction of Polish unions was more impressive than French counterparts; such conditions did not exist in France. Differences with core countries are also conspicuous. Had German unions mobilized to the degree observed in Poland, Government policy would have faced more considerable challenge.

It is nonetheless impossible to consider the reaction of the Polish labour movement to the debt crisis in isolation from non-membership of the single currency. Had Poland entered the Eurozone and achieved competitive advantage, it is probable that Polish labour would have adopted an attitude more akin to counterparts in the core. As in Germany, this would likely have been driven by the sentiments of union rank and files. The vein of right-populism within Polish society, from which union leaders were not immune, demonstrates the existence of these attitudes in Poland. Given the nationalist-populist orientation of Solidarność, the union being allied with the nationalist PiS party, the Polish labour movement might have been particularly susceptible.

Had Poland adopted the euro and failed to achieve competitiveness within the zone, the Polish labour movement would have faced the challenge of constructing coalitions to contest austerity; this was the task which confronted southern European counterparts after the outbreak of crisis. It is likely that Polish labour would also have struggled with this endeavour. Not only is union density low in Poland, but the extent to which industrial relations structures are Europeanized is limited. Given the fate to which labour movements in periphery countries succumbed, one doubts that outcomes would have differed in Poland.

Conclusion: Splendid isolation?

As in other countries, the capacity of Polish labour to respond to integration in a strategic manner was underwhelming. Though this was a result of political problems which were not present in other cases, Polish tripartism being politicized to an unusual degree, similar issues with planning were evident. It can thus be concluded that CEE tripartite bodies also have difficulties responding to Europeanization in a coherent manner. Given that many CEE countries have corresponding institutions, results in Poland are likely to be generalizable. In the Polish case, the structural influence which explained subsequent outcomes was absence from the Eurozone. This points to the crucial influence of single currency membership in determining the effects of competition and/or coopera-tion undertaken by labour; a precondition of several key processes which I have theorized in previous chapters is membership of the Eurozone.

The Polish case also indicates the capacity of a non-Eurozone labour movement to exhibit solidarity with counterparts in the periphery. Given that non-Eurozone countries differ considerably, it is difficult to extrapo-late this finding. Similar anti-austerity demonstrations took place in non-Eurozone CEE contexts such as Czech Republic and Romania (Dufresne and Pernot, 2013: 20), yet comparable protests in Slovenia, a country which is a member of the single currency, suggest that this was a regional trend. The evolving attitude of Polish unions towards bargaining coor-dination is also worthy of comment. If this is sustained, it will facilitate efforts at European cooperation; recalcitrance among some CEE unions has long been an impediment to the development of these strategies.

I have now reviewed the cases of labour movements in core, periphery, intermediate and non-Eurozone countries. Having done this, I turn attention to the question of the extent to which labour movements com-pete and/or cooperate in response to European integration.

PART III

Answering the question

I theorize is to be considered a dualization regime, it is thus necessary to link its existence with the interests of sections of the workforce. The majority of this chapter is dedicated to this goal, yet before this task may be undertaken it is necessary to reacquaint ourselves with differences among studied countries. It should be noted that I am concerned with relative changes since the onset of crisis in 2007/8. Though this book examines developments since the 1999 launch of the euro, it was not until the crisis that effects on labour markets became fully manifest; appreciation of the consequences of EMU, and the associated role of labour competition and/or cooperation, requires evaluation of recent trajectories.

The situation in periphery countries is particularly inauspicious. In Spain, unemployment grew to 20 per cent after the outbreak of crisis and eventually exceeded 25 per cent. Workers on non-standard contracts were disproportionate victims of unemployment, a result of their particular disposability, yet insiders were far from insulated from the changes which took place from 2008. Labour market reforms effected in these years, the most notable of which was implemented in 2012, eroded the dismissal protection enjoyed by such employees. Workers on non-standard contracts were also vulnerable to heightened job insecurity. A proliferation of precarious forms of employment, associated with labour market reforms which permitted such contracts, made work on the margins of the labour market yet more insecure.

Conditions are considerably better in the core of the Eurozone. In Germany, unemployment declined after the initial onset of recession and remained at low levels. There was also no deregulation of dismissal protection. Certain measures even fortified such legislation; a number of 2013 Federal Labour Court decisions strengthened protection afforded to temporary workers. The ascent of non-standard employment also relented. From 2008 to 2013, the percentage of workers employed on contracts of limited duration declined from 14.7 per cent to 13.4 per cent, while the proportion of fixed-term contracts converted to permanent rose from 30 per cent to 39 per cent between 2009 and 2012 (Vogel, 2013).

The situation in intermediate countries is between those found in core and periphery. In France, although the onset of the crisis did not lead to the unemployment levels experienced by periphery countries, labour market performance was mediocre. Unemployment remained around 10 per cent and began to climb in 2012. There was also a certain diminution in employment security. Labour market reforms downgraded the protection enjoyed by permanent and temporary workers, and there was an increase in certain forms of contractual precarity; such insecurity was nonetheless not as pronounced as levels found in the periphery.

In my non-Eurozone country, Poland, the status quo largely endured. There was a light rise in unemployment after the onset of crisis, yet this growth was modest compared to periphery countries and later relented. Levels of security also remained stable. The regulation of permanent employee dismissal protection went untouched, though there was a slight change in protection afforded to temporary employees and an increase in levels of false self-employment. Polish labour market stability could be linked to many factors, yet non-membership of the euro was crucial.

Does the European insider–outsider division benefit certain workers?

I have sketched above the contours of a European insider–outsider regime. The presence of these patterns does not necessarily imply the existence of a system of dualization however. For this to occur, it is requisite for such divisions to be in the interest of certain parties; the extent to which these partitions convenience certain workers must therefore be appraised. A note on terminology is important. In the discussion below, in which I argue that the European insider–outsider division partly advantages workers in core and intermediate countries, references to such employees include both insiders and outsiders. The degree to which these workers benefit from such processes admittedly differs, and this is an issue to which attention is paid in analytical sections. Reference to workers in periphery countries likewise includes insiders and outsiders; I am also careful to distinguish the varying extent to which these employees were disadvantaged by theorized processes.

When one considers the degree to which workers in different countries were advantaged and disadvantaged by the discrepancies in labour markets which emerged in Europe after the onset of crisis, the case of Spain is simple; these developments were clearly unfavourable for employees. Such processes were detrimental to the material position of Spanish workers. Different types of employees were affected in varying ways. Non-standard workers were more touched by unemployment while permanent employees suffered more from deregulation of dismissal protection, yet there is no doubt that the net effect was negative. These processes were also to the detriment of those organizations which represent Spanish labour. Mass unemployment weakened Spanish unions in terms of membership and mobilization capacity, while PSOE suffered considerable loss of support.

Such processes had much slighter implication for the Polish labour movement. Though attacks on labour in individual European countries are typically not to the advantage of labour movements in other European countries, discussed in greater detail below, the fact that Poland was absent from the Eurozone meant that there was slight consequence for the labour market. Retention of the złoty helped ensure that there was no significant upturn in unemployment and insecurity; the Polish labour movement also stood to gain little from poor conditions in the periphery of the Eurozone, as was arguably the case in other contexts.

The more stimulating question is the extent to which such partitions are consistent with the interests of labour movements in core countries. Radical scholars emphasize the extent to which deregulation and mass unemployment in individual European countries are to the disadvantage of labour movements across Europe; since the outbreak of the crisis a number of such accounts have appeared (Bieler and Erne, 2015; Stierle and Haar, 2012). Many of the arguments of these researchers are difficult to deny. The dwindling of labour strength in countries such as Spain weakens the capacity of workers to engage in European collective action, making European policies hostile to labour more likely. The onset of developments unfriendly to labour in periphery countries also makes similar processes more likely in core countries. Not only does it put competitive pressure on conditions in other member states, particularly within the Eurozone, but it puts wind in the sails of employers desirous of deregulation. Churchill's famous verdict on appeasement might be paraphrased; workers who are indifferent to austerity are like those who feed a crocodile, hoping it will eat them last.

Any attack on labour may therefore be to the disadvantage of workers in general yet, *pace* the arguments of radicals, in certain conditions sections of labour can profit rather agreeably from assaults on other workers. Literature on dualization attests to this fact (Emmenegger *et al.*, 2012; Palier and Thelen, 2010). In recent decades, across European economies, insiders have benefited from attacks on outsiders. Insouciance in the face of these processes may return to haunt insiders, and one could even argue that this day has come for such workers in periphery countries, yet it undoubtedly aids these employees in the medium term; it relents pressure on their position and allows them to continue to benefit from security in an age of increasing flexibility.

Processes of European dualization are admittedly not directly equivalent to processes in national political economies. In national contexts, the representatives of core workers have after all consented, albeit reluctantly, to deregulation of the margins of the labour market. The option of direct deregulation of dismissal protection is one which European public authorities are traditionally unable to utilize. This is now changing, one thinks of the terms of European rescues and Semester country-specific recommendations (Clauwaert, 2013; Prosser, 2016a), yet in these cases representatives of labour have minimal negotiating leverage. If a European form of dualization is to be theorized, it is thus necessary to interrogate processes which take place indirectly. National divides between the employed and unemployed provide precedent. The representatives of insiders have never explicitly consented to the creation of unemployment, rather their vigorous defences of the terms and conditions of members have indirectly led to this. The representatives of workers in core countries have equally never directly consented to a European insider–outsider division, yet this does not mean that such a partition cannot be somewhat in their interests nor that their actions are not associated with this development.

There are two main ways in which dualization on a European scale might advantage workers in core countries. First, there are benefits associated with the consolidation of domestic economies. Distribution of fruits of economic successes is admittedly bound up with social class, and as is well known there is a long-standing trend in the West for the income share of workers to decline, yet it is difficult to argue that domestic economic success involves no benefit for labour. As I elaborate below, the perception that German pre-eminence within EMU advantaged everyone in Germany exerted a critical influence on the extent to which German labour prioritized solidarity with the periphery. This conviction was often expressed in the language of crude populism, yet at root it contained more than an element of truth; German predominance within the single currency helped achieve secure employment for workers.

Second, on a more general level, the incidence of European dualization benefits workers in core countries because it postpones pressures for austerity and deregulation in domestic contexts. Parallels with national insider–outsider divisions are palpable. At national level, insiders have chiefly benefited from attacks on outsiders because it ensures that their own position goes untouched (Palier and Thelen, 2010). It is easy to see how such a process could take place on a European scale. In an age of weak economic growth, demands on labour are generally intensifying. In a single economic unit such as the Eurozone, it was therefore inevitable that serious pressure would be exerted on labour and that, somewhere in the area, comprehensive labour market reform would have to be undertaken. By tacitly consenting to austerity and deregulation on the periphery of the Eurozone, insiders in core countries save their own skins. This may be a problematic strategy in the long term yet, as literature on national processes of dualization reminds us, this is feasible in the medium term. The famed dictum of Keynes, namely that in the long run we are all dead, comes to mind.

If we are to better appreciate dynamics behind the creation of the European insider–outsider division and lay foundations for an understanding of the manner in which labour movements react to integration, it is also necessary to appreciate the extent to which labour movements intended for such a scenario to materialize. This hinges on two processes which were selected so as to assess this question: the collective agreements concluded by unions in the first decade of the euro and the attitude of labour movements towards austerity in periphery countries.

It is difficult to argue that unions in core countries intended to undercut periphery economies, and by implication create discrepancies in employment and job security, after the introduction of the euro. As contended in chapter 4, there are a number of factors which make this unfeasible: labour movements tend not to calculate on a long-term basis, there is limited evidence of the use of competitive benchmarks by German unions and wage restraint can be explained with reference to structural influences. It is possible that the imperative of gaining competitiveness over European rivals may have informed the strategies of certain sections of German labour at certain times, the occasional use of competitive benchmarks and select declarations by union leaders attesting to this, but to argue for a conscious strategy of neomercantilism would be unjustified. The intentional creation of a partition based on employment and job security, a further step removed from the mere establishment of superior competitiveness, is yet more implausible.

Whatever the intentions of labour movements in the core, divisions based on employment and job security nonetheless transpired from 2008. The response of core labour to this development was crucial. Just as insiders in domestic dualization regimes react to unemployment by resisting attempts to deregulate protection, and it is worth recalling that such employees also do not create such partitions by design, workers in core countries reacted disappointingly to the predicament of the periphery. Lack of union interest in German undervaluation was one instance of this. Even if there was very limited evidence to suggest that German unions had attempted to engineer competitive advantage within EMU, the issue of intra-Eurozone imbalances was a different one and it could reasonably have been expected that, in the spirit of European solidarity, this might have been addressed more assiduously.

Reluctance to reform the status quo may be associated with the interests of workers in core countries. As with insiders in domestic dualization regimes, there were significant benefits associated with prevailing conditions for such groups and they lacked incentive to pursue reform. Because existing bargaining patterns helped ensure German superiority within the Eurozone, thereby promoting economic success, the prospects of German labour were partly tied to the existing regime. It is admittedly important to distinguish between the interests of different classes of worker within Germany. As a result of the particular stability of their situation, permanently employed workers benefited more considerably from such processes. These employees are also more numerous and better represented by unions and social-democratic parties; my argument mainly pertains to this group. Advantages for temporary workers and the unemployed are less palpable. Such citizens may profit from improving economic conditions and deferral of further assault on their position, yet the precarity of their existing status means gains are more modest.

This logic can be discerned in the attitude of German workers to the austerity programmes which were implemented in periphery countries from 2010. Though processes of austerity implied a risk to labour movements in the core, as attacks on individual European labour movements threaten the interests of all, there were also advantages for the economies of core countries. Devaluation of the euro was one benefit. Because austerity measures put downward pressure on the value of the currency, German exports were consequently cheapened. This led to better economic results for the country and improvement of the employment prospects of German workers. Austerity measures also consolidated the financial position of core countries; rather than being subjected to 'haircuts' which would involve losses, the emergency loans associated with austerity ensured that German banks who had lent to periphery countries continued to have prospect of repayment. It is true that there is a clear class dimension in this case, as the better-off profit from upturns in the finance sector, yet there are also ramifications for national economic success which are ultimately shared by workers.

Such factors help explain the ambivalent attitude of core labour movements towards austerity. From 2010, the representatives of workers in core countries offered lukewarm support to counterparts in the periphery of the Eurozone. The actions of social democrats can partly be explained by their status as political parties; such organizations have wider bases than unions and a broader obligation to act in the national interest. At times, SPD were also confronted by desperate circumstances; had the party opposed the provision of emergency loans, the euro might have collapsed. Despite less substantial constraints, the reaction of trade unions could have been more impressive. Though unions in core countries consistently denounced austerity, often in vigorous terms, the degree to which they adopted measures of concrete opposition was less remarkable. As Dribbusch (2015) observes, German engagement in pan-European solidarity actions was rather underwhelming; the case of the November 2012 European Day of Action and Solidarity, in which the participation of German unions was largely symbolic, is especially revealing (see table 8.1).

This lack of concrete action may be explained by the situation in which German labour found itself after 2010. Not only did unions and SPD have an interest in maintaining decent relations with a Government which was committed to austerity, this being particularly the case for SPD after it entered coalition government in 2013, but many of their constituents concurred with the strategy of the Merkel Government. Regular workers may have been partly motivated by nationalism, a sentiment instigated by tabloid papers such as *Bild*, yet it is difficult to deny that economic factors had no relationship with their preferences.

Table 8.1 Protests undertaken by trade unions against EU-imposed austerity measures

Country	Protests undertaken
Germany	Actions were largely symbolic. Works councils sent messages of solidarity and there were protests in large towns, yet these demonstrations were poorly attended.
Spain	Spanish unions were at the vanguard of pan-European opposition to austerity. Attempts were made to organize a European strike and, on European days of action, strikes were held in Spain. These strikes were well-observed and made reference to European challenges.
France	Observation of European actions was mixed. On the European Day of Action and Solidarity of 14 November 2012, more than 130 actions took place and a nation-wide figure of 113,000 protestors was reported (Dufresne and Pernot, 2013). On the other hand, there was no strike action and participation in demonstrations was mediocre.
Poland	A number of demonstrations in support of periphery countries were held by unions. These included a June 2011 protest prior to the Polish assumption of the presidency of the Council of the European Union and a September 2011 demonstration in Wrocław which coincided with a meeting of European finance ministers in the city. Participation was often impressive, though no strike action was taken and Solidarność failed to engage in 14 November 2012 protests.

The fact that there were certain benefits associated with austerity for the German economy meant that opposition was a lower priority than it might have been; the issue was a secondary one and major political capital was not expended upon it. Structural constraints on pan-European action may be called to attention. The capacity of unions to mobilize has been in decline for years, while impediments to European collective action are well-documented (Scharpf, 1999). Though the influence of these checks is undeniable, they do not fully explain the inaction of core labour; the more impressive reaction of labour movements in other countries shows this to be the case (see table 9.2). At this point, it is also necessary to remind ourselves how purposeful action from labour movements in Europe might have diluted or halted austerity. As contended in chapter 4, the cases of successful opposition to the Port Services Directive and Bolkestein Directive illustrate the potential power of European solidarity. Austerity may well have been a more formidable foe than the aforementioned measures, yet full-blooded European action, including sustained input from labour movements in core countries, would surely have led to some mollification of its terms.

It is true that EMU has had negative effects for workers in core countries. In Germany, wage moderation has long been endured and certain employees suffer contractual precarity. The accomplishment of internal devaluations in periphery countries may also put renewed pressure on workforces in the core. Notwithstanding these considerations, benefits of EMU for German workers, as monetary union existed in the 2010–15 period, were significant enough to preclude considerable solidarity with periphery countries. This interpretation is consistent with my understanding of actor cognition as short-term in scope. Developments in this time are also consonant with dualization scholarship (Emmenegger *et al.*, 2012; Palier and Thelen, 2010); such theorists posit that divisions between workers result from the reluctance of insiders to defend outsiders wholeheartedly, rather than conscious malevolence. This explanation is germane to the European insider-outsider division. Though austerity was not in the unambiguous interest of workers in the core, benefits associated with the existing system of EMU diluted grounds for opposition, leaving periphery workforces exposed. The structural position of labour movements in core countries may well have been pressing, yet such constraints characterize other insider-outsider divisions; there are few cases in which labour movements are free of restraint.

It is also necessary to reflect on the relationship of the French labour movement with these processes. Given that the French economy is in an intermediate position, falling between core and periphery, the case of the country is particularly interesting. The arguments I have made about German labour, regarding the benefits of national ascendancy in the Eurozone and associated difficulties of marshalling support for reform of an advantageous status quo, partly apply to French counterparts. Problems with French competitiveness are not as severe as those found in the periphery; perpetuation of EMU as it currently exists therefore cannot be said to be unequivocally against the interests of France. As in Germany, French success within the Eurozone also has benefits for workers; a respectable French position in the single currency guarantees a certain level of employment and relents pressure for deregulation. The national interest of France can also be associated with austerity; French banks owned periphery debt and national economic success, in turn associated with the interests of workers, was tied up with repayment.

These linkages are admittedly fainter than in the core; France has never occupied the position in the single currency enjoyed by a country such as Germany. There are also grounds on which French labour might oppose the prevailing system of EMU. As contended in chapter 6, membership of the Eurozone was associated with a certain rise in unemployment and loss of employment security in the French labour market (Hancké, 2016).

The argument that austerity in one country is an attack on all labour movements is therefore more applicable to France than Germany, given the more precarious position of the French economy.

The reaction of French labour to the crisis was consistent with these expectations. Despite exhibiting superior levels of solidarity than German workers, the extent of French support for labour movements in the periphery was mixed. Not only was the stance of President Hollande disappointing, but trade unions might have shown more solidarity; French unions reacted to the November 2012 European action with medium-sized demonstrations, rather than strikes. The reasons why this was the case resemble those found in Germany. Because the current regime was partly in the interests of French labour, or at least not plainly unfavourable to them, opposition was somewhat weakly prioritized.

The question of the degree to which labour movements in non-Eurozone and periphery countries opposed austerity is also crucial, for it throws further light on the extent to which the actions of workers in core and intermediate countries were tied up with national status in the Eurozone. The case of Poland is illuminating; the country is not a member of the single currency and Polish labour had less direct stake in relevant processes. Though the reaction of the left-wing SLD was underwhelming, Polish unions held a series of well-attended demonstrations; this response was impressive given structural weaknesses of Polish unions. Such a reaction was more considerable than that of the better-resourced German labour movement, which indicates that the reticence of German labour was rooted in benefits associated with pre-eminence within EMU. If one takes into account Polish non-membership of the euro, it can also be argued that the actions of Polish labour were more substantial than French counterparts; this suggests that the response of French labour had similar foundations to the reaction of the German movement.

The case of Spain is also key, given the position of the country on the periphery of the Eurozone. The existing shape of EMU and implementation of austerity was unambiguously counter to the interests of Spanish labour; one should therefore expect to see the attempts at pan-European opposition which were underdeveloped in core and intermediate countries. The reaction of the social-democratic PSOE was anomalous. Despite the fact that it was in the interests of PSOE to oppose austerity in Spain and Europe after defeat in the 2011 election, this goal was pursued to a disappointing degree. This is related to somewhat irregular factors, namely the extent to which PSOE was compromised by its 2010 introduction of austerity and the later shellshock of electoral defeat. The case of PSOE alerts us to the potential of such constraints to impede full-blooded opposition to austerity. This should temper our judgement of

SPD and PS, yet similar factors do not fully explain the stances of these parties; national positions within EMU must also be taken into account.

The actions of Spanish trade unions were more consistent with expectations. Not only did Spanish unions arrange largescale protests against austerity within Spain, but there were also efforts to organize on a European scale. Those European actions which took place were impeccably observed by unions. Reasons for lack of success of European protests were mainly related to factors external to Spain; the commitment of Spanish unions should not be doubted.

It is thus reasonable to speak of dualization on a European scale. Not only have considerable discrepancies in unemployment and employment security emerged between core and periphery countries, but these are underpinned by the interests of workers in core countries. These differences may not have taken shape as straightforwardly as divisions in national political economies, national-level representatives of insiders sometimes directly consenting to deregulation of dismissal protection for temporary workers, yet a palpable link with the interests of workers in core countries can be traced. The onset of such a system may not have been the intention of movements in the core, as engineering a scheme of such complexity would be beyond the capacity of any organization, yet once this regime was in place those who benefited from it had insufficient motivation to overturn it. The process was akin to those partitions between the employed and unemployed which have long characterized national labour markets (Lindbeck and Snower, 1988); these divisions, though they are associated with the interests of permanently employed workers, were never consciously designed.

It is also necessary to reflect on future trajectories. The competitive advantage of core countries may not endure in the long term; in recent years, as a result of internal devaluations in Southern Europe, discrepancies in ULCs among core and periphery have narrowed. This may lead to diminutions in unemployment rates between the regions, yet differences in employment security would likely remain. As contended in chapter 5, internal devaluations entrench low quality employment within periphery countries, leaving them in a subservient position vis-à-vis the core. It is also possible that the periphery will one day hold an advantage over the core in terms of unemployment and employment security, though this now seems remote. If this were to materialize, there is little reason to think that southern European labour movements would behave differently to northern counterparts. My argument is that EMU institutions and national membership profiles prompt such outcomes; it is not that some movements are morally superior to others.

Conclusion: Old problem, new form?

It is perhaps unsurprising that a European insider–outsider division has taken root. The EU has increasingly assumed the economic policy competences of a nation state and, as literature on dualization underlines (Emmenegger *et al.*, 2012), in these units such partitions between workers typically emerge. The phenomenon of dualization on a trans-national scale is nonetheless noteworthy and evokes certain processes which were called to attention in the past. One pertinent debate is the long-standing Marxist concern that, under imperialism, workers in col-onizing countries benefit at the expense of the colonized. Lenin outlined this process (1999):

> The Roman proletarian lived at the expense of society. Modern society lives at the expense of the modern proletarian. Marx specifically stressed this profound observation of Sismondi. Imperialism somewhat changes the situation. A privileged upper stratum of the proletariat in the impe-rialist countries lives partly at the expense of hundreds of millions in the uncivilised nations. (p. 125)

The idea that one national working class can benefit at the expense of workers in other lands provides fruitful insight. It was a notion which Bukharin also trumpeted, though later Marxists called attention to problems with the concept; such issues included plausible mechanisms by which wealth was transferred to working classes in imperial countries (Brewer, 2001: 127). Specific problems with the Marxist-Leninist inter-pretation are not here of primary relevance, rather I am interested in the potential of the idea to frame concerns about the potential of workers in one country to benefit at the expense of foreign counterparts. Later literatures, which address topics such as neoimperialism (Baran, 1968), have made related claims.

The potential of such ideas is most auspicious and I claim the European division theorized in this chapter to be a modern descendent of the par-tition conceptualized by Marxist-Leninists. We should admittedly be sensitive to differences between the ages of Lenin and the contemporary EU. The more integrated European economy arguably provides greater occasion for the establishment of such divides, yet is only comprised of advanced economies; the European division is therefore distinctive because it exists within a developed economic bloc. Modern Europe is also not marked by the deep racism of formal imperialism, which encour-aged particular callousness towards the colonized. Ethnic stereotypes of our own times should nonetheless be called to attention. Depictions of feckless Greeks found in publications such as *Bild* are much milder than the scientific racism of the early twentieth century, yet they play a key role in perpetuating the suspicion with which core workers regard counterparts in the periphery.

Examination of the circumstances in which one national workforce benefits at the expense of another might represent a productive avenue as work on transnational labour relations moves ahead. There are many areas in which such a concern could be pursued; relations between workers of different nationalities in EWCs, MNCs and countries in transnational trading blocs are a few examples. In chapter 10, in which I outline an agenda for future research, I discuss the potential of such projects in greater detail.

Care must nonetheless be taken when evaluating the nature of relevant links. As results have shown, the European insider–outsider division came about largely by accident and was perpetuated by the inability of core labour movements to prioritize solidarity with the periphery, rather than by the active malice of these workers. Future investigation on the incidence of transnational dualization may examine more closely the manner in which divisions function. I have argued that the benefits of such partitions are related to better employment prospects and deferral of attacks on core workers; other researchers might discover the existence of other advantages. The conditions in which such divisions are perpetuated might also interest scholars. I have contended that the European divide primarily resulted from the weak emphasis which core labour movements put on solidarity with counterparts in periphery countries; others might discover alternative mechanisms.

Such questions will interest researchers in a range of fields. My key concern is nonetheless the manner in which labour reacts to integration; the case of the European insider–outsider division, because it demonstrates substantive consequences of processes of competition and/or cooperation, prepares the ground for investigation of this broader issue.

9

How do labour movements respond to European integration?

In this chapter, I move towards a new theory of the manner in which labour movements respond to European integration. I contend that, rather than being based on cooperation, the behaviour of labour tends to facilitate competition between national regimes. Owing to the nationally embedded nature of labour movements, which is itself in the interests of certain workers, bargaining processes tend to lead to an unplanned yet incremental drift towards zero-sum outcomes which benefit national workforces in stronger structural positions. Strategies which aim to correct discrepant outcomes, which become particularly necessary at times of crisis, are generally unsuccessful. Not only are attempts at European cooperation weakly prioritized by labour movements, which is related to the tendency for certain workers to benefit from the status quo, but difficulties associated with collective action mean they can be easily vetoed. Such developments can be linked with the current stage of integration. The introduction of the euro has heightened competition among national regimes and increased the probability of crises, while spikes in nationalism have made workers less disposed to support disadvantaged counterparts.

A series of further issues is raised by this argument. Not only do I reflect upon implications for theories of the Europeanization of social democracy, but I consider the extent to which the actions of labour movements were generally representative of workers. The chapter concludes with an assessment of implications of findings for related academic debates; these literatures concern theories of institutions and the employment relationship.

Towards a new theory of the response of labour to integration

Prior to the theory of labour behaviour which is set out in this chapter, it is necessary to remind ourselves of difficulties with prevailing approaches.

Though competitive (Rhodes, 1998a; Scharpf, 1999; Streeck, 1996) and cooperative (Erne, 2008; Falkner, 1998; Ladrech, 2000) aspects of labour behaviour have previously been theorized, a problem with existing scholarship is its inability to forge adequate relationships with substantive outcomes. Such literature also tends to evaluate previous stages of European integration. If the terms in which labour movements exert influence are to be established, it is necessary to appraise substantive outcomes in the contemporary EU.

On the basis of analysis undertaken in previous chapters, designed with such goals in mind, I submit that labour movements respond to integration in a manner which instigates competition between national regimes. Before this hypothesis is outlined in detail, the degree to which my reasoning is bound up with case selection means that it is necessary to stress limits to my argument. Given that labour movements react to integration in multiple ways, potential for case studies is near boundless; separate studies will also yield different results. Such a discussion evokes the well-known fable of the blind men and the elephant. This ancient tale relates the story of a group of blind men who, having never encountered an elephant, feel different parts of its body. The separate impressions of the men lead to disagreement, before the group learn the source of the discrepant interpretations.

All scientific disputes do not correspond to this parable. Debates among evolutionists and creationists, in which the conclusions of one party mutually exclude others, are one such example. This study, which hinges on case selection and arrives at findings which do not exclude competing interpretations, is more compatible with the tale. Disagreements with authorities who emphasize the propensity of labour to cooperate should be read with this in mind. My claim is merely that my argument is representative of the behaviour of labour movements in contemporary Europe; it is not that competing works are false. Given use of distinct case studies and difference in contemporary political conditions, separate conclusions are inevitable.

A key cause of the competitive relations I hypothesize is the national structures in which labour movements are embedded. Owing to the nationally entrenched nature of labour markets, which is itself in the interests of certain workers, an unplanned yet incremental drift towards regime competition occurs. This process is unlikely to take a planned form. In the first case study, in which collective bargaining practices of unions after the introduction of the euro were investigated, the capacity of unions to calculate was particularly constrained (see table 9.1). The most controversial recent allegation of union sectionalism, namely the charge that German unions had consciously engaged in a strategy of neomercantilism, was found to have slim foundation. This goal may have informed the thinking of certain actors in the country, yet it was

Table 9.1 How did trade unions behave in period one?

	Did unions engage in competition?	Did unions engage in cooperation?	What were the effects?
Germany	There is little sustained evidence that unions engaged in conscious competition with European counterparts, notwithstanding certain declarations from union leaders. The wage moderation which took place in these years likely resulted from structural influences.	German unions have long been at the vanguard of efforts to achieve European bargaining coordination. Despite these attempts, difficulties associated with coordination and comparability prevent greater influence (Glassner and Pochet, 2011).	Owing to wage moderation in exposed and non-exposed sectors, Germany achieved competitive advantage in the Eurozone. It is difficult to associate this with trade union intent.
Spain	There is little evidence that unions engaged in conscious competition with European counterparts. Though inter-sectoral negotiators were mindful of international developments, such awareness was vague and did not inspire systematic competition.	Spanish unions have been less involved in European bargaining coordination. Though this is the result of structural influences, it is also associated with union attitudes towards Europeanization (Köhler and González Begega, 2007: 138).	Despite attempts at moderation at peak level, fragmentation at lower levels led to loss of competitiveness within the Eurozone.

	Did unions engage in competition?	Did unions engage in cooperation?	What were the effects?
France	Owing to low rates of density, unions were mainly excluded from wage negotiations; the state assumed a leading role in wage-setting.	French unions have been involved in efforts to achieve European bargaining coordination. Despite these attempts, difficulties associated with coordination and comparability prevent greater influence (Glassner and Pochet, 2011).	A state-led incomes policy allowed France to achieve an intermediate level of competitiveness within the Eurozone. Trade unions had little to do with this.
Poland	There is little evidence that unions engaged in conscious competition with European counterparts. Though inter-sectoral negotiators were mindful of international developments, such awareness was vague and did not inspire systematic competition. Political division among unions also precluded such strategies.	Polish unions have been less involved in European bargaining coordination; this is partly related to perceptions of low-cost advantage. Owing to recent economic development, such attitudes are evolving.	Polish absence from the single currency precluded the processes which took place in Eurozone members.

insufficiently systematic to be considered a 'strategy'; it was forestalled by difficulties associated with goal formulation and the power of structural influences on wage-setting. Results in other countries tended to be consistent with these findings. In Spain and Poland, calculated attempts to procure advantage did not take place for similar reasons. Though in France wage-setting took a more premeditated form, the role of labour in this process was marginal. There may be exceptions in certain contexts, for example in Italy social pacts have explicitly referred to developments in other member states (Parsons and Pochet, 2008: 347), yet the occurrence of this finding across countries means it may be extrapolated. In cases in which conscious competition takes place, problems associated with lower-level compliance also remain.

Such results are congruent with existing theories of institutions; scholars of institutions know that actor strategies are often short-term in nature and that their formulation is subject to contestation, especially when multiple actors are involved. The capacity of structural influences to frustrate actor strategies is also well-attested. More broadly, it is reasonable to expect that the prevalence of consciously competitive strategies among unions will be limited. There may well be exceptions, for example it might be easier to employ such tactics in a firm-level context in which fewer actors are involved and structural influences are less constraining, but it is unlikely that these will be widespread. Such strategies are associated with problems outlined above and are forestalled by the existence of class solidarity among unions (Hyman, 2001). The constraints on actor agency which I underline are indeed more considerable than those emphasized by other authorities (Erne, 2008; Johnston, 2016). These scholars are scarcely unaware of limits on actor volition, yet the ability of unions to consciously respond to integration is sometimes stressed.

Theorized developments are likely to result from structural influences. As a consequence of difficulties associated with the execution of actor strategies, outlined above, there is an incremental drift towards zero-sum outcomes which reflect structural factors. For obvious reasons, such a process is likely to benefit those labour movements in stronger institutional positions. This effect was patent in results. Though it was found that conscious strategies to obtain competitive advantage in the Eurozone were not adopted by unions in core countries, there was a drift towards outcomes which benefited these movements. In the case of Germany, the tendency of wage-setting institutions to deliver moderation enabled the country to gain competitive advantage. A related process was evident in France, though in this case the extent of the advantage was less impressive. The inverse happened in Spain; as a result of structural weaknesses in the country, there was a move towards lack of competitiveness. In Poland, the relevant structural influence was non-membership of the euro; this insulated the country from processes which took place in other contexts.

Outcomes associated with structural characteristics of national regimes put different labour movements in asymmetric positions of power. As a result of institutional advantages, labour movements in core countries found themselves in a privileged position by the end of the 2000s. According to accounts which emphasize the tendency of labour to act collectively (Erne, 2008), discrepancies in institutional power should partly be offset by strategies which aim to maximize joint outcomes. In the first case study, bargaining coordination networks nonetheless achieved little effect. Such initiatives had the potential to produce mutual benefits for participants, yet exerted a weak influence on the behaviour of negotiators. This was the result of structural constraints, yet also reflected discrepant benefits of collective action; there were insufficient incentives for wholehearted engagement.

Though the first investigated process did not yield evidence of the purposeful competition conceptualized in chapter 3, it would be unreasonable to absolve unions of all responsibility for the regime competition which occurred in these years. Aside from limited forms of conscious competition uncovered by scholars (Bofinger, 2015), unions were reluctant to engage in corrective forms of cooperation. Competition in the first period was primarily the result of institutional influences yet, had unions shown greater appetite for bargaining coordination, it is likely that corrosive effects of structural pressures would have been mollified.

In the second studied process, levels of cooperation were also found to be restricted. Although labour movements in both Germany and France condemned austerity and even undertook certain concrete actions, it is difficult to argue that opposition was a priority for movements in either country. This is evidenced by the extent of union participation in cross-European acts of solidarity. Gestures of support were made, in France shows of unity even moved beyond the token, yet the effort which was exerted paled in comparison to the energies which were dedicated to national goals.

This lack of concern was the result of factors which included the hostility of regular workers towards southern countries, the desire of unions not to sour relations with governments and certain benefits of austerity for core and intermediate economies. The outcome was that, while opposition to austerity was expressed by unions, the degree to which it was prioritized was slight. The reaction of social democrats in these countries was similar; if anything, such parties were more disinterested than unions. This leads to the conclusion that, in those cases in which differences in structural resources produce asymmetric outcomes, labour movements in stronger positions are unlikely to cooperate meaningfully with weaker counterparts. Declarations might be issued and limited actions undertaken, yet dedication of more considerable resources is improbable. The behaviour of the Polish labour movement is consistent with this argument. Though the absence of Poland from the Eurozone meant that counterparts in Southern Europe could be supported with less restraint, which may explain the more significant opposition of Polish labour to austerity, the issue was not of sufficient salience to prompt more considerable engagement.

Labour movements in disadvantaged structural positions are likely to have related problems marshalling pan-European solidarity. This is illustrated by the case of Spain. The weak post-2011 opposition of PSOE to austerity is rather anachronistic, resulting from the earlier implementation of austerity by the party, yet resistance was unambiguously in the interests of Spanish unions and consequently became a primary goal. Attempts to organize pan-European opposition nonetheless met mixed results; the European strike which UGT and CCOO helped initiate was observed only in a few periphery countries. Though this could be associated with the under-Europeanized nature of Spanish unions, the response of European partners was a more significant factor. Because of the ambiguous attitude of core and intermediate labour towards austerity and their consequently weak reaction, attempts by Spanish unions to achieve successful European action were effectively vetoed. I conclude that, in cases in which labour movements in disadvantaged structural positions attempt to marshal pan-European solidarity, mixed reactions of movements in more privileged positions are likely to frustrate such efforts.

In the second period, labour movements faced major constraints. Not only were there limits to their influence over public authorities, but the more charitable views of leaders were negated by the conservatism of members and voters. Retrospective analysis also tends to underestimate the pressing nature of contemporary challenges; in this time events occurred at a pace which made coherent responses onerous. Notwithstanding these caveats, the agency of labour movements was elevated in the second period; as stressed in chapter 3, this interval was a 'critical juncture' in which actor agency is more significant (Capoccia and Kelemen, 2007). A more rigorous interpretation of the actions of labour movements is thus apt. Failure to demonstrate solidarity with colleagues in the periphery, which was especially marked in core countries, played an important part in the deterioration of conditions in the region. Lack of solidarity was equated with *de facto* competition in chapter 3. Such competition was softer in form, yet it should be considered in these terms; it consolidated the advantage of one group of workers at the expense of another.

Through unplanned drifts to the advantage of movements with stronger structural resources and the weak extent to which solidarity

Table 9.2 How did labour movements behave in period two?

	Did labour movements show solidarity with periphery countries?	What could have been expected?
Germany	Support was rather underwhelming. Though German unions disagreed vocally with austerity, levels of participation in European protests were disappointing. Austerity was also denounced by SPD, yet certain actions of the party could be perceived as supportive of the policy.	Impressive mobilization of unions in Southern Europe set a reasonable benchmark for responses to European protests; German unions failed to meet this standard. There are less clear precedents for European opposition by social-democratic parties. SPD faced constraints and had a duty to maintain Eurozone stability, yet the stance of Die Linke suggests that bolder opposition to austerity was possible.
Spain	Support was impressive. Spanish unions were at the vanguard of attempts to organize European protests and general strikes were held in Spain on European days of action. The earlier implementation of austerity measures by PSOE nonetheless restricted the extent of social-democratic opposition to European austerity.	The actions of Spanish unions set standards for movements in other countries. Given that the later anti-austerity stance of PSOE was discredited by the Zapatero Government's earlier introduction of austerity, the case of the party is somewhat anomalous.
France	Support was mixed. French unions engaged in European protests to a respectable degree, yet participation was small compared to numbers demonstrating against French reforms. Within PS, there was considerable grassroots support for Southern Europe; external realities nonetheless meant that President Hollande increasingly followed the line of the German Government.	Impressive mobilization of unions in Southern Europe set a reasonable benchmark for responses to European protests; the reaction of French unions was fair, yet it failed to meet this standard. PS leaders faced constraints and had a duty to maintain Eurozone stability, yet the attitude of party grassroots suggests that bolder opposition to austerity was possible.

(*continued*)

Table 9.2 (Cont.)

	Did labour movements show solidarity with periphery countries?	What could have been expected?
Poland	Support was at times significant. Trade unions engaged in a series of actions in support of Southern Europe; this was particularly noteworthy given organizational weaknesses of Polish unions. On the other hand, opposition to austerity was not a priority for the left-wing SLD party.	Impressive mobilization of unions in Southern Europe set a reasonable benchmark for responses to European protests. Notwithstanding a good performance, Polish unions did not meet this standard; this must be understood with reference to Polish non-membership of the Eurozone and union weakness. SLD faced internal problems at the time of the crisis, yet the reaction of the new-left Razem party suggests that bolder opposition to austerity was possible.

is consequently prioritized, labour movements therefore react to integration in a manner which instigates competition between national labour markets. The influence of structures may be foremost, yet labour agency is not negligible; this was particularly demonstrated in period two. Such developments can be linked with the current stage of integration. The introduction of the euro has heightened competition among national regimes and increased the probability of crises (Höpner and Schäfer, 2010; Streeck, 2014), while spikes in nationalism have made workers less disposed to support disadvantaged counterparts (Polyakova and Fligstein, 2016); these changes are elaborated in chapter 10. In my opinion, a strength of this approach is its explanation of broader developments; findings are based on case studies which assessed macro-processes and established links with key substantive outcomes. Though it is undeniable that cooperation takes place, the influence of such campaigns is likely to be less potent. The conclusion of Erne (2008), who drew equivalence between the vigour of these forces, is problematic; the competitive processes theorized in this work are significantly more salient than countervailing trends.

My framework is likely to be more effective at explaining the manner in which national unions respond to integration, particularly at inter-sectoral and sectoral level, yet it will aid understanding in a series of other contexts. At European sector level, it might facilitate comprehension of the motivations of national participants in SSDCs; these institutions have also suffered from problems related to collective action. At European firm level, the approach may help researchers examining the negotiation of international framework agreements (IFAs) or participation in EWCs. The insights of my theory are nonetheless likely to be less applicable the further one moves from the macro level; the lower number of actors involved at firm level may mean that consciously competitive strategies are viable or that, consistent with literature which has arrived at such findings (Erne, 2008), cooperation between unions takes place. I have nonetheless outlined hypotheses which can be tested in future studies and, in chapter 10, an agenda for further research is elaborated.

A note on the extent to which the theory 'travels' outside of Europe is also necessary. Though the literature and cases with which I engage are inextricable from the European context, certain insights might be applied to international settings. Basic premises of my theory, related to drift towards scenarios which advantage labour movements with stronger structural resources and difficulties associated with cross-national solidarity, are pertinent to debates about the internationalization of labour movements; such themes have featured in scholarship which concerns globalization and cross-national labour relations. Future studies in contexts outside of Europe, whether they investigate continent-wide developments or relationships between workers in different national subsidiaries of MNCs, might attempt to operationalize relevant issues.

Europeanized social democracy?

Though the theorization of labour movements which I have undertaken is bound up with the behaviour of social-democratic parties, it is also necessary to reflect on specific implications for European social democracy. A preliminary result was that the degree to which social democrats exhibited solidarity with periphery countries was generally weaker than unions; this was the case in all countries. This result is far from surprising, scholars having long known that the broader bases of social-democratic parties and their need to govern in the national interest tend to make them less radical than unions, yet it is related to two more significant findings.

First, the current form of European integration appears to be driving a wedge between social-democratic parties and unions. In the last decade, European economic governance has become progressively centralized yet has retained its neoliberal, technocratic form. This has put social-democratic parties under increasing pressure to make difficult economic policy choices, so as to support the goals of European public authorities. This trend emerged in the Eurozone countries which were examined. In Spain and France, the decision of governing social democrats to support European economic policy led to profound grassroots unhappiness. In Germany, SPD faced a similar dilemma, though the privileged German position within the Eurozone meant that the decision provoked less rebellion. Unsurprisingly, such processes have increased tensions with unions, particularly in countries outside of the core of the Eurozone, and is one of the key forces which drives unions and social-democratic parties apart. It is unclear whether such a separation is happening generally, as literature is ambivalent on this question (Allern and Bale, 2017), yet results suggest that the nature of contemporary EU economic governance is one driver of such a process.

Second, and related to the first point, there are few signs of a meaningful process of Europeanization of social democracy. There was little vertical evidence of such a development. Though PES was not inactive during the crisis, little evidence of influence emerged in national case studies; representatives of national social-democratic parties make scant mention of the party in relevant material. There is also limited indication that such a process occurred horizontally. National social-democratic parties have considerable bilateral links, yet the impact of such associations on policy processes appears minor. The most striking example of this was the failed 2012 pact between President Hollande and SPD, yet there are numerous other incidences; the relative failure of PSOE and SLD to develop significant bilateral relationships, in comparison to the achievements of more energetic national union movements, is also telling. Other case studies may reveal more considerable Europeanization of social democracy, and it is undeniable that signs of this process continue to exist, yet results are consistent with scholarship which is sceptical of such a development (Holmes and Lightfoot, 2014; Lightfoot, 2005).

A further issue concerns the extent to which the actions of unions and social-democratic parties were representative of constituents. As they have progressed through this book, I suspect that readers with radical sympathies have cultivated the notion that a bolder response to the crisis might have been feasible. Such a perspective is understandable; some processes chronicled in this work do not show unions and social democrats in a good light. In periphery countries there was an inability to marshal effective opposition, while in other contexts there was indifference to the plight of the periphery. Dissatisfaction with the performance of labour movements is now a trend in Europe; it is linked with the belief that, if only established unions and social-democratic parties were able to more faithfully represent constituents, socio-economic outcomes would be fairer and more effective. There are three problems: (i) the extent to which the positions of labour movement leaderships were estranged from those of members; (ii) the issue of the attitudes of workers who are under-represented in unions and social-democratic parties; and (iii) the question of whether more radical movements would have delivered better outcomes.

One result is clear: leaderships of unions and social-democratic parties tended to be more committed to European solidarity than memberships. The case of Spain is peculiar given the disadvantaged status of the country within the Eurozone, which promoted synergy between the views of leaders and members, yet this was undoubtedly the case in Germany and Poland. In these countries, ordinary workers were more prone than leaders to advocate austere treatment of periphery countries; such positions reflected the kinds of views found in tabloid presses. The picture in France was more mixed. The small and militant character of union membership meant that the dispositions of members were more congruent with leaderships, while a substantial proportion of PS members were dismayed by the austere line of President Hollande. Whatever the vagaries of the French case, there is nonetheless a tendency for rank and files to be less sympathetic to benighted counterparts. The radical retort to this trend might invoke 'false consciousness' or blame presses, yet both of these objections are problematic. The dispositions of workers should normally be accepted as they are found; doing otherwise patronizes workers and is difficult to reconcile with logical principles such as Occam's razor. Criticisms of tabloid presses also tend to underplay the extent to which the content of such publications reflects the views of readers.

Related to this issue is a second question of the attitudes of those workers who are under-represented by unions and social-democratic parties. Labour movements are more representative of the interests of permanent workers who work in traditional industries; groups who tend to be under-represented include the highly paid and workers employed in very precarious conditions. Though it is difficult to make generalizations about the dispositions of such diverse constituencies, it is reasonable to conclude that the attitudes of these groups were not distinguished by generosity to periphery countries. This can be deduced from analysis of opinion polls in Germany, France and Poland; average citizens in these countries tended to be unsympathetic to the plight of the periphery. The idea that ordinary workers were more uncharitable to periphery countries than labour movement leaderships may be uncomfortable for some progressives, yet it is one which is concurrent with evidence; it is also consistent with scholarship which finds that, on an issue such as migration, elites are more liberal than populaces (Bearce and Hart, 2017).

A third issue concerns the extent to which more radical labour movements might have implemented responses more in keeping with

European solidarity than moderate counterparts. Given that unions have greater ability to avoid compromising decisions than political parties, which is related to narrower membership bases and lack of obligation to govern in the national interest, this question is particularly pertinent to social-democratic parties. It is admittedly the case that radical parties such as Die Linke advocated greater solidarity with periphery countries than advocated by social-democratic parties such as SPD. As indicated in table 9.2, social democrats had much to learn from the positions of radicals. On the other hand, the extent to which this would have changed had a party such as Die Linke entered office might be debated. Once in power, the reality of pressure from voters, European public authorities and financial markets may have made initial intentions unfeasible. The case of Syriza is instructive. Though this party took power in a periphery country, the policies to which it agreed in government were not fundamentally different from those it had decried while in opposition. Radicals may have made valid criticisms of counterparts on the moderate left, yet the extent to which such parties would have governed more effectively may be doubted. In countries outside of the periphery, these movements would also have been constrained by hostile public opinion, including that of ordinary workers.

What implications for other literatures?

Arguments advanced in this chapter also have interesting ramifications for theories of (i) institutions and (ii) the employment relationship. These literatures were not primary concerns in this work, and my research design was not made with this scholarship specifically in mind, yet certain results are pertinent to such debates; limitations associated with the indirect manner in which findings have emerged should nonetheless be remembered.

A key literature for which results are relevant is institutional theory; this scholarship is concerned with the manner in which economic institutions function. There is recurrent debate about the extent to which actors are able to effect institutional change. Though it is recognized that the influence of actors is unusually elevated during periods of 'critical juncture', classic accounts stress the capacity of institutions to remain stable and the correspondingly limited role of actors (Hall and Soskice, 2001). In reaction to this, works have emerged which underline processes by which actors achieve change; the arguments of Streeck and Thelen (2005), which theorize ways institutions evolve incrementally, are especially renowned. The theory of discursive institutionalism, which emphasizes the potential of ideas to drive change, is an interesting innovation (Schmidt, 2008).

Findings in this work nonetheless point to the enduring capacity of institutions to constrain. In my two cases, there was a propensity for actor agency to be subservient to structural pressure. The capacity of actors to consciously plan competitiveness followed this logic. Unions in Germany and Spain sometimes attempted to formulate long-term plans for competitiveness within the Eurozone, yet difficulties associated with planning and powerful structural influences on wage-determination frustrated these strategies. Expressions of solidarity with labour movements in periphery countries also followed such a pattern. Though movements in France, Germany and Poland made gestures of support to colleagues in the periphery, which were rooted in notions of solidarity and might be stressed by discursive institutionalists, the strength of these gestures was constrained by wider structural imperatives. Because the position of these countries in the Eurozone was not disadvantageous, there was limited incentive for labour movements to support counterparts in Southern Europe. Such findings can be linked with the transnational form of the European project. As scholars have long recognized, integration involves loss of national institutional control over economic processes; this further reduces the capacity of actors to overcome structural constraints. Results suggest that this problem is more acute than ever. These insights may be of particular note to scholars interested in lower-level processes of institutional change in European labour markets. Work on this topic has several achievements (Morgan and Hauptmeier, 2014), yet arguably fails to recognize the potential for structural constraints to draw actors back to long-term equilibriums.

Aside from implications for these controversies, results also indicate two more specific challenges for accounts which theorize actor agency. First, greater attention might be paid to the extent to which actor strategies are congruent with wider structural imperatives. Findings demonstrate that strategies which are incompatible with structural influences tend to be unsuccessful. The fate of efforts to express solidarity with the periphery make this clear; labour movements within core and intermediate countries made such attempts, yet tensions between these strategies and structural positions meant that they failed. Though work on institutional theory has already drawn attention to the need for actor strategies to align with structural conditions (Fligstein and McAdam, 2012: 20–1), results confirm this necessity and indicate its particular pertinence to the study of European labour movements.

Second, and associated with the first point, theorists might pay greater attention to the extent to which actor strategies are prioritized. In the course of my study, it was found that the degree to which actor initiatives were made a priority was a crucial predictor of their success. The reaction of labour movements to austerity made this clear. Certain individuals within French, German and Polish movements may have argued that solidarity with the periphery should be a foremost objective for their organizations, yet this goal was eventually pursued to a half-hearted degree. Had the aim of solidarity been adopted as a top priority by labour movements, it is plausible that reservations of rank and files would have been overcome and austerity would have been diluted. This would admittedly have involved the expenditure of considerable political capital; one could even argue that the price was too high given the existence of other organizational objectives.

Findings related to the low degree to which solidarity was prioritized have interesting implications for theories of actor behaviour. Scholars have reflected on questions related to the manner in which actors formulate strategies, yet results indicate that the problem of goal prioritization is of unusual pertinence; such an issue is also tied up with the question of scarcity of resources, which is particularly relevant in contemporary Europe. This subject deserves greater contemplation, chiefly involving the manner in which such a question might be operationalized, and in chapter 10 I reflect further on this issue.

My work is also relevant to theories of the employment relationship. These approaches, which conceptualize sources of conflict between management and labour (Heery, 2016), have underpinned analysis of the Eurozone crisis. Unitarism, which stresses harmony of interest among employers and workers, is associated with the view that the crisis is a dispute between countries. Radical scholars, who emphasize systematic differences in class interests under capitalism, adopt an opposite interpretation. In analysis of the crisis, Bieler and Erne (2015) assert that 'this is not a struggle between different countries … [but] about class struggle between capital and labour' (p. 20).

I am sympathetic to the pluralist perspective; this position regards the interests of management and labour as distinct, though prone to converge in some cases. Such an interpretation has underpinned the argument that, though the interests of capital and labour in individual countries were far from identical, on certain occasions commonalties of interest facilitated cross-class alliances. Pluralism most economically explains the modest reaction of core workers to developments in the periphery; radical authors rely on explanations related to nationalism and the press, which lie in tension with logical principles such as Occam's razor. In terms of specific relevance of my results to theories of the employment relationship, I suggest that scholars might pay more attention to the manner in which inter-state competition diminishes internal conflicts of interest between capital and labour. This work examined processes in which countries competed against one another and found that there were important areas in which domestic workers and employers shared a common interest; the competitiveness of German industry within EMU was one example. Because workers who lost from such processes were in different countries, and were therefore only indirectly linked with those employees who gained, the establishment of commonalities of interest between workers in different member states was particularly onerous. Class collaboration was also facilitated by the manner in which EMU encouraged competition among countries, even if nationalism heightened perceptions of shared interest. As theories of the employment relationship are developed, scholars might pay attention to the propensity of competition between states to reduce common interests among workers in competing states, yet enhance grounds for domestic cooperation between capital and labour.

In addition to implications for debates such as this, the argument that labour movements respond to integration in a competitive manner raises general questions about the European project. Addressing this issue will not only strengthen the theoretical basis of my work, but will also enrich understanding of the role of non-state actors in the integration process. In the final chapter, I undertake this endeavour.

10

Intergovernmentalism, disintegration and the importance of European unity

Having outlined a new approach to the manner in which labour movements respond to European integration, the task of conceptualizing the relationship between the behaviour of labour movements and theories of integration remains. This chapter commences with a theorization of the role of labour in the integration process. Rather than facilitating Europeanization, as certain theories predict, I contend that relations among separate labour movements are more compatible with intergovernmentalist readings of integration. Though neofunctionalism was an appropriate way of understanding the behaviour of labour in the 1990s, the competitive nature of EMU and recent rise of nationalist-populism means that intergovernmentalism is now more apposite.

Implications of findings for disintegration theory are also appraised. I reflect upon the capacity of labour sectionalism to contribute to disintegration and advance a theory of actor stasis; this approach conceptualizes the potential of actor inaction to lead to disintegration. An agenda for future research is then outlined. In addition to suggesting that the cases of other Eurozone countries are examined in the light of theories advanced in this book, I discuss the degree to which new research questions might develop knowledge of asymmetric relations between labour movements. Further research in areas related to theories of institutions and European integration is also encouraged.

Finally, I evaluate ways in which the EU might be reformed so as to strengthen institutional grounds for labour cooperation. Although arguments in this book present the EU in a mixed light, I stress that the endurance of the European project is unequivocally in the interests of labour; I therefore end by suggesting ways in which labour movements might help fortify the EU.

Labour movements, the contemporary EU and intergovernmentalism

As outlined in chapter 2, there are two basic approaches to the study of European integration: neofunctionalism and intergovernmentalism. Neofunctionalism is predicated on 'spillover'. Proponents of the theory, which have included scholars of social policy (Falkner, 1998), forecast that actors will incrementally transfer loyalties to the European level (Haas, 1958; Niemann and Ioannou, 2015). In contrast to neofunctionalists, advocates of intergovernmentalism emphasize the extent to which integration is controlled by member states and the related reluctance of governments to cede power to the supranational level (Bickerton *et al.*, 2015; Hoffmann, 1966; 1982). Intergovernmentalism has also inspired work in the field of social policy; a number of scholars have emphasized impediments to social integration (Scharpf, 1999; Streeck, 1994).

Findings in this book are broadly supportive of intergovernmentalism; in the course of my study, processes of spillover were consistently eclipsed by competitive pressures. In sections below, I delineate these influences and propose that, as a result of the nature of EMU and a rise in nationalist-populism, a theoretical approach to the study of labour which is rooted in intergovernmentalism is most apposite. Notwithstanding this general trend, it is important to acknowledge certain processes congruent with the spillover hypothesis which emerged in the course of this study. Some pressures for the Europeanization of collective bargaining were found; certain projects, typically instigated by European federations, aimed to coordinate the bargaining demands of unions in member states. These initiatives influenced the behaviour of national negotiators, albeit in a secondary manner.

Following the outbreak of crisis, there was also notable solidarity between European labour; movements across the continent mobilized in support of counterparts in the periphery. This process occurred in core countries. In Germany, despite the existence of considerable popular hostility to countries in Southern Europe, the leaderships of German unions made gestures of solidarity with these countries which were not insignificant. Such actions were based upon links forged in previous attempts at European cooperation; European confederations such as ETUC played a key role in expressions of unity. Examples of solidarity between social-democratic parties also transpired. PS and SPD created a (temporary) anti-austerity alliance and PSOE had a number of European links, though unity was less extensive than levels observed among trade unions. In the course of my study, a number of instances of spillover therefore emerged; this is consistent with investigations which have found evidence of spillover in fields as diverse as European social dialogue (Falkner, 1998), collective bargaining coordination (Gollbach and Schulten, 2000) and the Europeanization of social democracy (Ladrech, 2000).

Despite these examples, instances of spillover were eclipsed by patterns of competition which are more consistent with intergovernmentalist arguments. Such influences manifested themselves in competition between collective bargaining regimes and restricted solidarity after the outbreak of crisis. With respect to the first of these, my study found limited pressure for Europeanization of collective bargaining following the introduction of the euro. Notwithstanding the examples which are cited above, there was little significant movement towards European coordination of bargaining. It is necessary to remind ourselves that, though this development now sounds somewhat fanciful, it was once a feasible goal. EMU is after all an integrated economic regime, equivalent to the national systems around which bargaining structures historically crystallized; figures within ETUC once considered European sectoral wage determination a possibility (Coldrick, 1998).

Though such a development cannot be ruled out in the future, it did not materialize in the period under investigation. Rather than initiating processes of spillover which ended in meaningful cooperation, EMU tended to promote regime competition. After the introduction of the euro, unions in countries as diverse as Spain and Germany concluded agreements which put pressure on competitors. Even if this was unintentional, it had the effect of encouraging reliance on national bargaining institutions and forestalling spillover. My argument is most cogently illustrated by the discrepant effects of processes of spillover and competition. Though attempts to coordinate bargaining achieved certain effects, consequences were dwarfed by the impact of competitive behaviour rooted in national institutions. The latter led to marked discrepancies in ULCs and the ultimate outbreak of debt crisis. Such developments are anticipated by theories of negative spillover (Scharpf, 1999), which note the propensity of integration to prompt undesirable social outcomes.

The extent of solidarity between labour movements after the outbreak of crisis was also limited. A key tenet of neofunctionalism is that the loyalties of elites and citizens will shift to European level; this prediction is now not advanced as confidently as it once was, yet it remains an important element of spillover theory. Some evidence of this process emerged among elites. Across studied countries, leaderships of trade unions exhibited solidarity with counterparts in periphery countries; such support was heartfelt and based on bonds forged through European integration.

Despite the existence of solidarity between labour movement leaderships, the potential of this unity was negated by indifference and hostility to periphery countries among rank and files. There were some demonstrations of solidarity, the 14 November 2012 European Day of Action and Solidarity attracting significant support in intermediate and periphery countries, yet inclinations to the contrary were more potent. Across member states outside of the periphery, there was a perception that periphery countries had authored their own downfall. Such pressures constrained labour movements. Though leaderships sometimes wished to demonstrate more significant solidarity, popular objection to this course of action, expressed via lack of participation in anti-austerity actions and disapproval of policies favourable to the periphery, meant that this was unfeasible. Such trends affected both unions and social-democratic parties; SPD relinquishment of support for Eurobonds, following voter dislike of the idea, is a definitive instance. The extent to which there was a shift in popular loyalty to the European project was therefore limited, and one could even argue a regression took place over the course of decades, leading to a situation in which European labour was weakened in the face of assault.

Rather than a scenario in which there is incremental progress towards shared institutions and identity among European labour movements, one witnesses a picture more consistent with the intergovernmentalist reading; power remains vested in national institutions and there is considerable reluctance to relinquish competences. The relationship of labour movements with the European project has attracted this interpretation in previous periods, yet two characteristics distinguish the contemporary situation. First, there is the influence of EMU. Though the neoliberal nature of European economic integration was theorized by a previous generation of intergovernmentalists (Streeck, 1994), the full effects of EMU were yet to become apparent. Since the introduction of the single currency, the potential for advantage within the Eurozone has initiated more considerable competition among national regimes. This competition may have been largely unintentional, yet its effects have been significant; pressures for spillover have been further eclipsed, even if such influences continue to exist in an insipid form.

Second, there is the influence of nationalist-populism. Decades of European integration have never prompted the disappearance of nationalism, yet such sentiments have undergone a recent resurgence (Polyakova and Fligstein, 2016). In years since the outbreak of debt crisis, populations in core and periphery countries have regarded each other with increasing suspicion. This has been associated with the emergence of right-populist parties. These movements have not only made considerable gains in a number of European countries, but have also influenced the mainstream. Such trends have impeded the capacity of labour movements to cooperate. Though elites continue to desire such collaboration, popular nationalism has made more considerable solidarity unfeasible. This lack of co-feeling between European workforces, which was less apparent in the 1990s, has constrained labour movements and is a key driver of developments theorized in this work.

My argument about the extent to which labour movements in Europe respond to pressures for spillover is therefore a pessimistic one, yet it needs to be stressed that the field of social policy is merely one domain. In a number of areas, among the most notable of which are trade and monetary policy, the EU has long shown impressive propensity for spillover. In recent times, in reaction to the debt crisis, fiscal policy has also been centralized in a manner which is consistent with neofunctionalism (Niemann and Ioannou, 2015). This process has also included elements related to social policy; the European Semester system makes a number of recommendations for the reform of labour markets. If one regards the neoliberal measures in which the Semester specializes as constituting social policy, it might be argued that significant spillover has taken place; most would nonetheless consider such spillover to be negative (Scharpf, 1999). On the other hand, there are signs that the European Semester is being reformed to make it friendlier to labour; a social policy 'scoreboard' has been introduced and Polish unions were found to be well-disposed to certain Semester output. Such developments are arguably limited in consequence, yet possibilities associated with the Semester are discussed below.

What role for labour in the disintegration process?

A further important issue concerns the potential role of labour in European disintegration. As outlined in chapter 2, recent accounts have grappled with the dynamics of the disintegration process. Most do not prophesize an outright collapse of the EU, exceptions nonetheless existing (Simms and Less, 2015), but raise the prospect of partial exits from parts of the union such as the Schengen zone and Eurozone. Promising avenues for the study of disintegration have been identified. Vollaard (2014) advocates the ideas of Bartolini (2005); this approach conceives of the external consolidation and internal structuring of states as mutually dependent. Notwithstanding the existence of this scholarship, there is little discussion of the role of labour, or non-state actors in general, in the process of disintegration. Owing to this omission, I assess the role labour might play in European disintegration; this will also be relevant to other non-state actors.

As contended above, a distinguishing trait of the labour movements examined in this book is inaction. Despite the existence of substantial European economic integration, which triggered spillover in other policy fields (Niemann and Ioannou, 2015), labour failed to react to such pressures; there was no real Europeanization of collective

bargaining after the introduction of the euro and, following the outbreak of crisis, solidarity with benighted counterparts was in short
supply. It is not widely discussed in literature, yet the propensity of
actors to Europeanize undeniably exerts a steadying force on the
European polity; actors with Europeanized structures and orientations
are more prone to adopt positions conducive to European unity. As EU
competences expand, which has occurred over the lifespan of EMU, it
is vital that the loyalties of actors shift accordingly. Such reflexes are
likely to be crucial during crises. Just as economic stabilizers forestall
pressures for recession, Europeanized actors will restrain pressures
for disintegration which can accompany crisis. This point is related to
Bartolini's (2005) argument concerning the necessity of internal state
organization.

The proclivity for actor inaction which has been observed in this book
therefore has vital implications for the functioning of the EU and merits
theorization; I term it stasis and contend that it potentially facilitates disintegration. Stasis takes place when actors fail to react to pressures for
integration. It may be asserted that the labour movements examined in
this work do respond to integration in certain ways yet, as I have argued
and other studies indicate (Streeck, 1994), the scale of this response
tends to be underwhelming. Stasis is a potential driver of disintegration.
Though such inaction may not seem to handicap the EU in good times,
for example during the Delors years few were troubled by trade union
recalcitrance, in such periods it stockpiles future problems and, in ages in
which there are pressures for disintegration, it represents a serious threat
to the integrity of the EU.

Following the reinvigoration of the European project by the
Delors Commissions (1985–95), the extent to which a corresponding
Europeanization of trade unionism took place had limits; progress was
particularly insubstantial compared to economic integration. This did
not give major grounds for concern at the time yet, consistent with my
argument that actors should respond to wider pressures for integration,
it was to prove problematic in the longer term. As a range of authorities have demonstrated (Hancké, 2013; Hassel, 2014; Johnston, 2016),
discrepancies in ULCs which resulted from the endurance of national
bargaining practices were a key cause of debt crisis. Had industrial
relations institutions been Europeanized to the extent that meaningful
coordination of collective bargaining had taken place, it is possible that
crisis would have been averted. The restricted extent of Europeanization
of labour movements also had key consequences for the capacity of the
EU to react to debt crisis. Because trade unions and social-democratic
parties had undergone limited Europeanization, there was little solidarity with benighted sister movements after the outbreak of crisis. This
lack of unity was a major problem for the EU; had workers in core and

intermediate countries been more sympathetic to counterparts in the periphery, the crisis would have been easier to manage.

Labour movement stasis therefore hamstrung the EU. Over a number of decades, labour failed to react to pressures for spillover and, in the longer term, this impeded the ability of the EU to function. If more considerable Europeanization of labour movements had occurred, marked imbalances within EMU may have been averted and solidarity with southern European colleagues might have been more considerable. These findings represent a contribution to disintegration theory. Though theories of disintegration have identified the broad terms in which the phenomenon takes place, there has been little detailed analysis of the manner in which such processes are likely to proceed. Via assessment of the tendency for labour movement inaction to impede the functioning of the EU, especially during times of crisis, the theory of stasis contributes to this endeavour.

The process of stasis which I have theorized is deduced only from the study of labour movements. Notwithstanding this limitation, there are reasons for thinking that the theory may be generalizable to other non-state actors. As an extensive literature has outlined, the degree to which non-state actors respond to European integration is mixed. Some actors have undergone considerable Europeanization in response to integration, such as certain business lobbies, yet the profile of others is more akin to that of labour movements; examples include groups such as farmers, churches and employers' associations. The theory of stasis is likely to be applicable to the latter groups. Though the conditions in which this process takes place and potential damage to the EU will vary, rudiments are likely to be similar. In a section below in which ideas for future research are discussed, I reflect on ways in which differences between actors might be better understood and this agenda advanced.

Driving the agenda forward: some suggestions for future research

Findings made in this work raise a series of related questions; in the following section, an agenda for future research is outlined. There are a number of ways in which the core hypothesis of this book, namely that European labour movements are more likely to compete than cooperate, might be further developed. Examination could be undertaken of the extent to which specific arguments made by this work correspond with the cases of other European countries. Though I consider my four countries to be representative, arguments would be nuanced were investigation into further cases to be undertaken. Inspection of other core countries (Austria and Netherlands) would likely yield compelling results. There is a more centralized bargaining system in Austria; it may therefore emerge that moderation took a more intentional form. Given that alternative factors were found to pre-empt consciously competitive strategies, the systematic presence of such tactics is nonetheless unlikely. Investigation in these contexts may also find that the dispositions of unions and social-democratic parties towards periphery countries were distinctive; it would be interesting to discover the extent to which labour movements were influenced by German counterparts.

Examination of alternative intermediate, periphery and non-Eurozone countries would also be fruitful. Belgium is the only other intermediate country, yet its peculiarities might shed further light on the behaviour of labour movements in such contexts; this is particularly the case given that Belgian unions are less marginalized than French counterparts. There are a series of other periphery countries (Cyprus, Greece, Ireland, Italy and Portugal) and assessment of their cases would lead to interesting findings. Studies of these contexts might reveal different responses to the introduction of the euro, as there are distinct labour market structures in these countries, and separate capacities to resist attacks on working conditions. The predicament of PSOE, hamstrung by the introduction of austerity while in government, underlines the extent to which cases are context dependent. The group of non-Eurozone countries is the most numerous and diverse, containing countries as dissimilar as Croatia, Hungary and the UK, yet study of these cases may lead to further understanding of the behaviour of labour movements in non-Eurozone contexts. Particular challenges would depend on the country in question; it is difficult to generalize owing to the diversity of this category.

A key issue is the extent to which broader research questions, inspired by the thesis of this work yet investigating different variables, would validate my arguments. Specifically, future studies could examine the extent to which relations between different European labour movements are characterized by unplanned drifts towards sectional outcomes and the related issue of whether corrective strategies tend to be unsuccessful. These hypotheses underpin my contention that competition is more likely than cooperation. There are a number of ways in which such concerns might be further operationalized. Substantive indicators such as wages might be added and independent variables such as labour influence over public authorities could be investigated.

A rich seam of material might be found at lower levels. At sector level, examination of the extent to which arguments are consistent with the dynamics of European collective bargaining networks would represent an interesting undertaking. Such studies might investigate the extent to which unions are willing to enter into cooperation, the hypothesis that difficulties associated with such action are related to benefits for certain unions and the conditions in which corrective strategies are efficacious. At firm level, research into EWCs could pursue similar lines of investigation. The results of such projects would inevitably differ from those of this study. Particularly at firm level, contexts will be distinctive and fewer actors will be involved; strategies which consciously attempt to undercut rivals, which this study found tended to be unfeasible on a national scale, may be more viable.

Future studies, whether conducted at macro level or micro level, will arrive at distinct results. Notwithstanding these differences, it is my hope that such investigation will advance knowledge of transnational labour relations. Research in countries outside of Europe would be welcome. This work has argued that the Eurozone is characterized by relations among core and periphery labour movements which are akin to certain Marxist conceptions of imperialism. Though rudimentary differences between formal imperialism and the Eurozone have been outlined, it may be that the situation is more akin to the classic Marxist formulation in contexts in the developing world. The point is that there will be differences according to place and, if a better understanding is to be developed of the conditions in which labour movements benefit (or not) at the expense of counterparts, it is vital that researchers become sensitive to discrepancies.

Certain studies may arrive at findings which are not in accordance with the arguments of this work. This is a normal part of academic debate; I have attempted to formulate hypotheses which are falsifiable and, in certain cases, it is probable that this will occur. Given that we are at a stage of European integration at which a question mark hangs over the future of the union, fresh investigation which emphasizes the capacity of actors to cooperate might be welcome. As outlined below, ideas in this book were conceived at a point (2014/15) at which a key problem in European politics was the propensity of certain countries to exploit others. Events have progressed since this time; the most pressing matter now appears to be preservation of the EU itself. Though the issue of core–periphery inequality remains crucial, a priority of future research may be to discover the conditions in which European harmony can be achieved. The conflictual tendencies which this work calls to attention undoubtedly characterize integration, yet there is also a propensity for member states and actors to cooperate. Given the straits in which the EU today finds itself, it may be time to emphasize these inclinations; scholars of labour movements might consider the manner in which unions overcome new European collective action problems and/or the potential of soft coordination associated with the European Semester. If such work is undertaken, substantive consequences of cooperation should be examined carefully; this is a weakness of existing scholarship.

Other findings made by this study may also inspire future research; results which concern institutional theory, related to the question of whether the goals of actors are prioritized, are pertinent. As outlined in chapter 9, an important discovery was that the extent to which actors prioritize specific aims is critical to the likelihood of success; when goals are secondary priorities for actors, chances of favourable outcomes are lessened. Future research might therefore examine the extent to which it is feasible for actors to pursue multiple goals. Though various literatures have examined the manner in which actors respond to scarcity (Hobson and Lynch, 2016), the question of the management of organizational objectives is crucial enough to merit dedicated literature. Issues related to the pursuit of multiple aims are also vital to the work of trade unions and social-democratic parties, especially true of the latter given the broader nature of their constituencies, and research would yield insightful findings about these organizations. Work could be conducted using quantitative and/or qualitative methodologies and might develop awareness of the conditions in which the pursuit of multiple objectives is feasible (or not). Though it is difficult to anticipate what results might be, acquaintance with relevant factors would markedly advance knowledge of the manner in which actors respond to scarcity; this would represent an important contribution to institutional theory.

It is also my hope that this work will inspire further study of the relationship between theories of European integration and the behaviour of labour; this issue has attracted limited recent investigation and my arguments about labour movements and intergovernmentalism are attempts to stimulate debate. Accounts which grapple with the question of whether the behaviour of labour movements is indicative (or not) of spillover would be welcome. Though studies have been undertaken in previous years (Falkner, 1998; Marginson and Sisson, 2004) and this book has attempted to work in this tradition, there is a dearth of contemporary scholarship. Analysis of lower levels of governance, including EWCs and Europeanization of collective bargaining, would be insightful and could be conducted using quantitative and qualitative methodologies. Such research might reach generalizable conclusions about the extent of labour spillover in contemporary Europe. This study has attempted to arrive at a clear verdict on this question and to link conclusions to contemporary political conditions; work which directly engages with my hypotheses would be of great interest. Conclusions could be extrapolated from micro-level studies, though projects with a broader scope might be better equipped to achieve such objectives.

Future investigation might also consider the role of non-state actors more generally. As I have stressed, the terms in which non-state actors respond to integration is an area in which there could be more research. Drawing inspiration from studies such as this one, scholars might examine the manner in which actors such as NGOs, employers' associations and consumer lobbies react to Europeanization. If an appropriate quantity of results were accumulated, there could be work on a typology of the behaviour of non-state actors.

Knowledge of the manner in which non-state actors react to integration could also aid research into theories of disintegration. Development of the concept of stasis was an attempt to move towards better understanding of the manner in which labour movements contribute to processes of disintegration. Though it is hoped that this hypothesis will aid comprehension of the role which other non-state actors play, it may be that the conclusions of others differ from my own. Whatever these results, further investigation into the relationship between non-state actors and disintegration will only develop knowledge of this area. Given that theories of disintegration may increase in relevance in coming years, this is an important undertaking.

What future for Europe?

To reflect on European politics at the time I write, in early 2018, is to do so against a backdrop of no little unpredictability. Following years of economic crisis, the Brexit vote and the rise of populist parties, the EU faces a degree of uncertainty it has never before encountered; it is conceivable that the union will not exist in five years' time. Though my argument has been that division between labour movements is a key reason why the EU is malfunctioning, in the section which follows I contend that it is vital that the EU is saved and suggest ways in which the EU might be reformed so as to strengthen institutional grounds for labour cooperation. This work would not be complete without such a section, yet it is imperative to stress the limits of such counsel.

Aside from the issue of the restricted circulation of academic books(!), the political economy tradition in which I write emphasizes the limits of actor volition. As is well known, such scholars tend to stress the importance of existing structures; the varieties-of-capitalism approach underlines how institutions constrain paths available to actors (Hall and Soskice, 2001) while historical institutionalists argue that socio-economic structures reflect the logic of past processes (Mahoney, 2000). It is true that the influence of actors is considered pronounced during so-called critical junctures; these are periods, often prompted by war or revolution, in which new institutions are established. The main critical juncture of EMU nonetheless took place at the time of the Maastricht Treaty. This is therefore a horse which has bolted, notwithstanding smaller opportunities for reform in periods such as 2011–12.

Even if these words were to be widely read by European policymakers, their impact might be limited. This is a pessimistic note on which to commence such a section, yet realism means that this must be underlined. Issuance of counsel nonetheless remains a key duty of the socially concerned scholar; if everyone were to cease advocating new ideas because they considered their prospects modest, our world would be a bleak place indeed.

Discussion of ways in which labour movements might contribute to the European project, in a manner which reinforces both, involves other challenges. Not only are future events notoriously difficult to predict, but contemporary European politics is particularly fickle. One long-term possibility is EU collapse, which I contend below would be highly undesirable for labour movements. A more optimistic vision involves the reform of European economic governance to incorporate objectives related to growth. Certain authorities envisage an EU without the euro, Höpner states that 'Europe would be better off without the Euro' and commends the European monetary system of 1979–98 (2014: 665), yet implementation difficulties mean that most favour reform of the euro. A number of strategies have been outlined; ideas such as Eurobonds, growth orientated monetary and fiscal policies and transfer payments to periphery countries are commonly suggested. The fortification of social integration, including the introduction of a European minimum wage, is associated with these proposals. *A Marshall Plan for Europe*, which was issued by DGB during the debt crisis (see chapter 4), is one of the best articulations of such visions.

Notwithstanding practical problems associated with these proposals, to which I allude above, there are three ways in which labour movements might contribute to a progressive European economic policy regime. First, better coordination of collective bargaining would be likely to fore-stall trade imbalances and exert a redistributive influence. Though the European public authorities have long been wise to the need to avoid such imbalances, there is a general aversion to achieving such objectives through collective bargaining coordination. Given the role of uncoordinated bargaining practices in instigating the crisis, demonstrated by this study and others, this may be a serious error.

In a progressive system of European economic governance, meaningful coordination of collective bargaining might take place. Trade unions have attempted to coordinate bargaining for many years, yet have encountered problems related to differences in economic environment and collective bargaining systems. Many such problems could be overcome were greater public support to be provided to unions. If collective bargaining conferences were financed by the European public authorities, possibly through the network of SSDCs which already exist, it is likely that there would be a substantial amelioration of outcomes. Tripartite bargaining conferences might also be held. If these meetings included formalized processes of consultation, à la the European Semester, their effectiveness would be further enhanced. In such a process, social partners and public authorities might discuss collective bargaining results and objectives in the light of economic policy goals. Certain unions might resist mandate transfer, yet these objections could be overcome.

Second, a progressive European economic policy regime might include a strengthened European social dialogue. Many had high hopes for the dialogue after the conclusion of the Social Protocol, yet initial expectations have not been realized and an incremental weakening has taken place (Prosser, 2016b). Though fortification of the dialogue should involve more legally binding sectoral and inter-sectoral agreements on topics which improve substantive conditions in labour markets, equally important is social partner involvement in economic governance. Even if a macroeconomic dialogue has existed for a number of years, the degree of labour participation in economic decision-making has been very slight. Given the extent to which European economic governance has now been centralized, it is crucial that labour partakes more extensively in this process. Though a more realistic short-term goal is greater labour engagement in the European Semester process, a prospect discussed below, comprehensive labour participation in economic governance should be a longer-term aim. This would involve social partners being granted rights in the determination of EU monetary and fiscal policy; a labour seat on the ECB governing council would be one progressive measure.

I am nonetheless conscious of the fact that similar ideas have been advanced for many years and, certain accomplishments notwithstanding, have achieved limited success. I do not believe that this reflects their feasibility. These are moderate ideas which attempt to move economic governance in a social-democratic direction; one might even say that popular unhappiness with the EU makes such measures urgent. Crucially, such initiatives would also strengthen the structural basis for labour cooperation. My argument in this work has been that the institutional logic of EMU encourages competition between labour movements. Effective reform would do much to improve matters, even if national membership profiles would remain a source of tension.

Given historic difficulties with the achievement of reform and the extent to which bolder change depends upon benign political conditions, it is also necessary to discuss a third, more modest goal. This is the strengthening of labour participation in the European Semester. The Semester is the annual process by which the economic policies of member states are coordinated; it is now a well-established part of European economic governance and it is crucial that labour are able to shape it. Though ETUC has lobbied for greater union voice and certain reforms have been made which increase the influence of labour, for example a social policy 'scoreboard' has been introduced, much is left to do. Securing enhanced participation in the Semester must continue to be a goal of European labour. Unions should demand influence at all stages of the Semester process, while PES might make greater effort to ensure that the Semester incorporates social goals. These reforms are in the general interest of the EU. Not only would such measures help reconcile workers to the European project, but greater labour influence on European governance may help prevent macroeconomic imbalances.

This book, in certain of its parts, has flattered neither European labour movements nor the EU. The former have been depicted as lacking in European spirit, while the latter has been portrayed as an impersonal force, guilty of inflicting hardship on millions in Southern Europe. This orientation reflects the environment in which this project was conceived. In 2014/15, the years in which ideas for this book took shape, the effects of austerity dominated debate about the EU. The research design of this work, which emphasizes division among member states and corrosive effects of EMU, reflects these concerns. Hindsight also impresses upon me the extent to which the European left was comparatively united in opposition to austerity; in intellectual communities, as opposed to political circles in which hard choices had to be made, there was often little to differentiate the verdicts of social democrats and radicals.

Events have moved on since this project was conceived. In this time, it has become clear that the survival of the European project is now at stake; freedom of movement crises and the Brexit vote, not to mention continued problems with EMU, represent existential threats. In such circumstances, a new partition has appeared on the left; this is between those who are convinced of the need to save the EU and those to whom the prospect of the demise of the union is a matter of relish or indifference. The 2017 French presidential election, in which a pro-EU centre-left struggled to keep a Eurosceptic far-left at bay, was illustrative of this division.

My sympathies lie with moderates. Reasons why the EU is worth saving have not been at the fore of this book, and I must therefore outline why I consider it vital for labour movements that the EU endures. The primary reason is the need to guarantee European stability. Issues of war and peace are not typically invoked in works of political economy, yet the prospect of an EU collapse and consequent descent of Europe into nationalism means that this issue is unusually pertinent. This book has underlined the capacity of national labour movements to compete with one another. Though such processes were encouraged by EMU, I would suggest that pacifying effects of EU political structures, which discourage conflict between member states and their labour movements, more than countervail these tensions. It is also crucial to remember that strained relations among different sections of workforces, whether within or between nation states, are endemic; this has been recognized by literatures which range from Marxist theories of imperialism (Brewer, 2001) to work on dualization (Emmenegger *et al.*, 2012; Rueda, 2007). If the EU were to collapse, competitive propensities of labour movements might begin to serve states with nationalist foreign policies. This would represent a far more sinister development than anything theorized in this work and would evoke the Europe of the first half of the twentieth century.

There are other reasons why it is firmly in the interests of labour for the EU to endure. Though economic growth associated with the union has tended to favour wealthier classes, it has also enriched the poorer. The development of Southern Europe which took place in decades prior to the crisis, which transformed such countries and substantially benefited lower socioeconomic groups, was associated with EU membership. The achievements of European social policy are far from negligible. Decent conditions have been established in labour markets; research shows that, rather than dealing in minimums, European regulation commonly exceeds existing national standards (Falkner *et al.*, 2005). The criticisms of the EU which have been made in this work should therefore not be read as a call for the demise of the union, nor as inference that progressives should be indifferent to such a development, but rather as inspiration for reform.

These circumstances involve a conundrum; the endurance of the EU is in the interests of workers yet, as this book has argued, there is a tendency for labour movements to engage in competitive behaviour. Primary responsibility for resolution of this problem rests with European public authorities; reforms must be undertaken which strengthen institutional grounds for cooperation. Labour movements nonetheless have a role to play. Given longstanding efforts of leaderships to improve links with European colleagues, which meant that there was significant solidarity among elites during the crisis, action at this level might not be a priority. Challenges at lower levels appear more considerable. Owing to a rise in nationalism, workers have become increasingly susceptible to discourses which stigmatize counterparts in other member states; a number of examples emerged in this work. If collaboration between labour movements is to remain feasible, it is vital that this trend is reversed.

In addition to engagement with initiatives which fortify social Europe, labour movements might aim to improve popular commitment to integration. Certain recent efforts, in which union officials have helped dispel stereotypes about Southern Europe, could act as inspiration for more comprehensive programmes. In future projects, trade unions might run campaigns which aim to educate members and citizenry about benefits of European cooperation. Social-democratic parties could engage in similar endeavours. It will require courage for labour movements to participate in such agendas, for as the German case shows it is difficult for labour movements to articulate pro-European values in the face of populist critique; the crisis of integration nonetheless makes such strategies imperative. Labour movements may be prone to competitive behaviour, yet countervailing strategies can help neutralize negative effects.

Given that this work has delineated many of the ways in which Europe is malfunctioning, some may be surprised at the defence of the EU which has made been in conclusion. These positions are not contradictory. The intergovernmentalist framework which this work favours does not aim for the demise of the EU – many who pursue this goal conceive of the union in paranoid neofunctionalist terms – but merely seeks to understand its actual manner of functioning. Some degree of conflict between actors within a polity is inevitable; as outlined above, distributional struggles are endemic. In a multi-national polity such as the EU, more considerable skirmishes which are susceptible to exacerbation through nationalism are foreseeable.

If the EU and/or Eurozone were to collapse, it is highly improbable that such conflicts would subside; history suggests that they would exacerbate. The containment of disputes among nation states is the historic achievement of European integration. Though it is inevitable that tensions will continue to exist within a European polity, common European structures allow for them to be managed without reversion to war. This infrastructure has admittedly been tested in recent years and inefficiencies associated with EMU, which will not be easy to reform, have made such problems worse. If reform is successful, and there is every indication that progress can be made, there can be a return to the more harmonious Europe of decades past. I consider one thing axiomatic; a Europe in which the EU has disintegrated is likely to be far worse for workers.

Appendix 1

List of semi-structured research interviewees

Organization	Form and nationality of organization	Date interview conducted	Interview format
CFDT	French trade union	June 2016	Face-to-face
CFE-CGC	French trade union	June 2016	Face-to-face
CFTC	French trade union	June 2016	Face-to-face
CGT	French trade union	October 2017	Telephone interview
FO	French trade union	June 2016	Face-to-face
Parti Socialiste (PS)	French social-democratic party	July 2017	Telephone interview
Lewiatan	Polish employers' association	July 2016	Face-to-face
OPZZ	Polish trade union	August 2016	Face-to-face
Platforma Obywatelska (PO)	Polish centre-right political party	August 2016	Face-to-face
Sojusz Lewicy Demokratycznej (SLD)	Polish centre-left political party (Interview with academic expert rather than party representative)	August 2017	Telephone interview
Solidarność	Polish trade union	August 2016	Face-to-face

Organization	Form and nationality of organization	Date interview conducted	Interview format
CCOO	Spanish trade union	November 2016	Face-to-face
CEOE	Spanish employers' association	November 2016	Face-to-face
Partido Socialista Obrero Español (PSOE)	Spanish social-democratic political party	November 2016	Face-to-face
UGT	Spanish trade union	November 2016	Face-to-face
DGB	German trade union	February 2017	Face-to-face
Gesamtmetall	German employers' association	February 2017	Face-to-face
IG Bau	German trade union	February 2017	Face-to-face
IG Metall	German trade union	February 2017	Face-to-face
Sozialdemokratische Partei Deutschlands (SPD)	German social-democratic political party	February 2017	Face-to-face
Ver.di	German trade union	February 2017	Face-to-face

Glossary

CCOO   Confederación sindical de comisiones obreras (CCOO) is one of the two main Spanish trade union confederations. Though CCOO is historically linked to the Spanish Communist Party, in recent decades it has shown a willingness to engage in social dialogue.

CFDT   Confédération française démocratique du travail (CFDT) is a moderate French trade union confederation. CFDT has been prepared to compromise with employers and public authorities and is the largest union confederation in France.

CFE-CGC   Confédération française de l'encadrement – Confédération générale des cadres (CFE-CGC) is a French trade union confederation for managerial staff which is smaller in size.

CFTC   Confédération française des travailleurs chrétiens (CFTC) is a French Catholic trade union confederation which is smaller in size.

CGT   Formed in 1895, Confédération générale du Travail (CGT) is a French trade union confederation which is renowned for its militant character and links with the French Communist Party. CGT continues to adopt adversarial stances towards employers and public authorities, though is no longer the largest union confederation in France.

Corporatism   This refers to negotiations between employers, trade unions and public authorities. Such pacts were pioneered by authoritarian regimes in inter-war years, though have been used repeatedly in post-war democratic states. Corporatism is synonymous with tripartism, notwithstanding minor differences between the two (Prosser and Perin, 2015).

Die Linke   Founded in 2007 by a coalition which included former East German Communists, Die Linke is a radical left-wing German political party. The party has consistently had a presence in the Bundestag.

DGB   Deutscher Gewerkschaftsbund (DGB) is the main German trade union confederation. The extent to which DGB has engaged in corporatist negotiations is modest, yet the confederation is influential at national and European level.

Dualization   The concept of dualization refers to a tendency for labour markets to become divided between insiders and outsiders. In recent decades, the position of insiders has remained secure while outsiders have been vulnerable to unemployment and temporary contracts. This results from the enhanced capacity of insiders to defend themselves, which is associated with higher rates of unionization and representation by social-democratic parties.

Economic and Monetary Union (EMU)   EMU was established by the 1992 Maastricht Treaty and set out procedures for the institution of a single European currency. There were profound implications for labour markets. Not only did initial convergence criteria prompt pacts which moderated wages, but centralization of monetary policy meant that national policymakers could no longer devalue currencies; the remaining option of 'internal devaluation' has involved deregulation of labour markets.

European social dialogue   Refers to talks between European employers' associations and trade unions (the social partners). Dialogue takes place at European inter-sectoral and sectoral levels and social partners have a treaty-based right to conclude European collective agreements.

ETUC   Founded in 1973, the European Trade Union Confederation (ETUC) is the main trade union organization at European level. ETUC coordinates activities of member unions, lobbies European public authorities and is recognized as a social partner.

EWCs   Given legal status by a 1994 EU directive, European works councils (EWCs) provide for the information and consultation of workers within European firms. The directive was revised in 2009, yet the efficacy of EWCs has been criticized.

Exposed/non-exposed sector   This refers to the exposure of sectors to international competition. In exposed sectors, competitive pressures typically moderate wage rises. Such an effect does not exist in non-exposed sectors.

FO   Formed in 1948 following a split from CGT, Force Ouvrière (FO) is a French trade union confederation which has remained radical in orientation. FO is the third largest union confederation in France.

La France Insoumise   A French new-left party, which was founded in 2016 to support the 2017 presidential election campaign of Jean-Luc Mélenchon.

Gesamtmetall   The employers' association in the German metalworking sector and negotiating partner of IG Metall.

IG BAU   A German trade union for building, forestry, agricultural and environmental workers.

IG Metall   A German metalworking sector trade union, which has been a key actor in German industrial relations since its 1949 formation. As a result of its position in the exposed sector, IG Metall is renowned for its propensity to engage in wage moderation.

Intergovernmentalism   This is an approach to the study of European integration which emphasizes the capacity of states to control the integration process. The theory was initially associated with Hoffmann (1966; 1982), though the liberal intergovernmentalism of Moravcsik (1993) better conceptualized domestic influences.

Internal devaluation   Owing to EMU's removal of the option of currency devaluation, the primary remaining means of adjustment involves making labour costs cheaper; this is known as 'internal devaluation'.

Neofunctionalism   This is an approach to the study of European integration which emphasizes the tendency of processes of 'spillover' to lead to greater integration. As a result of the propensity of integration to inter-lock politico-economic functions, neofunctionalists forecast that actors will incrementally transfer loyalties to the European level. Early neofunctionalists consequently predicted a federal Europe.

Occam's razor   A logical principle which is associated with the philosopher William of Ockham. It states that 'entities should not be multiplied unnecessarily'. In other words, 'when you have two competing theories that make exactly the same predictions, the simpler one is the better'.

OPZZ   Founded in 1984 as an official response to the creation of Solidarność, Ogólnopolskie Porozumienie Związków Zawodowych (OPZZ) is one of the two main trade union confederations in modern Poland. It is sympathetic to the post-Communist SLD political party.

Parti Socialiste   A social-democratic French political party, Parti Socialiste (PS) has provided a series of presidents and prime ministers. Elections in 2017 nonetheless saw PS suffer heavy defeats, which has put the future of the party in question.

PES   The Party of European Socialists (PES) is a social-democratic European political party, which promotes cooperation between its member parties. In the European Parliament, PES is represented by the Progressive Alliance of Socialists and Democrats.

Podemos   Formed in 2014 due to popular anger with established parties, Podemos is a new-left Spanish political party. The party had substantial initial success, yet support for it appears to have plateaued.

PSOE   Partido Socialista Obrero Español (PSOE) is a Spanish social-democratic political party. PSOE has been politically dominant in democratic Spain, forming several governments under the leadership of Felipe González and José Zapatero, yet has suffered a series of recent electoral setbacks.

Razem   A Polish new-left party, Partia Razem was founded in 2015 following concern that there was no genuinely left-wing party in Poland. Razem has yet to achieve representation in Parliament.

Semester process   The European Semester is an annual process which aims to coordinate the economic, fiscal and labour market policies of member states. The Semester was introduced in 2010, following the outbreak of the debt crisis.

SLD   Formed from the disbanded Polish Communist Party, Sojusz Lewicy Demokratycznej (SLD) is the main left-wing party in post-Communist Poland. The party has provided prime ministers and a president, though currently has no representation in Parliament.

SPD   Formed in 1875, Sozialdemokratische Partei Deutschlands (SPD) is a German social-democratic political party. SPD has led and participated in several post-war German Governments, though in recent years critics have accused it of embracing neoliberalism.

Social partners   This term collectively refers to employers' associations and trade unions.

Solidarność Originating in 1980 protests against the Polish Communist Government and possessing a consequent claim to be the most famous trade union in the world, NSZZ Solidarność is one of the two main trade union confederations in modern Poland. The union is distinguished by its Catholic-nationalist political stance.

Tripartism   see corporatism.

UGT   Unión General de Trabajadores (UGT) is one of the two main Spanish trade union confederations and is allied with the social-democratic PSOE political party. The moderate political stance of UGT has made it disposed to engage in social dialogue.

ULCs   Unit labour costs (ULCs) measure the average cost of labour per unit of output and are calculated as the ratio of total labour costs to real output. In simpler terms, they establish the real cost of labour.

Ver.di   A German services sector trade union, formed by a 2001 merger of five unions.

References

ABC. (2012) 'Cuatro de cada diez españoles teme perder su trabajo en los próximos meses', 13 June. Available at: www.abc.es/20120613/economia/abci-empleo-informe-perdida-201206131108.html (accessed 4 March 2018).

Ágh, A. (2004) *The Europeanization of the ECE Social Democracy: The Case of HSP in an ECE Context*. ECPR 2004 Joint Sessions of Workshops, Uppsala University. Workshop 2, The Political Representation of Social Interests in Central and Eastern Europe.

Allern, E.H. and Bale, T. (eds) (2017) *Left-of-Centre Parties and Trade Unions in the Twenty-First Century*. Oxford: Oxford University Press.

Amable, B. (2014) 'Who wants the Contrat de Travail Unique? Social support for labor market flexibilization in France', *Industrial Relations: A Journal of Economy and Society*, 53(4), pp. 636–62.

Andrade, J. (2012) *El PCE y el PSOE en (la) transición: la evolución ideológica de la izquierda durante el proceso de cambio político*. Siglo XXI de España Editores.

Anduiza, E., Cristancho, C. and Sabucedo, J.M. (2014) 'Mobilization through online social networks: the political protest of the indignados in Spain', *Information, Communication & Society*, 17(6), pp. 750–64.

Armingeon, K. and Baccaro, L. (2012) 'The sorrows of young Euro: the sovereign debt crisis of Ireland and southern Europe', in Bermeo, N. and Pontusson, J. (eds) *Coping with Crisis: Government Reactions to the Great Recession*. New York: Russell Sage Foundation, pp. 162–97.

Balbona, D.L. and Begea, S.G. (2016) 'Crisis económica y coaliciones anti-austeridad en España Viejos y nuevos repertorios de protesta (2010–2014)', *Sociología del Trabajo*, 87, pp. 45–67.

Baran, P.A. (1968) *The Political Economy of Growth*. New York: Monthly Review Press.

Bartolini, S. (2005) *Restructuring Europe: Centre Formation, System Building, and Political Structuring between the Nation State and the European Union*. Oxford: Oxford University Press.

Bearce, D.H. and Hart, A.F. (2017) 'International labor mobility and the variety of democratic political institutions', *International Organization*, 71(1), pp. 65–95.

Bentolila, S.P., Dolado, J.J. and Jimeno, J.F. (2012) 'Reforming an insider-outsider labor market: the Spanish experience', *IZA Journal of European Labor Studies*, 34(4), pp. 1–29.

Bercusson, B. (1996) *European Labour Law*. 2nd edn. London: Butterworths.

Bergounioux, A. and Grunberg, G. (1992) *Le long remords du pouvoir: le Parti socialiste français (1905–1992)*. Paris: Fayard.

Berruyer, O. (2012) 'Analyse du 1er tour de l'élection présidentielle (2/2)', *Les Crises*, 3 May. Available at: www.les-crises.fr/presidentielle-2012–1t-2/ (accessed 7 March 2018).

Bickerton, C.J., Hodson, D. and Puetter, U. (2015) 'The new intergovernmentalism: European integration in the post-Maastricht era', *JCMS: Journal of Common Market Studies*, 53(4), pp. 703–22.

Bieler, A. and Erne, R. (2015) 'Transnational solidarity? The European working class in the Eurozone crisis', in Panitch, L. and Albo, G. (eds) *Transforming Classes [Yearbook: Socialist Register 2015]*. London/New York: Merlin Press/ Monthly Review Press, pp. 157–77.

Blanpain, R. and Windey, P. (1996) *European Works Councils: Information and Consultation of Employees in Multinational Enterprises in Europe*. Leuven: Peeters.

Blatter, J. and Haverland, M. (2012) *Designing Case Studies: Explanatory Approaches in Small-N Research*. Basingstoke: Palgrave Macmillan.

Blyth, M. (2013) *Austerity: The History of a Dangerous Idea*. Oxford: Oxford University Press.

Bobke, M. and Müller, T. (1995) 'Chancen für eine Neugestaltung des Systems der Arbeitsbeziehungen auf der europäischen Ebene', *WSI-Mitteilungen*, 10, pp. 654–61.

BOE (2003) 'Resolución de 31 de enero de 2003, de la Dirección General de Trabajo, por la que se dispone la inscripción en el Registro y publicación del Acuerdo Interconfederal para la Negociación Colectiva 2003 (ANC 2003)', *Agencia Estatal Boletín Oficial del Estado, Boletín Oficial del Estado: lunes 24 de febrero de 2003*, Núm. 47. Available at: www.boe.es/boe/dias/2003/02/24/ pdfs/A07539–07548.pdf (accessed 4 March 2018).

Bofinger, P. (2015) 'German wage moderation and the EZ crisis', *VoxEU*, 30 November. Available at: https://voxeu.org/article/german-wage-moderation-and-ez-crisis (accessed 4 March 2018).

Bohle, D. and Greskovits, B. (2007) 'Neoliberalism, embedded neoliberalism and neocorporatism: towards transnational capitalism in Central-Eastern Europe', *West European Politics*, 30(3), pp. 443–66.

Bohle, D. and Greskovits, B. (2012) *Capitalist Diversity on Europe's Periphery*. Ithaca: Cornell University Press.

Bourgeot, R. (2013) 'Labour costs and crisis management in the Euro Zone: a reinterpretation of divergences in competitiveness', La Fondation Robert Schuman: the Research and Studies Centre on Europe, 23 September. Available at: www.robert-schuman.eu/en/european-issues/0289-labour-costs-and-crisis-management-in-the-euro-zone-a-reinterpretation-of-divergences-in (accessed 7 March 2018).

Brewer, A. (2001) *Marxist Theories of Imperialism: A Critical Survey*. 2nd edn. Taylor & Francis e-Library.

Brzoza-Brzezina, M., Makarski, K. and Wesołowski, G. (2014) 'Would it have paid to be in the eurozone?', *Economic Modelling*, 41(C), pp. 66–79.

Calmfors, L. and Driffill, J. (1988) 'Bargaining structure, corporatism and macro-economic performance', *Economic Policy*, 3(6), pp. 13–61.

Capoccia, G. and Kelemen, R.D. (2007) 'The study of critical junctures: theory, narrative, and counterfactuals in historical institutionalism', *World Politics*, 59(3), pp. 341–69.

Carruth, A.A. and Oswald, A.J. (1987) 'On union preferences and labour market models: insiders and outsiders', *The Economic Journal*, 97(386), pp. 431–45.

Chastand, J.-M. (2014) 'Les précaires en première ligne du chômage', *Le Monde*, 27 November. Available at: www.lemonde.fr/emploi/article/2014/11/27/les-precaires-restent-aux-premieres-loges-du-chomage_4529871_1698637.html (accessed 7 March 2018).

Clauwaert, S. (2013) 'The country-specific recommendations (CSRs) in the social field: an overview and (initial) comparison to the CSRs 2011–2012 and 2012–2013 and 2013–2014, background analysis 2013.02', Brussels: ETUI. Available at: www.etui.org/fr/Publications2/Background-analysis/The-country-specific-recommendations-CSRs-in-the-social-field (accessed 6 March 2018).

Coldrick, P. (1998) 'The ETUC's role in the EU's new economic and monetary architecture', *Transfer*, 4(1), pp. 21–35.

Courage, S. (2017) '"Mort du PS": pourquoi les socialistes ont si peur du spectre DSK', *L'Obs*, 7 November. Available at: www.nouvelobs.com/politique/20171107.OBS7047/mort-du-ps-pourquoi-les-socialistes-ont-si-peur-du-spectre-dsk.html (accessed 7 March 2018).

Crimmann, A., Wießner, F. and Bellmann, L. (2010) 'The German work-sharing scheme: an instrument for the crisis', *Conditions of Work and Employment Series No. 25*. Geneva: International Labour Office. Available at: www.ilo.org/wcmsp5/groups/public/---ed_protect/---protrav/---travail/documents/publication/wcms_145335.pdf (accessed 6 March 2018).

Crouch, C. (1993) *Industrial Relations and European State Traditions*. Oxford: Clarendon Press.

Crowley, S. (2004) 'Explaining labor weakness in postcommunist Europe: historical legacies and comparative perspective', *East European Politics and Societies*, 18(3), pp. 394–429.

Dany, G., Gropp, R.E., Littke, H. and von Schweinitz, G. (2015) 'Germany's benefit from the Greek crisis', IWH Online – Leibniz Institüt für Wirtschaftsforschung Halle. Available at: www.iwh-halle.de/d/publik/iwhonline/io_2015–07.pdf (accessed 6 March 2018).

De Spiegelaere, S. (2016) *Too Little, Too Late? Evaluating the European Works Councils Recast Directive*. Brussels: ETUI.

DGB (2012) *A Marshall Plan for Europe: Proposal by the DGB for an Economic Stimulus, Investment and Development Programme for Europe*. Berlin: DGB. Available at: www.scribd.com/document/176415988/A-Marshall-Plan-for-Europe-Proposal-by-the-DGB-for-an-economic-stimulus-investment-and-development-programme-for-Europe (accessed 4 March 2018).

Dølvik, J.E. and Visser, J. (2009) 'Free movement, equal treatment and workers' rights: can the European Union solve its trilemma of fundamental principles?', *Industrial Relations Journal*, 40(6), pp. 491–509.

Dribbusch, H. (2015) 'Where is the European general strike? Understanding the challenges of trans-European trade union action against austerity', *Transfer: European Review of Labour and Research*, 21(2), pp. 171–85.

Dufresne, A. and Pernot, J.M. (2013) 'Les syndicats européens à l'épreuve de la nouvelle gouvernance économique', *Chronique Internationale de l'IRES*, 143(4), pp. 3–29.

Dunlop, J.T. (1958) *Industrial Relations Systems*. New York: Holt.

Dyson, K.H. and Featherstone, K. (1999) *The Road to Maastricht: Negotiating Economic and Monetary Union*. Oxford: Oxford University Press.

Eichhorst, W. and Marx, P. (2011) 'Reforming German labour market institutions: a dual path to flexibility', *Journal of European Social Policy*, 21(1), pp. 73–87.

El País (2010a) 'UGT y CC OO convocan huelga general para el 29 de septiembre', 15 June. Available at: https://elpais.com/economia/2010/06/15/actualidad/1276587182_850215.html (accessed 6 March 2018).

El País (2010b) 'Las manifestaciones cierran una jornada de huelga desigual', 29 September. Available at: https://elpais.com/elpais/2010/09/28/actualidad/1285661849_850215.html (accessed 6 March 2018).

El País (2012a) 'Are Spain's temporary workers about to lose again?', 5 March. Available at: http://elpais.com/elpais/2012/03/05/inenglish/1330952298_341418.html (accessed 6 March 2018).

El País (2012b) 'Cientos de miles de manifestantes cierran la protesta de la huelga general del 14-N', 14 November. Available at: https://politica.elpais.com/politica/2012/11/13/actualidad/1352838703_548795.html (accessed 6 March 2018).

Emmenegger, P. (2009) 'Barriers to entry: insider/outsider politics and the determinants of job security regulations', *Journal of European Social Policy*, 19(2), pp. 131–46.

Emmenegger, P., Häusermann, S., Palier, B. and Seeleib-Kaiser, M. (eds) (2012) *The Age of Dualization: The Changing Face of Inequality in Deindustrializing Societies*. Oxford: Oxford University Press.

Emmenegger, P. (2014) *The Power to Dismiss: Trade Unions and the Regulation of Job Security in Western Europe*. Oxford: Oxford University Press.

Erne, R. (2008) *European Unions: Labor's Quest for a Transnational Democracy*. Ithaca: Cornell University Press.

Erne, R. (2015) 'A supranational regime that nationalizes social conflict: explaining European trade unions' difficulties in politicizing European economic governance', *Labor History*, 56(3), pp. 345–68.

Ertel, M., Stilijanow, U., Iavicoli, S., Natali, E., Jain, A. and Leka, S. (2010) 'European social dialogue on psychosocial risks at work: benefits and challenges', *European Journal of Industrial Relations*, 16(2), pp. 169–83.

Esping-Andersen, G. and Regini, M. (2000) *Why Deregulate Labour Markets?* Oxford: Oxford University Press.

ETUC (2010) *Euro-Demonstration 29 September 2010: 'No to Austerity – Priority for Jobs and Growth!'*. Available at: www.etuc.org/euro-demonstration-29-september-2010-no-austerity-%E2%80%93-priority-jobs-and-growth#Actions (accessed 6 March 2018).

Eurofound (2018) *Working Life in Spain*, 18 October. Available at: www.eurofound.europa.eu/country/spain#actors-and-institutions (accessed 6 March 2018).

European Commission (2012) 'Macroeconomic imbalances – France, European economy', Occasional Papers No. 105. Brussels: European Commission.

European Commission (2014) 'Macroeconomic imbalances Germany 2014', European Economy Occasional Papers No. 174. Brussels: European Commission DG ECFIN.

EurWORK (2005) *Social Partners Debate Bargaining Framework for 2005*, 12 January. Available at: www.eurofound.europa.eu/observatories/eurwork/articles/social-partners-debate-bargaining-framework-for-2005 (accessed 6 March 2018).

EurWORK (2009) *Belgium: Wage Formation*, 30 March. Available at: www.eurofound.europa.eu/observatories/eurwork/comparative-information/national-contributions/belgium/belgium-wage-formation (accessed 6 March 2018).

EurWORK (2011) *Unions Join Euro-Demonstration in Wrocław*, 16 November. Available at: www.eurofound.europa.eu/observatories/eurwork/articles/industrial-relations/unions-join-euro-demonstration-in-wroclaw (accessed 6 March 2018).

EurWORK (2012) *European Works Council*, 19 March. Available at: www.eurofound.europa.eu/observatories/eurwork/industrial-relations-dictionary/european-works-councils (accessed 7 March 2018).

EWCDB (2018) *Stats and Graphs*. Available at: www.ewcdb.eu/stats-and-graphs (accessed 6 March 2018).

Fakt (2011) 'Żart z netu. Adoptuj sobie Greka! Po to by..', 23 September. Available at: www.fakt.pl/wydarzenia/swiat/zart-z-netu-adoptuj-sobie-greka-po-to-by/p9xlchz (accessed 6 March 2018).

Fakt (2015) 'Grecy się awanturują, a mają lepiej niż my', 8 July. Available at: www.fakt.pl/wydarzenia/polityka/grecy-maja-lepiej-niz-polacy-ceny-w-grecji/g6bj24d (accessed 6 March 2018).

Falkner, G. (1996) 'European Works Councils and the Maastricht Social Agreement: towards a new policy style', *Journal of European Public Policy*, 3(2), pp. 192–208.

Falkner, G. (1998) *EU Social Policy in the 1990s: Towards a Corporatist Policy Community*. London: Routledge.

Falkner, G., Treib, O., Hartlapp, M. and Leiber, S. (2005) *Complying with Europe: EU Harmonization and Soft Law in the Member States*. Cambridge: Cambridge University Press.

Flassbeck, H. (2016) 'Wages and prices in Germany – or why Europe will not escape from deflation within the next twenty years. Part 2', *Flassbeck Economics International*, 2 May. Available at: www.flassbeck-economics.com/wages-and-prices-in-germany-or-why-europe-will-not-escape-from-deflation-within-the-next-twenty-years-part-2/ (accessed 6 March 2018).

Fleischhauer, J. (2012) 'Willkommen in der Feuilleton-Ökonomie', *Der Spiegel*, 5 July. Available at: www.spiegel.de/politik/ausland/euro-krise-warum-die-position-der-spd-unvertretbar-ist-a-842704.html (accessed 6 March 2018).

Fligstein, N. and McAdam, D. (2012) *A Theory of Fields*. Oxford: Oxford University Press.

Fligstein, N. and Mara-Drita, I. (1996) 'How to make a market: reflections on the attempt to create a single market in the European Union', *American Journal of Sociology*, 102(1), pp. 1–33.

Forsal.Pl. (2013) 'Umowy śmieciowe w Polsce: Umowy cywilnoprawne coraz bardziej powszechne', 23 April. Available at: http://forsal.pl/artykuly/699684, umowy_smieciowe_w_polsce_umowy_cywilnoprawne_coraz_bardziej_powszechne.html (accessed 6 March 2018).

Frankfurter Allgemeine Zeitung (2015) 'Große Koalition: Gabriels Intervention', *Frankfurter Allgemeine Zeitung GmbH*. Available at: www.faz.net/aktuell/politik/inland/sigmar-gabriel-aendert-meinung-zu-griechenlands-schuldenkrise-13648436.html (accessed 6 March 2018).

Garz, M. (2013) 'Employment and wages in Germany since the 2004 deregulation of the temporary agency industry', *International Labour Review*, 152(2), pp. 307–26.

Gazeta Wyborcza (2011) '30 tysięcy ludzi demonstruje w marszu "Solidarności"', 29 June. Available at: http://warszawa.wyborcza.pl/warszawa/1,54420, 9865249,30_tysiecy_ludzi_demonstruje_w_marszu__Solidarnosci_.html (accessed 6 March 2018).

Gazeta Wyborcza (2015) 'Sześć faktów i mitów o greckim kryzysie', 2 July. Available at: http://wyborcza.pl/1,155290,18291672,Szesc_faktow_i_mitow_o_greckim_kryzysie.html (accessed 7 March 2018).

Gesamtmetall (2017) 'Die Tarifrunden in der Metall- und Elektro-Industrie seit 1990 (Tarifarchiv)'. Available at: www.gesamtmetall.de/sites/default/files/downloads/broschuere_-_tarifentgelte_1990–2017.pdf (accessed 7 March 2018).

Glassner, V. and Pochet, P. (2011) 'Why trade unions seek to coordinate wages and collective bargaining in the Eurozone: past developments and future prospects', *ETUI Working Paper 2011.03*. Available at: https://ssrn.com/abstract=2221845 (accessed 7 March 2018).

Gobierno de España, CEOE, CEPYME, CCOO, UGT (2004) 'Competitividad, empleo estable y cohesión social (declaración para el diálogo social 2004)', 8 July. Available at: http://personal.us.es/jesuscruz/declaraciondsocial.pdf (accessed 7 March 2018).

Godin, E. and Chafer, T. (eds) (2004) *The French Exception*. New York: Berghahn Books.

Gold, M. and Schwimbersky, S. (2008) 'The European Company Statute: implications for industrial relations in the European Union', *European Journal of Industrial Relations*, 14(1), pp. 46–64.

Gollbach, J. and Schulten, T. (2000) 'Cross-border collective bargaining networks in Europe', *European Journal of Industrial Relations*, 6(2), pp. 161–79.

Gonzalez, B. and Khalip, A. (2012) 'Journée européenne de mobilisation contre l'austérité', *BFMTV*, 14 November. Available at: www.bfmtv.com/international/journee-europeenne-de-mobilisation-contre-lausterite-319452.html (accessed 4 March 2018).

Guardian (2014) 'François Hollande gambles on excluding Socialist dissidents', 25 August. Available at: www.theguardian.com/world/2014/aug/25/francois-hollande-socialist-dissidents-reshuffle-france (accessed 7 March 2018).

Haas, E.B. (1958) *The Uniting of Europe: Political, Economic and Social Forces, 1950–1957*. London: Stevens & Sons.

Hall, P.A. and Soskice, D.W. (eds) (2001) *Varieties of Capitalism: The Institutional Foundations of Comparative Advantage*. Oxford: Oxford University Press.

Hancké, B. (2013) 'The missing link: labour unions, central banks and monetary integration in Europe', *Transfer: European Review of Labour and Research*, 19(1), pp. 89–101.

Hancké, B. (2016) 'What the new French labour law tells us about France and the euro', *LSE EUROPP blog*, 9 March. Available at: http://blogs.lse.ac.uk/europpblog/2016/03/09/what-the-new-french-labour-law-tells-us-about-france-and-the-euro/ (accessed 7 March 2018).

Hancké, B. and Soskice, D.W. (2003) 'Wage-setting, fiscal policy and political exchange in EMU', Report for Project 2000–203–1, 'Institutionen, Wirtschaftswachstum und Beschäftigung in der EMU', financed by Hans-Böckler Foundation. Available at: http://personal.lse.ac.uk/hancke/myweb/EMU%20report.pdf (accessed 7 March 2018).

Hassel, A. (1999) 'The erosion of the German system of industrial relations', *British Journal of Industrial Relations*, 37(3), pp. 483–505.

Hassel, A. (2014) 'Adjustments in the Eurozone: varieties of capitalism and the crisis in southern Europe', *LEQS Paper No. 76*. Available at: https://ssrn.com/abstract=2436454 (accessed 7 March 2018).

Heery, E. (2016) *Framing Work: Unitary, Pluralist, and Critical Perspectives in the Twenty-First Century*. Oxford: Oxford University Press.

Henkel, I. (2015) 'German public opinion is caught between scapegoating Greeks and love-bombing them', *LSE EUROPP blog*, 21 July. Available at: http://blogs.lse.ac.uk/europpblog/2015/07/21/german-public-opinion-is-caught-between-scapegoating-greeks-and-love-bombing-them/ (accessed 7 March 2018).

Heyes, J. and Lewis, P.C. (2014) 'Employment protection under fire: labour market deregulation and employment in the European Union', *Economic and Industrial Democracy*, 35(4), pp. 587–607.

Hobson, K. and Lynch, N. (2016) 'Diversifying and de-growing the circular economy: radical social transformation in a resource-scarce world', *Futures*, 82, pp. 15–25.

Hoffmann, S. (1966) 'Obstinate or obsolete? The fate of the nation-state and the case of western Europe', *Daedalus*, 95(3), pp. 862–915.

Hoffmann, S. (1982) 'Reflections on the nation state in western Europe today', *JCMS: Journal of Common Market Studies*, 21(1), pp. 21–37.

Holmes, M. and Lightfoot, S. (2014) 'Limits of consensus? The party of European socialists and the financial crisis', in Bailey, D.J., de Waele, J., Escalona, F. and Vieira, M. (eds) *European Social Democracy During the Global Economic Crisis: Renovation or Resignation*. Manchester: Manchester University Press, pp. 215–32.

Höpner, M. (2014) 'Europe would be better off without the Euro: a comparative political economy perspective on the Euro crisis', *Labor History*, 55(5), pp. 661–6.

Höpner, M. and Schäfer, A. (2010) 'A new phase of European integration: organised capitalisms in post-Ricardian Europe', *West European Politics*, 33(2), pp. 344–68.

Horn, G.A. (2016) 'Lohnpolitik: Die Gewerkschaften sind die falschen Sündenböcke', *Makronom*. Available at: http://makronom.de/lohnpolitik-die-gewerkschaften-sind-die-falschen-suendenboecke-gustav-horn-15466 (accessed 8 February 2017).

Hudson, M. (1980) '"Concerted action": wages policy in West Germany, 1967–1977', *Industrial Relations Journal*, 11(4), pp. 5–16.

Hyman, R. (2001) *Understanding European Trade Unionism: Between Market, Class and Society*. London: Sage.

IFOP (2015) *Les Français et l'attitude à adopter face à la Grèce*. Available at: www.ifop.com/?option=com_publication&type=poll&id=2928 (accessed 7 March 2018).

Jensen, C.S., Madsen, J.S. and Due, J. (1999) 'Phases and dynamics in the development of EU industrial relations regulation', *Industrial Relations Journal*, 30(2), pp. 118–34.

IG Metall (2004) *Tarifvertrag über Entgelte und Ausbildungsvergütungen*. Available at: www2.igmetall.de/homepages/era-wissen/file_uploads/m-tv-entgelt-2004-era-bawue.pdf (accessed 7 March 2018).

Jabko, N. (2006) *Playing the Market: A Political Strategy for Uniting Europe, 1985–2005*. Ithaca: Cornell University Press.

Jakopovich, D. (2011) 'The construction of a trans-European labour movement', *Capital & Class*, 35(1), pp. 63–79.

Jódar, P., Vidal, S. and Alós, R. (2011) 'Union activism in an inclusive system of industrial relations: evidence from a Spanish case study', *British Journal of Industrial Relations*, 49(s1), pp. s158–s180.

Johnston, A. (2016) *From Convergence to Crisis: Labor Markets and the Instability of the Euro*. Ithaca: Cornell University Press.

Johnston, A. and Hancké, B. (2009) 'Wage inflation and labour unions in EMU', *Journal of European Public Policy*, 16(4), pp. 601–22.

Jones, E. (2015) 'Getting the story right: how you should choose between different interpretations of the European crisis (and why you should care)', *Journal of European Integration*, 37(7), pp. 817–32.

Kalleberg, A. (2009) 'Precarious work, insecure workers: employment relations in transition', *American Sociological Review*, 74(1), pp. 1–22.

Katka, K. (2011) '"Solidarność" udaje Greka', *Gazeta Wyborcza*, 29 June. Available at: http://wyborcza.pl/1,76842,9860923,_Solidarnosc__udaje_Greka.html (accessed 4 March 2018).

Keller, B. (1995) 'Perspektiven Europäischer Kollektivverhandlungen – Vor und Nach Maastricht', *Zeitschrift für Soziologie*, 24(4), pp. 243–62.

Keller, B. (1996) 'Nach der Verabschiedung der Richtlinie zu Europäischen Betriebsräten: von Enttäuschten Erwartungen, Unerfüllbaren Hoffnungen und realistischen Perspektiven', *WSI-Mitteilungen*, 49(8), pp. 470–82.

Keller, B. (1997) *Europäische Arbeits- und Sozialpolitik*. Munich: Oldenbourg.

Keller, B. (2003) 'Social dialogues: the state of the art a decade after Maastricht', *Industrial Relations Journal*, 34(5), pp. 411–29.

Keller, B. and Sörries, B. (1999) 'The new European social dialogue: old wine in new bottles?', *Journal of European Social Policy*, 9(2), pp. 111–25.

Köhler, H.D. and González Begega, S. (2007) 'Still learning from Europe: Spanish participation in European works councils', in Whittal, M., Knudsen, H. and Huijgen, F. (eds) *Towards a European Labour Identity: The Case of the European Works Council*. London/New York: Routledge, pp. 132–49.

Knutsen, P. (1997) 'Corporatist tendencies in the Euro-polity: the EU-Directive of 22 September 1994 on European Works Councils', *Economic and Industrial Democracy*, 18(2), pp. 289–323.

Külahci, E. and Lightfoot, S. (2014) 'Governance, Europarties and the challenge of democratic representation in the EU: a case study of the Party of European Socialists', *Acta Politica*, 49(1), pp. 71–85.

Ladrech, R. (2000) *Social Democracy and the Challenge of European Union*. Boulder: Lynne Rienner Publishers.

Ladrech, R. (2009) 'Europeanization and political parties', *Living Reviews in European Governance*, 4(1). Available at: www.europeangovernance-livingreviews.org/Articles/lreg-2009–1/download/lreg-2009–1Color.pdf. (accessed 17 July 2018).

Larsen, T. and Andersen, S. (2007) 'Autonomous Framework Agreements: a new way of regulating Europe', *European Journal of Industrial Relations*, 13(2), pp. 181–98.

Le Monde (2013) 'Réforme des retraites: les syndicats envisagent d'autres mobilisations', 10 September. Available at: www.lemonde.fr/politique/article/2013/09/10/les-manifestations-contre-la-reforme-des-retraites-ont-rassemble-entre-155–000-et-360–000-personnes_3475310_823448.html?xtmc=manifestation_syndicats_reforme_france_loi&xtcr=2 (accessed 7 March 2018).

Le Monde (2015) 'Yanis Varoufakis, d'Athènes à Frangy-en-Bresse', 17 July. Available at: www.lemonde.fr/politique/article/2015/07/17/yanis-varoufakis-d-athenes-a-frangy-en-bresse_4686993_823448.html (accessed 7 March 2018).

Lecher, W. (1994) 'Europäische Betriebsräte – ein empirisch gestützter deutsch-französischer Vergleich', in Lecher, W. and Platzer, H.-W. (eds) *Europäische Union – Europäische Arbeitsbeziehungen? Nationale Voraussetzungen und Internationaler Rahmen*. Cologne: Bund-Verlag, pp. 255–72.

Lecher, W., Nagel, B. and Platzer, H.W. (1999) *The Establishment of European Works Councils: From Information Committee to Social Actor*. Aldershot: Ashgate.

Lenin, V.I. (1999) *Imperialism: The Highest Stage of Capitalism*. Chippendale: Resistance Books.

Libération (2012) 'Ensemble, nous pouvons faire bouger les choses', 26 March. Available at: www.liberation.fr/france/2012/03/26/ensemble-nous-pouvons-faire-bouger-les-choses_805618 (accessed 4 March 2018).

Lightfoot, S. (2005) *Europeanizing Social Democracy? The Rise of the Party of European Socialists*. Abingdon: Routledge.

Lindbeck, A. and Snower, D.J. (1987) 'Efficiency wages versus insiders and outsiders', *European Economic Review*, 31(1–2), pp. 407–16.

Lindbeck, A. and Snower, D.J. (1988) *The Insider-Outsider Theory of Employment and Unemployment*. London: MIT Press.

Lindbeck, A. and Snower, D.J. (2001) 'Insiders versus outsiders', *The Journal of Economic Perspectives*, 15(1), pp. 165–88.

Ljungqvist, L. and Sargent, T. J. (1998) 'The European unemployment dilemma', *Journal of Political Economy*, 106(3), pp. 514–50.

López-Santana, M. (2006) 'The domestic implications of European soft law: framing and transmitting change in employment policy', *Journal of European Public Policy*, 13(4), pp. 481–99.

McMenamin, I. (2004) 'Varieties of capitalist democracy: what difference does East-Central Europe make?', *Journal of Public Policy*, 24(3), pp. 259–74.

Mahoney, J. (2000) 'Path dependence in historical sociology', *Theory and Society*, 29(4), pp. 507–48.

March, L. (2015) 'Beyond Syriza and Podemos, other radical left parties are threatening to break into the mainstream of European politics', *LSE EUROPP blog*, 24 March. Available at: http://blogs.lse.ac.uk/europpblog/2015/03/24/beyond-syriza-and-podemos-other-radical-left-parties-are-threatening-to-break-into-the-mainstream-of-european-politics/ (accessed 7 March 2018).

Marginson, P. (1992) 'European integration and transnational management: union relations in the enterprise', *British Journal of Industrial Relations*, 30(4), pp. 529–45.

Marginson, P. (1998) 'European Works Councils: the role of the negotiated option', in Lecher, W. and Platzer, H.-W. (eds) *European Union – European Industrial Relations? Global Challenges, National Developments and Transnational Dynamics*. London: Routledge, pp. 223–33.

Marginson, P. and Sisson, K. (2004) *European Integration and Industrial Relations: Multi-Level Governance in the Making*. Houndsmill: Palgrave Macmillan.

Marks, G. (1993) 'Structural policy and multi-level governance in the EC', in Cafruny, A. and Rosenthal, G. (eds) *The State of the European Community*. London: Longman, pp. 391–410.

Marks, G., Hooghe, L. and Blank, K. (1996) 'European integration from the 1980s: state-centric v. multi-level governance', *Journal of Common Market Studies*, 34(3), pp. 341–78.

Marks, G., Neilsen, F., Ray, L. and Salk, J. (1998) 'Competencies, cracks and conflicts: regional mobilization in the European Union', in Marks, G., Scharpf, F., Schmitter, P. and Streeck, W. (eds) *Governance in the European Union*. London: Sage, pp. 40–63.

Martinez Lucio, M. and Weston, S. (2000) 'European Works Councils and flexible regulation: the politics of intervention', *European Journal of Industrial Relations*, 6(2), pp. 203–16.

Marx, P. (2011) 'Labour market dualisation in France: assessing different explanatory approaches', *9th Annual ESPAnet Conference: Sustainability and Transformation in European Social Policy*. Valencia, Spain.

Mattila, M. and Raunio, T. (2006) 'Cautious voters-supportive parties: opinion congruence between voters and parties on the EU dimension', *European Union Politics*, 7(4), pp. 427–49.

Meardi, G. (2002) 'The Trojan horse for the Americanization of Europe? Polish industrial relations towards the EU', *European Journal of Industrial Relations*, 8(1), pp. 77–99.

Meardi, G. (2006) 'Social pacts on the road to EMU: a comparison of the Italian and Polish experiences', *Economic and Industrial Democracy*, 27(2), pp. 197–222.

Meardi, G. (2014) 'Employment relations under external pressure: Italian and Spanish reforms during the great recession', in Hauptmeier, M. and Vidal, M. (eds) *Comparative Political Economy of Work: Critical Perspectives on Work and Organisations*. Basingstoke: Palgrave Macmillan, pp. 332–50.

Meardi, G. and Trappmann, V. (2013) 'Between consolidation and crisis: divergent pressures and sectoral trends in Poland', *Transfer*, 19(2), pp. 195–204.

Meardi, G., Gardawski, J. and Molina, O. (2015) 'The dynamics of tripartism in post-democratic transitions: comparative lessons from Spain and Poland', *Business History*, 57(3), pp. 398–417.

Meyer, H., and Rutherford, J. (eds) (2012) *The Future of European Social Democracy: Building the Good Society*. Basingstoke: Palgrave Macmillan.

Middelaar, L.J. (2014) *The Passage to Europe: How a Continent Became a Union*. New Haven: Yale University Press.

Miller, L. (2015) 'Leszek Miller: Biedni, ale wolni…', *Super Express*, 7 July. Available at: www.se.pl/wiadomosci/opinie/leszek-miller-biedni-ale-wolni_639884. html (accessed 7 March 2018).

Miller, R.W. (1987) *Fact and Method: Explanation, Confirmation and Reality in the Natural and the Social Sciences*. Princeton: Princeton University Press.

Miller, S. and Potthoff, H. (1986) *A History of German Social Democracy: From 1848 to the Present*. New York: Berg Publishers.

Molina, O. and Rhodes, M. (2007) 'The political economy of adjustment in mixed market economies: a study of Spain and Italy', in Hancké, R., Rhodes, M. and Thatcher, M. (eds) *Beyond Varieties of Capitalism: Conflict, Contradictions and Complementarities in the European Economy*. Oxford: Oxford University Press, pp. 223–52.

Morgan, G. and Hauptmeier, M. (2014) 'Varieties of institutional theory in comparative employment relations', in Wilkinson, A., Wood, G. and Deeg, R. (eds) *Oxford Handbook of Employment Relations: Comparative Employment Systems*. Oxford: Oxford University Press, pp. 190–221.

Moravcsik, A. (1993) 'Preferences and power in the European Community: a liberal intergovernmentalist approach', *JCMS: Journal of Common Market Studies*, 31(4), pp. 473–524.

Müller, T., Schulten, T. and Zuckerstätter, S. (2015) 'Wages and economic performance in Europe', in Van Gyes, G. and Schulten, T. (eds) Wage Bargaining under the New European Economic Governance: Alternative Strategies for Inclusive Growth. Brussels: ETUI, pp. 259–82.

Muñoz de Bustillo, R. and Antón, J.I. (2011) 'From the highest employment growth to the deepest fall: economic crisis and labour inequalities in Spain', in Vaughan-Whitehead, D. (ed.) *Work Inequalities in the Crisis: Evidence from Europe*. Cheltenham: Edward Elgar, pp. 393–444.

Muñoz Sánchez, A. (2012) *El amigo alemán: el SPD y le PSOE de la dictadura a la democracia*. Barcelona: RBA Libros.

Nakano, S. (2014) 'Maastricht social protocol revisited: origins of the European industrial relations system', *JCMS: Journal of Common Market Studies*, 52(5), pp. 1053–69.

NBP (2009) *Report on Full Membership of the Republic of Poland in the Third Stage of the Economic and Monetary Union*. Available at: www.nbp.pl/en/publikacje/e_a/euro_report.pdf (accessed 7 March 2018).

Niemann, A. and Ioannou, D. (2015) 'European economic integration in times of crisis: a case of neofunctionalism?', *Journal of European Public Policy*, 22(2), pp. 196–218.

Nikolinakos, N.T. (2006) *EU Competition Law and Regulation in the Converging Telecommunications, Media and IT Sectors*. Alpen aan den Rijn: Kluwer Law International.

Palier, B. and Thelen, K. (2010) 'Institutionalizing dualism: complementarities and change in France and Germany', *Politics & Society*, 38(1), pp. 119–48.

Ortiz, L. (2002) 'The resilience of a company-level system of industrial relations: union responses to teamwork in Renault's Spanish subsidiary', *European Journal of Industrial Relations*, 8(3), pp. 277–99.

Ost, D. (2006) *The Defeat of Solidarity: Anger and Politics in Postcommunist Europe*. Ithaca: Cornell University Press.

Pardo, R.P. (2012) 'EU membership and the Europeanization of Spanish political parties', *International Journal of Iberian Studies*, 25(1), pp. 3–19.

Parsons, N. (2005) *French Industrial Relations in the New World Economy*. London and New York: Routledge.

Parsons, N. (2018) 'Social conferences in France: building consensus through social dialogue?', *Work in progress*.

Parsons, N. and Pochet, P. (2008) 'Wages and collective bargaining', in Dyson, K. (ed.) *The Euro at Ten: Europeanization, Power and Convergence*. Oxford: Oxford University Press, pp. 341–58.

Piazza, J. (2001) 'De-linking labor: labor unions and social democratic parties under globalization', *Party Politics*, 7(4), pp. 413–35.

Polska Times (2011) 'Wielka demonstracja "Solidarności" w Warszawie', 30 June. Available at: www.polskatimes.pl/artykul/421317,wielka-demonstracja-solidarnosci-w-warszawie-galeria,id,t.html (accessed 7 March 2018).

Polskie Radio (2012) *Protesty OPZZ. 'Chcemy zasiłków, jak w Grecji'*, 14 November. Available at: www.polskieradio.pl/5/3/Artykul/724305,Protesty-OPZZ-Chcemy-zasilkow-jak-w-Grecji (accessed 7 March 2018).

Polyakova, A. and Fligstein, N. (2016) 'Is European integration causing Europe to become more nationalist? Evidence from the 2007–9 financial crisis', *Journal of European Public Policy*, 23(1), pp. 60–83.

Portet, S. (2005) 'Poland: circumventing the law or fully deregulating?', in Vaughan-Whitehead, D. (ed.) *Working Employment Conditions in New Member States*. Geneva: International Labour Office, pp. 273–337.

Prosser, T. (2011) 'European social dialogue through "soft" law?', *European Journal of Industrial Relations*, 17(3), pp. 245–60.

Prosser, T. (2014) 'Financialization and the reform of European systems of industrial relations', *European Journal of Industrial Relations*, 20(4), pp. 351–65.

Prosser, T. (2016a) 'Dualization or liberalization? Investigating precarious work in eight European countries', *Work, Employment and Society*, 30(6), pp. 949–65.

Prosser, T. (2016b) 'Economic union without social union: the strange case of the European social dialogue', *Journal of European Social Policy*, 26(5), pp. 460–72.

Prosser, T. (2018) 'Social dialogue in the Polish hospitals and metal sector', *Report for SPEEED project*.

Prosser, T.J. and Perin, E. (2015) 'European tripartism: chimera or reality? The "new phase" of the European social dialogue in the light of tripartite theory and practice', *Business History*, 57(3), pp. 376–97.

PSOE (2012a) *Óscar López denuncia que Rajoy no tuviera 'nada que ofrecer'*. Available at: www.psoe.es/actualidad/noticias-actualidad/oscar-lopez-denuncia-que-rajoy-no-tuviera-nada-que-ofrecer-de-su-primer-ano-de-gestion-que-ha-sido-el-ano-del-recorte-y-del-engano--83963/ (accessed 7 March 2018).

PSOE (2012b) *Rubalcaba pide celebrar un encuentro de líderes socialdemócratas europeos para pedir un cambio de rumbo en la política económica*. Available at: www.psoe.es/actualidad/noticias-actualidad/rubalcaba-pide-celebrar-un-encuentro-de-lideres-socialdemocratas-europeos-para-pedir-un-cambio-de-rumbo-en-la-politica-economica--83977/ (accessed 7 March 2018).

PSOE (2013) *Óscar López: 2013 es un año 'para olvidar'*. Available at: www.psoe.es/actualidad/noticias-actualidad/oscar-lopez-2013-es-un-ano-para-olvidar-y-forma-parte-del-bienio-de-retroceso-del-pp-en-politicas-sociales-derechos-y-libertades--99433/ (accessed 17 July 2018).

PSOE (2015) *Moscoso del Prado: En septiembre, los partidos socialdemócratas vamos a coger el testigo y liderar el cambio en Europa*. Available at: www.psoe.es/actualidad/noticias-actualidad/moscoso-del-prado-en-septiembre-los-partidos-socialdemocratas-vamos-a-coger-el-testigo-y-liderar-el-cambio-en-europa--123394/ (accessed 7 March 2018).

Razem (2015) *Stanowisko w sprawie Grecji*. Available at: http://partiarazem.pl/stanowiska/stanowisko-w-sprawie-grecji/ (accessed 7 March 2018).

Rhodes, M. (1998a) 'Globalization, labour markets and welfare states: a future of "competitive corporatism"?', in Rhodes, M. and Mény, Y. (eds) *The Future of European Welfare*. London: Palgrave Macmillan, pp. 178–203.

Rhodes, M. (1998b) 'Defending the social contract: the EU between global constraints and domestic imperatives', in Hine, D. and Kassim, H. (eds) *Beyond the Market: The EU and National Social Policy*. London: Routledge, pp. 36–59.

Rigaux, M. and Dorssemont, F. (eds) (1999) *A Legal Analysis of the European Works Council: Towards a Revision of the Directive (EC) No. 95/45*. Antwerp: Intersentia Rechtsetenschappen.

Rodríguez-Teruel, J., Real-Dato, J. and Jerez, M. (2016) 'But still enthusiastic: the unchanged Europeanness of the Spanish parliamentary elite during the Eurozone crisis', *Historical Social Research*, 41(4), pp. 214–38.

Rosamond, B. (2000) *Theories of European Integration*. Basingstoke: Macmillan.

Rosamond, B. (2016) 'Brexit and the problem of European disintegration', *Journal of Contemporary European Research*, 12(4), pp. 86–71.

Rueda, D. (2007) *Social Democracy Inside Out: Partisanship and Labour Market Policy in Advanced Industrialized Democracies*. Oxford: Oxford University Press.

Scharpf, F.W. (1988) 'The joint-decision trap: lessons from German federalism and European integration', *Public Administration*, 66(3), pp. 239–78.

Scharpf, F.W. (1996) 'Negative and positive integration in the political economy of European welfare states', in Marks, G., Scharpf, F.W., Schmitter, P.C. and Streeck, W. (eds) *Governance in the European Union*. London: SAGE Publications, pp. 15–39.

Scharpf, F.W. (1999) *Governing in Europe: Effective and Democratic?* Oxford: Oxford University Press.

Schlecht, M. (2015) 'Wirtschaftskrise: Deutschlands Schuld an der Eurokrise', *Frankfurter Rundschau*, 6 September. Available at: www.fr-online.de/gastbeitraege/wirtschaftskrise-deutschlands-schuld-an-der-eurokrise, 29976308,31729098.html (accessed 17 July 2018).

Schmidt, V.A. (2003) 'French capitalism transformed, yet still a third variety of capitalism', *Economy and Society*, 32(4), pp. 526–54.

Schmidt, V.A. (2008) 'Discursive institutionalism: the explanatory power of ideas and discourse', *Annual Review of Political Science*, 11, pp. 303–26.

Schmitter, P.C. (1971) 'A revised theory of regional integration', in Lindberg, L.N. and Scheingold, S.A. (eds) *Regional Integration: Theory and Research*. Cambridge, MA: Harvard University Press, pp. 232–64.

Schulten, T. (1996) 'European Works Councils: prospects for a new system of European industrial relations', *European Journal of Industrial Relations*, 2(3), pp. 303–324.

Silver, B. (2008) *Forces of Labor*. New York: Cambridge University Press.

Simms, B. and Less, T. (2015) 'A crisis without end', *New Statesman*, 9 November. Available at: www.newstatesman.com/politics/uk/2015/11/crisis-without-end (accessed 7 March 2018).

Sinn, H.-W. (2013) 'It is wrong to portray Germany as the Euro winner', *Financial Times*, 22 July. Available at: www.ft.com/content/bbb2176a-ed70–11e2–8d7c-00144feabdc0 (accessed 7 March 2018).

SLD (2012) *SLD: Rząd kroczy drogą Grecji!*, 26 July. Available at: http://m.sld.org.pl/aktualnosci/683-sld_rzad_kroczy_droga_grecji.html (accessed 7 March 2018).

SLD (2013) *Oświadczenie Leszka Millera*, 18 May. Available at: http://m.sld.org.pl/aktualnosci/6487-oswiadczenie_leszka_millera.html (accessed 7 March 2018).

Solidarność (2011) *Manifestacja w Brukseli i w Warszawie*. Available at: www.solidarnosc.org.pl/gorzow/pl/article/show/category,14,id,122-.html (accessed 7 March 2018).

Standing, G. (1999) 'Global feminization through flexible labor: a theme revisited', *World Development*, 27(3), pp. 583–602.

Standing, G. (2011) *The Precariat: The New Dangerous Class*. London: Bloomsbury.

Stierle, S. and Haar, K. (2012) 'Troika for everyone, forever', *Corporate Europe Observatory*, 2 November. Available at: https://corporateeurope.org/eu-crisis/2012/11/troika-everyone-forever (accessed 7 March 2018).

Stierle, S. and Mayer, C. (2014) 'The lack of any effective opposition to the new German government should be a concern for the rest of the Eurozone', *LSE EUROPP blog*, 9 January. Available at: http://blogs.lse.ac.uk/europpblog/2014/01/09/the-lack-of-any-effective-opposition-to-the-new-german-government-should-be-a-concern-for-the-rest-of-the-eurozone/ (accessed 17 July 2018).

Stockhammer, E. and Sotiropoulos, D.P. (2014) 'Rebalancing the Euro area: the costs of internal devaluation', *Review of Political Economy*, 26(2), pp. 210–33.

Streeck, W. (1994) 'European social policy after Maastricht: the "social dialogue" and "subsidiarity"', *Economic and Industrial Democracy*, 15(2), pp. 151–77.

Streeck, W. (1996) 'Neo-voluntarism: a new European social policy regime?', in Marks, G., Scharpf, F.W., Schmitter, P.C. and Streeck, W. (eds) *Governance in the European Union*. London: Sage, pp. 64–94.

Streeck, W. (1997) 'Neither European nor Works Councils: a reply to Paul Knutsen', *Economic and Industrial Democracy*, 18(2), pp. 325–37.

Streeck, W. (1998) 'The internationalisation of industrial relations in Europe: prospects and problems', *Politics and Society*, 24(4), pp. 429–59.

Streeck, W. (2009) *Re-forming Capitalism: Institutional Change in the German Political Economy*. Oxford: Oxford University Press.

Streeck, W. (2014) *Buying Time: The Delayed Crisis of Democratic Capitalism*. London: Verso.

Streeck, W. and Thelen, K.A. (2005) *Beyond Continuity: Institutional Change in Advanced Political Economies*. Oxford: Oxford University Press.

Streeck, W. and Vitols, S. (1995) 'The European Community: between mandatory consultation and voluntary information', in Rogers, J. and Streeck, W. (eds) *Works Councils: Consultation, Representation and Cooperation in Industrial Relations*. Chicago: University of Chicago Press, pp. 243–81.

Stuttgarter Zeitung (2013) 'Interview mit IG-Metall-Chef Huber: "Das ist ein Fass ohne Boden"', 18 October. Available at: www.stuttgarter-zeitung.de/inhalt. interview-mit-ig-metall-chef-huber-das-ist-ein-fass-ohne-boden.3f3b77d0–2aae-4b0f-9293–42c52e11fed2.html (accessed 7 March 2018).

Super Express (2015) 'Dlaczego Grecja bankrutuje? Życie na kredyt i dodatek za mycie rąk', 29 June. Available at: http://superbiz.se.pl/wiadomosci-biz/dlaczego-grecja-bankrutuje-zycie-na-kredyt-i-dodatek-za-mycie-rak_634717.html (accessed 7 March 2018).

Der Tagesspiegel (1999) 'Appell für einen Kurswechsel der IG Metall', 1 August. Available at: www.tagesspiegel.de/wirtschaft/appell-fuer-einen-kurswechsel-der-ig-metall/84068.html (accessed 7 March 2018).

Tchorek, G. and Krzewicki, P. (2014) 'Wpływ akcesji do UE na strukturę polskiego eksportu', in Dubel, P. and Adamczyk. A. (eds) *Polska w Unii Europejskiej. 10 lat doświadczeń*. Warsaw: Poltext, pp. 33–60.

Thelen, K. (2014) *Varieties of Liberalization and the New Politics of Social Solidarity*. Cambridge: Cambridge University Press.

Tomczak, Ł. (2012) *Lewicowe partie polityczne w Polsce: programy, organizacja, strategie*. Szczecin: Szczecin University Press.

Traxler, F. and Brandl, B. (2009) 'Towards Europeanization of wage policy: Germany and the Nordic countries', *European Union Politics*, 10(2), pp. 177–201.

Trojstronna komisja ds społeczno gospodarczych (2017) *Uchwały Komisji*. Available at: www.dialog.gov.pl/archiwum/trojstronna-komisja-ds-spoleczno-gospodarczych/uchwaly-komisji/ (accessed 7 March 2018).

Turnbull, P. (2006) 'The war on Europe's waterfront: repertoires of power in the port transport industry', *British Journal of Industrial Relations*, 44(2), pp. 305–26.

TVP3 Warszawa (2012) *Manifestacja związkowców w ramach europejskiego dnia protestu*, 14 November. Available at: http://warszawa.tvp.pl/9096121/manifestacja-zwiazkowcow-w-ramach-europejskiego-dnia-protestu (accessed 7 March 2018).

Vogel, S. (2013) 'Fixed-term contracts may pave the way to permanent employment', *EurWork: European Observatory of Working Life*, 12 September. Available at: www.eurofound.europa.eu/observatories/eurwork/articles/fixed-term-contracts-may-pave-the-way-to-permanent-employment (accessed 7 March 2018).

Volkery, C. (2012) 'Window dressing for Hollande: the empty promise of Europe's "growth pact"', *Spiegel Online*, 27 June. Available at: www.spiegel.de/international/europe/the-eu-s-new-growth-pact-a-841243.html (accessed 7 March 2018).

Vollaard, H. (2014) 'Explaining European disintegration', *Journal of Common Market Studies*, 52(5), pp. 1142–59.

Völpel, E. (2013) 'Verdi-Chef über Arbeitnehmerrechte: "Deutschland, der kranke Mann"'. Available at: www.taz.de/!5074431/ (accessed 13 February 2017).

Wehr, A. (2012) 'Krise des Euro – was machen eigentlich die deutschen Gewerkschaften?'. Available at: www.dielinke.de/politik/disput/archiv/detail/archiv/2012/maerz/zurueck/archiv-4/artikel/krise-des-euro-was-machen-eigentlich-die-deutschen-gewerkschaften/ (accessed 12 February 2017).

Welz, C. (2008) *The European Social Dialogue under Articles 138 and 139 of the EC Treaty: Actors, Processes, Outcomes*. The Netherlands: Kluwer Law International.

Wirtschafts- und Sozialwissenschaftliches Institut in der Hans-Böckler-Stiftung (WSI). (2000) *2000 Monatsberichte Januar – Dezember*. Available at: www.boeckler.de/pdf/p_ta_monb_2000.pdf (accessed 7 March 2018).

Wolf, M. (2000) 'Von der "Konzertierten Aktion" zum "Bündnis für Arbeit"' *UTOPIE kreativ*, 117(6), pp. 669–80.

Wood, S. (2001) 'Business, government, and patterns of labor market policy in Britain and the Federal Republic of Germany', in Hall, P. and Soskice, D.W. (eds) *Varieties of Capitalism: The Institutional Foundations of Comparative Advantage*. Oxford: Oxford University Press, pp. 247–74.

Woś, R. (2014) *Dziecięca choroba liberalizmu*. Warsaw: Wydawnictwo Studio Emka.

Wprost (2012) 'Miller o współpracy z SPD: było chłodno, jest właściwie', 8 June. Available at: www.wprost.pl/kraj/327139/Miller-o-wspolpracy-z-SPD-bylo-chlodno-jest-wlasciwie.html (accessed 7 March 2018).

Wren-Lewis, S. (2015) 'German self-interest', *Social Europe*, 19 August. Available at: www.socialeurope.eu/german-self-interest (accessed 7 March 2018).

Yakubovich, C. (2002) 'Négociation collective des salaires et passage à la monnaie unique: une comparaison Allemagne, Espagne, France, Italie', *Premières Informations et Premières Synthèses*, 48(1), pp. 1–8.

Index

Note: Page numbers for tables appear in *italics.*

188